EXPERIENTIAL MARKETING

How to Get Customers to

SENSE, FEEL, THINK, ACT, and RELATE

to Your Company and Brands

BERND H. SCHMITT

Co-author of *Marketing Aesthetics*

THE FREE PRESS

*f*P

THE FREE PRESS
A Division of Simon & Schuster Inc.
1230 Avenue of the Americas
New York, NY 10020

THE FREE PRESS and colophon are trademarks
of Simon & Schuster Inc.

Designed by Carla Bolte

Manufactured in the United States of America

10   9   8   7   6   5   4

Library of Congress Cataloging-in-Publication Data
Schmitt, Bernd.
   Experiential marketing: how to get customers to sense, feel, think,
   act, and relate to your company and brands/by Bernd H. Schmitt.
      p.   cm.
   Includes bibliographical references and index.
   1. Brand name products—Marketing.   2. Corporate image.
   I. Title.
   HF5415.13.5343   1999
   658.8'27—dc21   99–18003
                              CIP

ISBN 0–684–85423–6

To my mother

(for SENSE and FEEL)

To my father

(for THINK, ACT, and RELATE)

To Hisako

(for HOLISTIC)

CONTENTS

PART TWO: TYPES OF EXPERIENCES

PREFACE

E
xperiential marketing is everywhere. In a variety of markets and industries (consumer, service, technology, and industrial), a wide variety of
organizations have turned to experiential marketing techniques to develop new products, communicate with customers, improve sales relations,
select business partners, design retail environments, and build web sites.[1] This
transformation is showing no signs of slowing down. More and more, marketers are moving away from traditional "features-and-benefits" marketing
toward creating experiences for their customers.

This book provides a strategic framework along with implementation
tools for this new approach to marketing. I have written about this subject in
academic and professional journals and presented the framework at various
conferences (in the United States and abroad), ranging from those on brand
management and positioning to strategic management and financial services.

One of the core ideas of the experiential marketing approach presented in
this book is the creation of different types of experiences for customers. I
view these types of experiences as SEMs (Strategic Experiential Modules).
Each SEM has its own distinct structures and marketing principles that as a
manager you need to be familiar with. As I will show, SEMs include sensory
experiences (SENSE); affective experiences (FEEL); creative cognitive experiences (THINK); physical experiences and entire lifestyles (ACT); and social-
identity experiences that result from relating to a reference group or culture
(RELATE).

Managers create these experiences by using ExPros, or experience providers. These include communications, visual and verbal identity, product

presence, co-branding, spatial environments, web sites and electronic media, and people.

The ultimate goal of experiential marketing is to create holistic experiences for customers. As we will see, the creation of SEMs and of holistic experiences raises a range of structural and strategic issues and the key organizational issue of how to build an experience-oriented organization.

This book, and especially chapter 4, builds on my prior book with The Free Press entitled *Marketing Aesthetics: The Strategic Management of Brands, Identity, and Image* (with Alex Simonson). In *Marketing Aesthetics* we argued that most of marketing is limiting because of its focus on features and benefits. We then presented a framework for managing sensory experiences. In the present book, I provide a much more detailed exposition of the limitations of the features-and-benefits (F&B) approach of traditional marketing. Moreover, I introduce a new model for managing sensory experiences. Finally, and most important, the book goes beyond sensory experiences by presenting a broad framework for managing all types of experiences, integrating them into holistic experiences, and addressing key structural, strategic, and organizational challenges.

I invite you now to follow me on the path of experiential marketing. If you are in a Proustian state of mind, I suggest you pick up a madeleine in your local grocery store or supermarket for the journey. Before we start, one brief comment about the writing style of the book. In my opinion, most management and marketing literature is too serious and too aggressive. War metaphors of the "Beat the competition into the ground" type are pervasive, but so is the opposite, the "brand is your friend" approach, especially in the age of relationship marketing. Few things in business and in life are that cut-and-dried. What I find missing in a lot of management and marketing literature is a sense of humor. Humor stimulates creativity and dialectical thinking, and it can provide a fresh perspective. Humor deflates pretense and opens new avenues of thought. So I have tried to infuse a sense of humor throughout this book.

One part of this humor is LAURA BROWN, whose voice you will encounter at the end of each chapter. Who is LAURA BROWN?

For now, think of LAURA BROWN as a kind of critical, thoughtful voice. She's the student in the last row who always asks the really hard questions. She's not impressed with the emperor's new clothes. She is Mephisto, the genie in the bottle, but, at the same time, the deus ex machina who saves the day. If you are more technically inclined, think of her as the cookie monster or the Melissa virus that forces you to keep your hard disk clean. The LAURA BROWNs of the world are important. Through their questioning, they keep us honest and focused on what matters. As I mentioned above, you will find LAURA BROWN's questions and commentary at the end of each chapter. And you will find a decisive answer to the question of who she really is in the "Epilogue."

ACKNOWLEDGMENTS

As a faculty member in the marketing department at the Graduate School of Business at Columbia University, I am standing on the shoulders of giants. The glorious past and present marketing scholars at Columbia University include, among many others, John Howard, John Farley, Don Lehmann and, last but not least, Morris Holbrook, who already wrote about experiential marketing and hedonic consumption more than twenty-five years ago. The book that I am presenting here is deeply influenced by their path-breaking contributions; in its conceptualization it is decidedly anti-Howardian, in terms of its managerial relevance positively Lehmannian, and in its exposition inspirationally Holbrookian. I trust that John Farley will be pleased to see that it is also truly international, incorporating research and management examples from around the world.

My younger colleagues in the marketing department at Columbia are another source of inspiration. I have greatly benefited from my discussions with Professors Sunil Gupta, Gita Johar, and Michel Pham, among others. A special thanks to my Columbia colleague Professor Asim Ansari, with whom I have had many delightful discussions. His thought-provoking ideas, creativity, and breadth of interests are truly infectious. In one of our heated inspirational debates, which are so much fun, he coined the term "strategic experiential modules" and has graciously allowed me to use it in this book. Another special thanks goes to Puneet Manchanda, a former doctoral student at Columbia Business School who now teaches at the University of Chicago, and to Nader Tavassoli, another former student and now a professor at MIT, who have given me sharp critical advice regarding essential concepts provided in this book.

ACKNOWLEDGMENTS

The MBA and Executive MBA students who took my classes on Corporate Identity and Brand Management at Columbia Business School will recognize the concepts used in this book. Since I was writing the book at the same time I taught these classes, I have learned a lot myself from the class discussions and benefited from testing the concepts with a group of unusually motivated and intelligent participants.

Another source of support throughout this project has been the China–Europe International Business School (CEIBS) located in Shanghai. I am grateful for the financial, logistics, and human resources that were provided to me.

Over the years, I have developed a rich network of contacts with advertising, brand, and identity firms around the world and, in particular, in New York City. I thank all of you for the constant inspiration and willingness to discuss often half-cooked ideas with me and to provide me with numerous business cases.

I have had terrific assistants in the process of conducting the research and writing of this book. First and foremost, I would like to thank Fei Hanying, who conducted background company research, organized the materials, and worked on the manuscript. Her skills in finding the right information, the right quotes, and the right exotic keys and commands on the keyboard are truly amazing. I often call her a computer whiz, but she assures me that it is merely good luck.

Ron Friedman compiled pertinent psychology literature; Uma Muhtu identified pertinent marketing literature; and Paula Appelbaum provided me with South American cases. A special thanks to Peter Demeyer, who compiled pertinent company research, and Monica Hamburg, who secured copyright permissions.

My editor at The Free Press, Robert Wallace, has provided invaluable encouragement and support throughout this project. His assistants, Caryn-Amy King and Daniel Zellman, have helped greatly in smoothing the editing process. I also thank Angella Baker and Iris Cohen.

Finally, a special thank you to Gail van der Merwe, my graphic designer and photographer, and Sally Lee, my research coordinator and web programmer. I have had the honor of welcoming Gail and Sally as my first two experiential "crew-saders" and as the initial signatories of the Experiential Manifesto (see www.exmarketing.com).

Originally, I wanted to dedicate this book, as a spin-off to the dedication in *Marketing Aesthetics,* to "the ultimate existential experiences in life." I decided against it; it seemed too slick. I have dedicated it instead to three real people who have enriched my personal experiential worlds in many ways. My mother taught me to appreciate the world of beauty and feelings in life; my father taught me how to think freely and act creatively, as well as the importance of social relations. My dear wife, Hisako, helps me to bring it all together holistically. The outcome of these experiential influences is this book. For a more formal discourse on "the ultimate existential experiences in life," you may turn to the "Epilogue."

New York City
August 1999

PART ONE

THE EXPERIENTIAL MARKETING REVOLUTION

1

FROM FEATURES AND BENEFITS
TO CUSTOMER EXPERIENCES

W e are in the middle of a revolution. A revolution that will render the principles and models of traditional marketing obsolete. A revolution that will change the face of marketing forever. A revolution that will replace traditional feature-and-benefit marketing with experiential marketing.

As the new millennium approaches, three phenomena are signaling an entirely new approach to marketing, if not to doing business as a whole. These three simultaneous developments are (1) the omnipresence of information technology, (2) the supremacy of the brand, and (3) the ubiquity of integrated communications and entertainment.

THREE MARKETING TRENDS AT THE TURN
OF THE NEW MILLENNIUM

The Omnipresence of Information Technology

Soon everything will be driven by information technology. Even if this change doesn't happen right away, it will, and very soon—definitely within most of our lifetimes. Indeed, the dictum of Razorfish, a strategic digital communications company founded in 1995, expresses the view of many futurists: "Everything that can be digital WILL BE."

Your standard road warrior outfit—a mobile phone in one pocket, a palm-top computer with database and appointment calendar in the other, and a heavy keyboard laptop in your briefcase—will soon be outdated. You may already have gotten used to the mind-boggling speed of technological development: From 4 megabytes of RAM to 8, then 16, 32, 64, and on and on. From a 400 MB hard disk to 1.2 gigabyte, then over 4. From a 120 processor to 133, then 266, then over 400.

But there's more to come. The future will not merely show improvements in speed and reduction in weight. It will also mean a transformation in media—from print to voice, for example—and media convergence.

We only need to look at how phenomenally voice recognition software has developed in order to see this new path. The keyboard as we now know it will likely disappear within a few years. You will be working with a considerably smaller device that will likely integrate a mobile phone and a voice-operated computer with access to anyone and anything anywhere, at low cost.

Just think of what the Palm III (not to mention the Palm V and the Palm VII) can already do. They can exchange business cards via infrared ports and browse the web. You can download Shakespeare or Cindy Crawford. You can use them as alarm clocks and, with plug-ins, as remote controls for your TV.

We are literally surrounded by technological innovation. A "constellation" made up of dozens of satellites is now orbiting the earth, designed to enable people to send and receive phone calls or electronic messages from any point on the planet, using handheld phones and pocket-size pagers.[1] A new technology known as distributed computing will allow devices that speak the Java programming language to communicate and cooperate with one another, thus putting the power of a supercomputer into the hands of the average user.[2]

Technology is finding more and more ways of entering our lives. As Nicholas Negroponte, founder of MIT's Media Lab and a columnist for *Wired* magazine, writes, "entirely new content will emerge from being digital."[3]

More fun is on the way. Smart sensors in products will measure and deliver information and help. These personalized and customized devices will

The author in his "Road Warrior" outfit

make your daily life information-rich and considerably more convenient. You will have smart cooking assistants that prepare food using recipes posted on the Internet. TV or computer-based programs will select customized news and deliver it whenever you wish. You will be able to order any music and any movie at any time. Soon you'll be able to alter their endings. Internet video services will offer users streaming video from TV shows. Smart processors in cosmetic and shampoo products will deliver the right mixture after diagnosing your haptic needs.

Techno-savvy futurists like Michael Dertouzos, Director of MIT's Laboratory for Computer Science, predict that within a few years you may see products like the "bodynet," a web of integrated devices—functioning as cell phone, computer, television, camera, etc.—that will be confined to an invisible envelope around your body.[4] Reality already meets predictions: in the summer of 1998 a Japanese company introduced its Eye Trek goggle mask that plays video in front of your eyes.[5]

Then there is virtual reality, another Japanese favorite. Kyoko Date was created by HoriPro and Visual Science Library (VSL), and was the first "virtual idol" in history. After eighteen months of work, the design teams created and animated an idealized teen who moves, talks, and even sings. (Think of her as an exotic dream girl like *Tomb Raiders'* Lara Croft, just a little more real.) Kyoko even has her own music video, which can be viewed on her web site, and she has released a few singles. A virtual identity was created for her, as well as a virtual personality: Kyoko was "born" in Tokyo; she is seventeen years old and a Scorpio. Her "father" runs a sushi bar, and she has a little sister. Her favorite colors are white and black; her favorite movie is *Toy Story;* her favorite artists are Mariah Carey and Enya.

Despite the fact that she is not real, Kyoko Date has a virtual fan club and a web site where devotees can share their feelings about her: "She makes me crazy!" "She is beautiful," "She is very sexy and makes cool music!" Within a few years, technology should enable Kyoko to appear on a live TV show and chat with other "artists." A motion picture is a distinct possibility.[6]

Why is this rapid technological development important? Because through these products you will be able to send and receive information in any medium (text, voice, picture, and other media) to practically anybody (real or virtual) anywhere. This will allow people and companies to connect and to share an experiential universe with one another at any time.

The Supremacy of the Brand

"Brand! Brand!! Brand!!! That's the message . . . for the late '90s and beyond," writes Tom Peters, the well-known management guru, in his book *The Circle of Innovation.*[7] Roper Starch Worldwide has identified the dominance of power brands as a key trend at the millennium. According to research by Citigroup and Interbrand, a firm well known for brand valuations, "companies which base their businesses on brands have outperformed the stock market during the past fifteen years."[8]

Just stroll through the hustle and bustle of Times Square in New York, or in the entertainment pinnacle of any other city in the world for that matter, and you feel the supremacy of the brand at once. From oversized billboards and dynamic product displays to high-tech screens, each brand is omnipresent.

Moreover, everything will soon be a brand. And through advancements in information technology, information about brands—in all different forms and media—will be available instantly and globally.

Consider also the branding that we already see happening in all aspects of life. *Titanic, Godzilla,* and *Star Wars* movies: all launched worldwide and merchandised worldwide. Bill Gates, Princess Diana, and President Clinton: all known, admired, or despised in London and Paris, Tokyo and Beijing, Buenos Aires and São Paulo, Los Angeles and New York. CNN, the Olympics, and the year 2000 are other "brands" that are widely marketed. Not surprisingly, Times Square 2000 has been planned by Landor Associates, one of the premier brand agencies of the world, and more and more celebrities are supplementing their PR agents with brand experts.

As we can see, even things we don't traditionally think of as brands are now being treated and marketed as such. Examples include business schools (Harvard, Stanford, Wharton, Columbia, etc.), museums (e.g., the Guggenheim or the Getty), medical practices (see chapter 2), and even nursing homes (see chapter 6). Consider TV stations, TV programs, and special reports. Major news stories and events are given titles. Really important stories even

Outdoor advertisements at Times Square, New York City, Winter 1998/99

have special music composed for them, and news brands are held together by consistent graphical presentations.

All these "brands" bring to mind distinct images, associations, and experiences. All may be merchandised and extended. All have brand equity. And all need to be managed and planned.

Brand extensions occur everywhere. Fashion brands, given the fast-paced nature of the industry, have always been more creative and image-conscious than those in other industries. But even by standards as recent as those of ten years ago, the following brand extensions would have been considered outrageous:

- A clothing retailer known for its casual, traditional menswear extending into paint

customers want to be entertained
stimulated, emotionally affected
and creatively challenged

Event marketing: forging an
emotional and memorable connection
w/ consumers where they live, work
and play
- less clutter - greater impact

feel - employ emotional stimuli
act - enhance physical experiences
relate - connect individual self to
    broader social and cultural contexts
    reflected in a brand

Marketing campaigns that:
   dazzle their senses
   touch their hearts
   stimulate their minds

want products, communications and
marketing campaigns that they
can relate to and that they can
incorporate into their lifestyles
   • deliver an experience

Experiential marketing focuses on
   customer experiences - which
   occur as a result of encountering,
   undergoing or living through situations
      - connect the company; brand to
      consumer lifestyle and place
      individual customer actions and
      the purchase occassion in
      broader social context
   - most powerful opportunities for influencing
   a brand occur during consumption
      - key determinant of customer satisfaction
      and brand loyalty

- Another clothing retailer extending its brand into bottled water
- A fashion designer famous for jeans extending into popcorn boxes
- A clothing retailer moving into toothpaste (at $15 a tube)
- A long-established Italian fashion house extending its brand into dog carriers (at $1,150 each!)

What possessed Ralph Lauren, DKNY, Calvin Klein, Paul Smith, and Gucci to dare such insane extensions? Are they just riding on a bubble economy? Are they aberrations of a turn-of-the-century disease, the "millennium fever"? Don't be fooled; there's nothing crazy about these extensions. The degree to which brands can be stretched and leveraged into new categories reflects their brand value and brand equity, and smart marketing is taking advantage of that. Even in Asia (amidst the 1997/98 financial crisis), I still saw lines of shoppers waiting in front of the Gucci, Prada, and D&G boutiques among the otherwise empty retail spaces. Interestingly enough, financial firms increasingly value these companies not by their standard assets or within narrowly defined categories (e.g., fashion and watches) but as true lifestyle brands, more similar to Nike and Coca-Cola than Geoffrey Beene and Seiko.

Even our language changes to reflect this lifestyle focus. Rest rooms (called simply "toilets" in many European countries) have become "lounges" at Barney's. Fitness rooms with StairMasters are now known as "cardio theaters." No cosmetic firm can command respect in the marketplace unless it is "cosmeceutical." And all the pharma firms have become "life science" outfits. And who knows what's in store for Amazon.com?

Not to fall behind, some industries are proving that they can be equally daring. For example, Swatch, the watch manufacturer, has just launched the Smart car in Europe, manufactured by Daimler Chrysler (see chapter 10). Richard Branson has long capitalized on this trend, offering under the Virgin label such diverse products and businesses as soft drinks and record stores; trains, airlines, and balloon flights; life insurance; and, as of October 1997, a collection of skin care, toiletries, hair care, fragrance, cosmetics, and aromatherapy products under the Virgin Vie label.

So what's next? Mr. Branson explains: "My vision for Virgin was ultimately summed up best by Peter Gabriel, who once said to me on a ski lift: 'It's outrageous Virgin is becoming everything. You wake up in the morning to Virgin Radio; you put on your Virgin jeans; you go to the Virgin megastore; you drink Virgin Cola; you fly to America on Virgin Atlantic. Soon you'll be offering Virgin births, Virgin marriages, Virgin funerals. I think you should re-name Virgin the In and Out Company. Virgin will be there at the beginning and there at the end."[9]

In the world in which the brands rule, products are no longer bundles of functional characteristics but means to provide and enhance customer experiences.

The Ubiquity of Communications and Entertainment

No more hiding. Just as everything is becoming branded, so will everything—you, your business, and every part of your products—become a form of communication. Communications will be ubiquitous, and they will all be linked to the brand.

These communications will have the potential to affect others (your customers, your investors, the press, and the community). They will have the potential of being publicly exposed and scrutinized. They will have the opportunity to do good or harm; to grow business or destroy it overnight.

What's more, communications will no longer be one-way. Customers and other constituencies of a company will be able to communicate directly with the company, thus influencing its image. Communications will be globally available.

In a global environment, the tone of communications is changing as well. Communications are no longer mostly information. "Everything is entertainment," writes high-tech management consultant Regis McKenna.[10] Companies and customers seem to be following the dictum of a recent ABC ad campaign: "Scientists say we use 10 percent of our brain. That's way too much." Café intellectuals and cultural anthropologists may sniff at it, but "capitalists" are getting better and better in dressing themselves as "customer-," "value-," and "community-oriented" and spare no efforts to provide fun and entertainment for their customers. Open the latest annual reports or browse the corporate information listing on a company's web site, and you will find terms like "value," "customer," "connection," and "stimulation" orbiting around you in bright colors. Or open the newspapers and turn on TV. Newspapers and TV programs that used to be packed with politics, economics, and highbrow culture are thick with dumb but entertaining stories on sports and Leonardo DiCaprio. But, as *The Economist* noted, "If Mr. DiCaprio makes you despair at breakfast, remember that 'dumb' is not necessarily stupid, and news that entertains may also be news that informs."[11]

ARE WE ENTERING A NEW CENTURY OF MARKETING?

What's going on here? What do all these trends have in common? What do they tell us about marketing in the years ahead? Are they indications of things to come, indications that we are entering not only a new century but also a new century of marketing?

In this book, I am proposing that these phenomena represent the early

ABC ad dismissing rational appeals

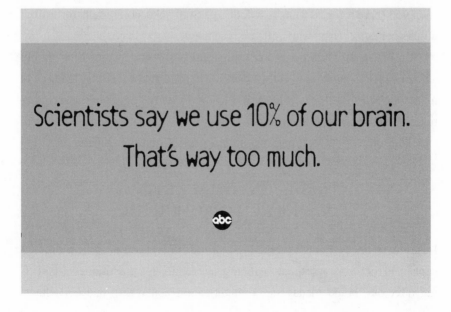

signs of an entirely new approach to marketing, if not to business as a whole. These phenomena provide the outlines of a type of marketing and management driven by experience. And within a short period of time, this new approach will replace the traditional approach to marketing and business.

As we enter the new century, companies have reengineered themselves and defined their core competencies, and they are now ready to capitalize on their newly acquired strengths and leverage their assets. The focus is on growth, revival, and expansion. Companies want to capitalize on the opportunities provided by the information revolution. They want to build their brands and create globally integrated, two-way communication with customers.[12]

"Welcome to the Experience Economy," write B. Joseph Pine II and James H. Gilmore, cofounders of Strategic Horizons LLP, a consulting firm based in Aurora, Ohio, in the *Harvard Business Review.* Using a long-term perspective, these authors have distinguished four stages in the progression of economic value: commodities, goods, services, and experiences. They write: "As services, like goods before them, increasingly become commoditized—think of long-distance telephone services sold solely on price—experiences have emerged as the next step in what we call the *progression of economic value.*"

As long as you sell coffee as a commodity, you can charge $1 per pound. When you sell it as a packaged product, it is 5 to 25 cents a cup; in a coffee shop you serve it for 50 cents to a dollar. At Starbucks, coffee sells for several dollars per cup.[13] (And wait unil you read about waters in chapter 9.)

Unfortunately, traditional marketing and business concepts offer hardly any guidance to capitalize on the emerging experiential economy. Traditional marketing was developed in response to the industrial age, not the information, branding, and communications revolution we are facing today. Let's take a look at some of the assumptions and practices of traditional marketing.

TRADITIONAL MARKETING: FOUR KEY CHARACTERISTICS

I use the term "traditional marketing" to refer to a canon of principles, concepts, and methodologies that marketing academicians, practitioners (marketing directors, brand managers, communication managers), and consultants have amassed throughout this century and, in particular, during the last thirty years. Strangely enough, these concepts have been around in marketing, essentially unchanged, for decades. Marketers are fond of saying, "Pay attention to the changes in the environment." Yet they themselves have mostly ignored the changes that directly impact their discipline.

The principles and concepts of traditional marketing describe the nature of products, the behavior of consumers, and competitive activity in the marketplace. They are used to develop new products, plan product lines and brands, design communications, and respond to competitive activities. Figure 1.1 and the following sections outline the key features of such traditional marketing.

1. Focus on Functional Features and Benefits

Traditional marketing is largely focused on functional features and benefits. Traditional marketers assume that customers (business customers or end consumers) in a variety of markets (industrial, consumer, technology, service) weigh functional features in terms of their importance, assess the presence of product features, and select the product with the highest overall utility (defined as the sum of weighted features). Everything that does not fit into this

FIGURE 1.1

Characteristics of Traditional Marketing

Traditional Marketing

Functional features and benefits (F&B)

Customers are rational decision-makers

Narrow definition of product categories and competition

Methods are analytical, quantitative, and verbal

framework gets labeled at best as "image" or "brand" effect, without any conceptual understanding of what that means. Or, in the worst cases, it is counted as "irrelevant," "meaningless" error variance.

FEATURES. What exactly are features? According to Philip Kotler, features are "characteristics that supplement the product's basic function."[14] Because customers are assumed to make choices based on features, product features are viewed as a key tool for differentiating a company's offerings from competitive offerings. Indeed, strategist Michael Porter describes product differentiation in a competitive context as developing a unique position on an attribute that is "widely valued by buyers."[15]

BENEFITS. Benefits arise from functional features. Benefits are performance characteristics that customers seek from products: For toothpaste: cavity prevention, tartar control, and whitening; for airlines: schedules, destinations, and frequent flyer miles; for personal computers: speed, connectivity, and portability.

The relation between features and benefits is typically not one-to-one, i.e., one feature offering one benefit. Typically, several features are necessary to provide one benefit. For example, picture clarity (a benefit in a TV set) may be the result of several product features (screen size, brightness, and contrast quality). Many marketers propose to start with benefits, then trace them back to product features and thus build a "House of Quality" that puts the customers' voice into the manufacturing process. While competing in the marketplace, the same manufacturer may stress different benefits for different users, thus engaging "in a powerful form of segmentation [that] involves classifying buyers according to the benefits they seek from the product."[16]

As Philip Kotler explains, using Procter & Gamble as an example, "P&G makes nine brands of laundry detergents (Tide, Cheer, Gain, Dash, Bold, Dreft, Ivory Snow, Oxydol, and Era) which are differentiated on the basis of the benefits that customers seek from laundry detergents. For example, Tide is 'so powerful, it cleans down to the fiber.' Ivory Snow is '99 and 44/100 percent pure' and therefore mild for diapers and baby clothes. Bold is the detergent with fabric softeners; it 'cleans, softens, and controls static.' Dash is P&G's value entry; it 'attacks tough dirt,' and does it 'for a great low price.' "[17]

Ask yourself: Are products simply the sum of all their features and benefits?

2. Product Category and Competition Are Narrowly Defined

In the world of a traditional marketer, McDonald's competes against Burger King and Wendy's (and not against Pizza Hut or Friendly's or Starbucks). Snapple competes against Minute Maid and Tropicana (and not against Arizona Iced tea or Nantucket Nectar, much less all the waters on the market). Chanel fragrances compete against Dior fragrances (and not against those of Lancôme or L'Oréal, or fragrance offered by a mass market retailer). Fine china manufacturers see their competition in other fine china manufacturers (and not in Crate & Barrel or Williams-Sonoma). For a traditional marketer, competition occurs primarily within narrowly defined product categories— the battleground of product and brand managers.

Ask yourself: Is this the right way to view categories and competition today?

3. Customers Are Viewed as Rational Decision Makers

Throughout this century, economists, decision scientists, and marketers have viewed customer decision-making processes as straightforward problem solving. As Engel, Blackwell, and Miniard explain, problem solving refers to thoughtful, reasoned action undertaken to bring about need satisfaction.[18] Customer decision-making processes typically are assumed to involve several steps.

- Need recognition. The customer perceives a gap between an ideal state of need satisfaction and the current state, which motivates him or her to reduce the gap. ("Aha. Toothpaste is running out, and I like to have clean teeth.")
- Information search. The customer searches for information, either externally by comparing alternative products in a store, by reading catalogs or other information, or by retrieving from memory previous satisfactory

choices. ("Let's see. Here's Colgate. There's Crest. And what's that? Let's take a close look at how they differ.")

- Evaluation of alternatives. The customer evaluates the ultimate choice set by performing a computation that resembles a multi-attribute model. He or she determines the importance of each attribute or benefit, assigns an importance weight, assesses and rates the degree to which the attribute is present in a brand, then multiplies the weight with each rating. The customer then compares the overall utility of each brand against each other brand. ("Hmm. Toothpaste cleans, may prevent cavities, tastes minty, and may have baking soda in it these days. Let's see how important each one is, and then look at whether a brand's got it. And then multiply the two for each attribute . . .")

- Purchase and consumption. The customer purchases the best alternative (if available) and uses it. Out of usage, the customer derives satisfaction by comparing expected performance with actual performance. If the customer is satisfied, he or she will purchase the product again.

Ask yourself: Is this how you buy toothpaste, a car, even a house? Is this how you buy anything?

4. Methods and Tools Are Analytical, Quantitative, and Verbal

Traditional marketing methodologies and tools are analytical, quantitative, and verbal. Consider the following frequently used methods:

- Regression models. The input to a regression model (and its stepchild, the logit model) typically consists of verbal ratings collected in interviews or surveys. The purpose is to predict purchase or choice based on a number of predictors and to assess their relative importance weights.

- Positioning maps. Input to a positioning map (and its stepchild, the correspondence analysis) consists of verbal pairwise similarity ratings among brand names and/or ratings on a number of mostly functional-features scales. Output consists of two-dimensional or three-dimensional spaces (quality *vs.* value; or functionality *vs.* luxury) in which one brand is positioned against another brand.

- Conjoint analysis. This type of analysis is used for assessing the monetary value of individual functional features within a bundle of offers. To arrive at the result, customers are asked to evaluate several products consisting of features or benefits bundles.

Clearly, there are situations in which these methodologies offer useful insights. The issue is not to critique individual research techniques but to think about the purpose and function of research within a corporation. Ask yourself: Do you expect to gain a competitive advantage by tweaking the customer importance weights used in a regression? Do you expect to gain strategic insights by examining the position of your brand against another along the broad, general dimensions of a positioning map? Can you justify a price increase or decrease after examining the "part worths" in a conjoint analysis?

Or consider the focus group. This sacred cow of market research is qualitative but almost entirely verbal. The focus-group facilitator walks in, presents a positioning statement or new product concept on an index card, and asks everyone to free-associate. Is this the right way to generate or test new product ideas?

TRADITIONAL MARKETING IS F&B MARKETING

After considering the essential features of traditional marketing, let us briefly consider the interrelations among them. Traditional marketing is first and foremost functional features-and-benefits (F&B) marketing. Everything else follows from there. That is, all of the above characteristics of traditional marketing (the narrow definition of categories and competition; the rational information-processing view of the consumer; the verbal-analytical tools) may be traced back to one fundamental assumption: for marketing purposes, products can and should be described in terms of functional features and benefits.

Because of F&B marketing, traditional marketers define product categories and competition in a narrow fashion. It is easy to compare one toothpaste against another because most toothpastes share the same features and benefits. They differ only in terms of importance to consumers and in terms of the degree to which a feature is present or a benefit is delivered.

Because of F&B marketing, consumers are viewed as rational information processors. Features and/or benefits (as rows) and the various brands (as columns) become the input matrix for an information processing system that performs various operations on the input—e.g., it weighs the features or benefits, assesses the presence of features/benefits in each brand, computes the overall utility of each brand, compares it against a standard (e.g., a necessary benchmark), and uses a formula to reach a decision. Anything other than functional features and benefits could not be processed in such a systematic, rational step-by-step fashion.

Finally, because of F&B marketing, marketing directors dedicate numerous hours, days, and weeks every year together with marketing consultants, researchers, and advertising managers to figure out the output of regression analyses, positioning maps, correspondence and conjoint analyses. The purpose: to find out the importance of weights and underlying dimensions of functional features and benefits.

Cole-Haan Shoes is running a print campaign that explicitly repudiates features-and-benefits marketing in favor of an emotional, experiential appeal. Under the headline "No factual mumbo jumbo please," the copy reads, "Ah, the heart. The emotional storage bin. Immune to all data and humdrum practicality. Not to mention it's a pretty darn good judge of greatness. At Cole-Haan, you can see its influence in the way we do things. Where just as many decisions are based on feelings and heartfelt intuition as mechanics and hard data. Of course, that's just our way of doing things, but we encourage you to give it a try. Pick up something with the Cole-Haan name on it and see how quickly your emotions get all stirred up inside. Cole-Haan. Stand for something."

TRADITIONAL MARKETING: THE GOOD, THE BAD, AND THE UGLY

Traditional marketing focusing on factual mumbo jumbo presents an engineering-driven, rational, analytical view of customers, products, and

Cole-Haan advertisement debunking F&B marketing

competition that is full of untested assumptions. It is not a psychologically based theory about customers and how they view and react to products and competition.

But let's not throw the baby out with the bathwater. There are definitely several positive attributes to traditional marketing that are worth preserving.

For example, a fundamental set of strategic concepts apply to traditional F&B marketing and will also apply to any other form of marketing. They are the backbone of good marketing decision making. Indeed, they have become part of business strategy in general and are used by strategic consultants and management strategists as well as in corporate decision making. They include, most importantly, the concepts of objective setting (e.g., do we go for profits or market share? are we focused on current users or do we intend to attract new users or competitors' users?), market segmentation (e.g., geographic, demographic, or psychographic), and strategic positioning.

But then, there's the bad. The almost exclusive use of F&B. The analytical focus; the obsession with measurement precision; doing things right rather than doing the right thing. The myopic view of competition. And all this at a time when the marketing environment is changing drastically from week to week.

Even traditional advertising leaves an unpleasant aftertaste. Traditional ad campaigns are a kind of trial-and-error approach to marketing and branding—run one campaign after the other until one sticks. As Nick Shore, a former adman and now CEO of nickandpaul, the brand agency, put it: "There is a mature and complex dialogue going on between consumers and brands, one that has evolved exponentially since the very concept of brand was invented. But advertising and its agencies have essentially stood still, rigidly insisting that brands are uni-dimensional entities communicable only in uni-dimensional ways, relying on formulas like 'unique selling proposition' or 'primary product benefit' that were developed by firms that hardly resemble their present day mega-merged ad factories."[19]

Finally, there's the ugly. Meaningless talk about strategy without considering implementation and focus on customers' true needs. Useless positioning statements that focus on broad dimensions like quality, innovation, service, product leadership, which by now are so commonplace that they mean nothing to customers anymore. That is, the ugly results from combining the good of strategic thinking with the bad of the F&B approach. This, however, is the essence of traditional marketing.

When I step back, when I leave the comfortable environment of theory and of marketing textbooks, when I consult for high-tech or cutting-edge service companies, when I stay at a W hotel, when I enter a Pottery Barn, visit Sephora cosmetics stores, or the G-Factory store in Soho (set up by Casio), when I use a Palm VII Organizer, look at the new Beetle, or pick up a Clif Bar in the supermarket, or when I watch the Budweiser lizard ads or the Gap khaki commercials on TV, I have a sense that traditional marketing has been left behind the times. Despite its methodological sophistication, traditional marketing has missed something very essential.

BUT HOW ABOUT "BRANDING"?

Didn't the "branding" movement, which has been so prominent in the nineties, change all that? Brand strategists certainly do not look at products just in terms of their functional features and benefits.[20] Brand equity, we have learned, lies in "assets (and liabilities) linked to a brand, its name and symbol."[21] Doesn't branding, then, extend beyond the limitations of F&B marketing?

Unfortunately, most brand theorists have treated brands as identifiers— and as identifiers only. Their equation reads: Brand = ID. That is, brands are markers that signify ownership and guarantee quality. They differentiate one product from another, or the branded product from a generic or commodity.

As we will see, this view of branding misses the very essence of a brand as a rich source of sensory, affective, and cognitive associations that result in memorable and rewarding brand experiences. Brand names and logos as such no longer drive customer choice in many industries. Customers expect breakthrough solutions, cutting-edge products, and brands that they can connect with and be stimulated by. Indeed, research conducted by brand agencies has shown time and again that familiarity and perceived quality or esteem are not enough. Millward Brown, a research agency, found that "bonding with the brand" accounts for the largest share of wallet. In a study identifying the best practices of brand leaders, Manning Selvage & Lee, a research firm, found that brand leaders do not just have a memorable name and great image—they also deliver experiences. In another survey of managers, the Jack Morton Survey on Experiential Communications, two thirds of the three hundred marketing executives surveyed forecast that spending on experiential communications will increase over the next five to ten years.

F&B and Brand = ID may still work in the PRC (People's Republic of China), where as recently as ten years ago consumers were washing their hair with hard soap and were afraid of putting cosmetics on their skin, and are just now starting to buy their food in supermarkets rather than traditional "wet markets."

But even consumers in emerging markets are becoming more sophisticated at an incredible rate. As James Watson, author of *Golden Arches East: McDonald's in East Asia,* concluded, the limited menu in Chinese McDonald's restaurants is no problem for consumers, since people in the PRC come for the experience, not the product.[22] Moreover, for new technologies, consumers expect experiential qualities: In a 1998 survey published in *China Daily,* 51 percent of respondents said they buy mobile phones by appearance; only 37 percent said they buy on price and 11 percent based on function.[23] And the mobile phone market in China is the second largest in the world. If experiences matter in markets like the PRC, it seems clear that traditional F&B marketing and branding just won't cut it in developed industries and markets.

THE RISE OF EXPERIENTIAL MARKETING

Today, customers take functional features and benefits, product quality, and a positive brand image as a given. What they want is products, communications, and marketing campaigns that dazzle their senses, touch their hearts, and stimulate their minds. They want products, communications, and campaigns that they can relate to and that they can incorporate into their lifestyles. They want products, communications, and marketing campaigns to deliver an experience. The degree to which a company is able to deliver a desirable customer experience—and to use information technology, brands, and integrated

MEASURING EXPERIENCES

Over the years, psychologists and marketing researchers have developed imaginative methodologies to explore customer experiences. These experiential methodologies use picture collections, photographic techniques, storytelling, and other methods to understand how customers think and feel about certain issues.

One of the most prominent and widely tested techniques is the Zaltman Metaphor Elicitation Technique, a patented research technique that has been tested with more than 20 firms and 2,500 customers and managers.[24] The technique is based on the premises that thought is primarily image based, not word based, that people communicate most information nonverbally, and that metaphors are key for eliciting knowledge.

The technique starts by asking participants to take photographs or collect images from magazines or newspapers related to a particular topic. Next, to get a better understanding of their experience (e.g., on how to use computer-mediated communications for personal purposes), a variety of methods are used to get participants to describe and elaborate on the images that they collected. These methods include:

- *Image sorting.* Participants sort the images based on similarities, and the researchers analyze the data based on the underlying meanings of these comparisons.
- *Visual elaboration.* Participants are asked to generate another picture that would reinforce (or contradict) the meaning of the current picture.
- *Sensory exploration of images.* Participants are asked to use nonvisual senses to convey the core meaning of the picture.
- *Vignette generation.* Participants describe a short movie that portrays their thoughts and feelings.
- *Creation of a digital image.* Participants' pictures are scanned into a computer, and the participants manipulate the pictures electronically.

These methods are useful for understanding experiences in general. In chapter 10, I will provide assessment tools for measuring the concepts provided in this book, which focus on different types of experiences.

Coca-Cola at the Tour de France and at the Eurocup (traditional market-ing)

communications and entertainment to do so—will largely determine its success in the global marketplace of the new millennium.

The progression from traditional marketing and branding toward experiential marketing can be illustrated nicely with recent campaigns by the Coca-Cola Company designed by Desgrippes Gobé, an international brand image creation firm. For the Tour de France 1996, Coca-Cola used a simple product-presence approach through the pervasive, ubiquitous use of its logo. In the Eurocup 1996, unique graphics were created to incorporate the Coca-Cola icons into the soccer sports event. In the Olympic Games in Atlanta, Coca-Cola presented a total experiential approach in its Olympic village and other events centered on the theme of "refreshment for the whole world."

Conceptually, how exactly does experiential marketing differ from the traditional F&B marketing and branding approach? The following section gives a brief overview of the key characteristics of experiential marketing.

Coca-Cola at the Atlanta Olympics (experiential marketing)

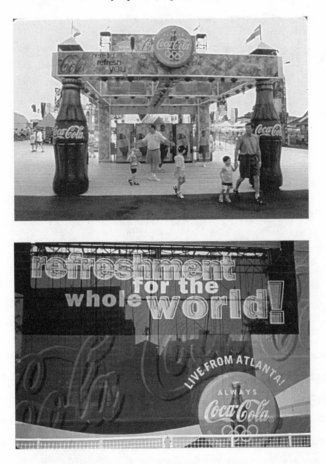

EXPERIENTIAL MARKETING: FOUR KEY CHARACTERISTICS

Experiential marketing differs from traditional marketing focusing on features and benefits in four major ways (see Figure 1.2).

1. Focus on Customer Experiences

In contrast to traditional marketing, experiential marketing focuses on customer experiences. Experiences occur as a result of encountering, undergo-

FIGURE 1.2

Characteristics of Experiential Marketing

ing, or living through situations. They are triggered stimulations to the senses, the heart, and the mind. Experiences also connect the company and the brand to the customer's lifestyle and place individual customer actions and the purchase occasion in a broader social context. In sum, experiences provide sensory, emotional, cognitive, behavioral, and relational values that replace functional values. In chapters 4 through 8, I will discuss each type of experience in more detail.

2. Examining the Consumption Situation

In contrast to focusing on narrowly defined product categories and competition, experiential marketers do not think shampoo, shaving cream, blow dryer, and perfume. Instead, they think "grooming in the bathroom" and ask themselves what products fit into this consumption situation and how these products, their packaging, and their advertising prior to consumption can enhance the consumption experience.

Experiential marketers create synergies. Virgin uses its experience in music to make transatlantic Virgin flights more fun, and to get customers to go to a movie theater, where they sample Virgin colas. As Richard Branson puts it, "We have put the Virgin experience together across retailing, entertainment, food, music, and travel . . ."[25]

Moreover, experiential marketers are keenly interested in the meaning of the consumption situation. As consumer researchers Russell Belk, Melanie Wallendorf, and John Sherry have noted, "contemporary consumers define certain objects or consumption experiences as representing something more than the ordinary objects they appear to be." Indeed, as the authors note further, consumers may grant "sacred status" to a variety of objects that are value expressive. "By expressing these values through their consumption, they participate in a celebration of their connection to the society as a whole and to particular individuals. For a society, defining as sacred certain artifacts that are value expressive provides social cohesion and social integration. For the individual, participating in these expressions provides meaning in life and a mechanism for experiencing stability, joy, and occasionally ecstasy through connection."[26]

Examining the consumption situation and sketching the (fuzzy) boundaries of categories and competition accordingly amounts to a radical shift in thinking about market opportunities—a shift that moves the marketing thinking "over"and "up" (see Figure 1.3). This type of thinking broadens the concept of a category ("moving over") and examines the meaning of the specific consumption situation in its broader sociocultural context ("moving up"). For an experiential marketer, McDonald's competes against any other form of fast food; even any other form of "quick bite" or "hangout." Suddenly we are talking not only Wendy's and Burger King but Friendly's, Denny's, and Starbucks. Moreover, we examine the macro picture: what does it mean to eat a hamburger at a time when nutrition facts are screaming in your face in the supermarkets and when Martha Stewart urges you to live a homey, healthy lifestyle? How should McDonald's be positioned and communicate in this world? In sum, we are moving away from thinking about an isolated product and instead following the sociocultural consumption vector (SCCV) to arrive at a broader space of meaning for the customer.

Thinking about product offerings using the SCCV also creates excellent

FIGURE 1.3

Moving "Over" and "Up"

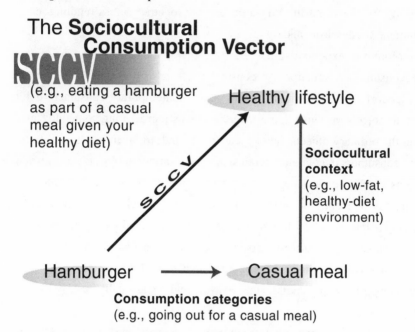

The **Socicultural** Consumption Vector

SCCV

(e.g., eating a hamburger as part of a casual meal given your healthy diet)

Healthy lifestyle

SCCV

Sociocultural context
(e.g., low-fat, healthy-diet environment)

Hamburger ⟶ **Casual meal**

Consumption categories
(e.g., going out for a casual meal)

opportunities for cross-selling. The customer does not evaluate each product as a stand-alone item, analyzing its features and benefits. Rather, the customer asks how each product fits into the overall consumption situation and the experiences provided by the consumption situation.

Ikea, the Swedish furniture company, lives from cross-selling based on the notion of a consumption situation. In 1998, Ikea had 140 stores in 29 countries. It was Sweden's third largest company after Ericsson, the communications group, and Astra, the pharmaceutical company. Swedish economist Stellan Bjoerg, the author of a book on Ikea, estimated that it could achieve a capitalization of more than SKr100bn (about USD12.4bn) if the group was listed. In its stores, furniture items and accessories are displayed as part of consumption situations, thus creating an imaginary lifestyle for the customer. And its brochures depict products that fall into consumption situations such as "going on a day trip," or "entertaining outdoors," where Ikea provides "everything you'll need to throw a few T-bones on the grill and invite the neighbors over."[27]

Another critical difference is that experiential marketers believe that the most powerful opportunities for influencing a brand occur in the post-purchase period, during consumption. These experiences during consumption are key determinants of customer satisfaction and brand loyalty. Most traditional marketing, however, focuses on persuasion—getting the customer to buy—and cares little about what happens after purchase. As Siegel & Gale, an identity firm specializing in user-friendly communications, has noted, companies spend much money on acquiring customers but fail to deliver on the brand promise, causing customer dissatisfaction and high brand switching.

3. Customers Are Rational and Emotional Animals

For an experiential marketer, customers are emotionally as well as rationally driven. That is, while customers may frequently engage in rational choice, they are just as frequently driven by emotions because consumption experiences are often "directed toward the pursuit of fantasies, feelings, and fun."[28] Moreover, it is useful to think of customers as *animals* whose physical and mental apparatus for generating sensations, thoughts, and feelings evolved by natural selection to solve the problems faced by their evolutionary ancestors.

Unfortunately, this broad view of the customer, which incorporates the latest concepts and findings from psychology, cognitive science, and evolutionary biology, has had little impact in the field of marketing. It contains an important message for today's marketers: don't treat customers just as rational decision makers. Customers want to be entertained, stimulated, emotionally affected, and creatively challenged.

4. Methods and Tools Are Eclectic

In contrast to the analytical, quantitative, and verbal methodologies of traditional marketing, the methods and tools of an experiential marketer are diverse and multifaceted. In a word, experiential marketing is not bound to one methodological ideology; it is eclectic. Just use what seems to be appropriate to get good ideas. Be explorative and worry about reliability, validity, and methodological sophistication later.

Some methods and tools may be highly analytical and quantitative (such as eye-movement methodologies for measuring the sensory impact of communications). Or they may be more intuitive and qualitative (such as brain-focusing techniques used for understanding creative thinking). They may be verbal, taking the traditional format of a focus group, in-depth interview, or questionnaire. Or they may be visual.[29] They may occur in an artificial lab environment or in the bar where consumers watch TV and drink beer. They are often ideographic (i.e., customized for the situation at hand) rather than nomothetic (providing the same standard format to all respondents). There is no dogma here; it all depends on the objective.

In summary, then, experiential marketing is distinct in four key ways: focusing on consumer experiences, treating consumption as a holistic experience, recognizing both the rational and emotional drivers of consumption, and using eclectic methodologies.

FROM BRAND=ID TO BRAND=EX

Experiential marketing also offers a new approach to branding. As described earlier, the traditional approach to branding treats a brand as a static identifier of a company's products through the use of names, logos, and ad slogans. This service as an identifier—Brand=ID—is indeed a core function of a brand. But brands are not just identifiers. Brands are first and foremost providers of experiences.

As a result, the ubiquitous logo-blasting approach to identify the product and to gain mass attention is often inappropriate. In today's world, it is not enough to plaster your brand name on dozens of products and line extensions. It's not enough to roll out merchandise from T-shirts and toys to pins and key chains. It is not even enough to have swoosh-shaped door handles (if you are Nike) or CC-shaped door handles (if you are Chanel) in your retail space. All these elements—the products, the merchandising materials, the design elements in your store—may be necessary and may be a good idea. But they need to enhance the brand. They need to appeal to all five senses, and the heart and the mind. They need to relate the brand to something the consumer cares about, thus incorporating it into the consumer's daily life. As shown in Figure 1.4, this requires the use of all communication elements and of events and contacts to provide an integrated holistic experience: Brand=Ex.

SUMMARY

The purpose of this book is to provide managers with a new look at the goal of marketing. Most managers (and academics) have not been trained to think of marketing and branding in terms of experiences. Managers tend to assume that rational consumers are seeking benefits based on functional product features, and that they engage in comparison shopping and decision making by comparing functional features and benefits among different products.

This model of the "feature- and benefit-driven consumer," however, is only part of the picture. Increasingly, marketers understand that consumers

FIGURE 1.4

Two Approaches to Branding

Two Approaches to
Branding

Brand=ID

Brands as **identifiers**

Brand names, logos, and **slogans**

Awareness and **image**

Brand=EX

Brands as **experience providers**

Names, logos, slogans, events, and other **customer contacts**

Sensory, affective, creative relations, and **lifestyles** with the brand

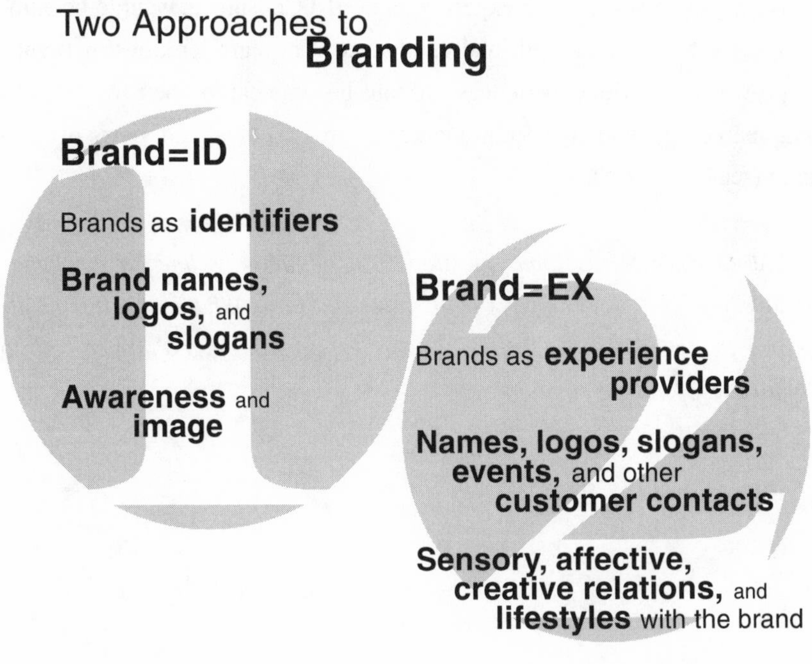

FIGURE 1.5

The Essence of the Two Marketing Paradigms

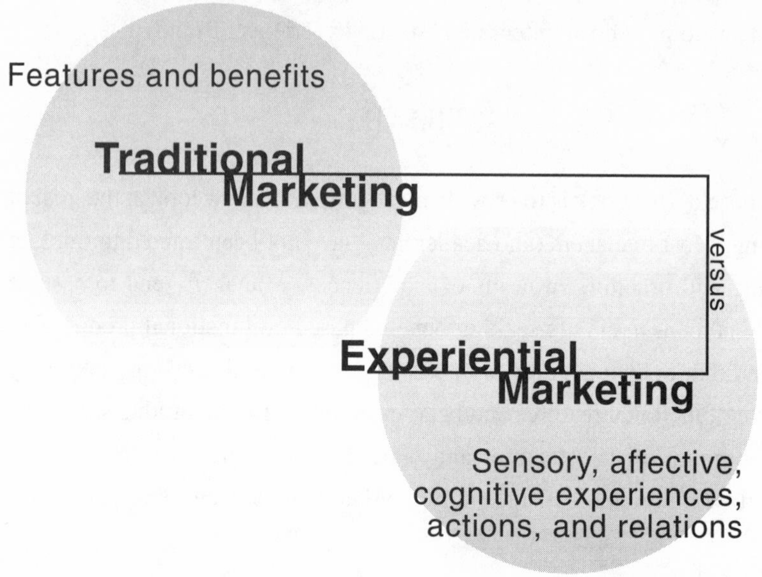

Features and benefits

Traditional
Marketing

versus

Experiential
Marketing

Sensory, affective,
cognitive experiences,
actions, and relations

are living human beings with experiential needs: Consumers want to be stimulated, entertained, educated, and challenged. They are looking for brands that provide them with experiences and thus become part of their lives. Traditional marketing and experiential marketing are two divergent views of marketing (see Figure 1.5).

But LAURA BROWN has some questions: All this may be fine for consumer products, but what if a company is an industrial firm? What if it is a consulting firm, or a medical practice? How does experiential marketing come into play for these kinds of companies?

2

THE BREADTH AND SCOPE OF EXPERIENTIAL MARKETING

Experiential marketing is being used by more and more businesses to forge experiential connections with customers. Everywhere you look today, you see examples of experiential marketing. In a wide variety of product and service categories, features-and-benefits marketing is being discarded in favor of a more vital, experiential approach.

"Understanding the customer experience" has been identified as a capital topic in utmost need of scholarly study by the executives of the membership companies of the Marketing Science Institute, an organization in Cambridge, Massachusetts, that brings together sponsoring companies with leading marketing researchers.

Experiential marketing is particularly relevant to multinationals in their drive to build global brands. As *Newsweek* stated: "Pity the poor multinational marketing executive, grappling with the task of selling hamburgers or cans of soda by the millions." Yet, the article continues, in facing the challenge, many companies are relying on a new approach: "The folks at Gillette, Coke and MasterCard call it 'experiential marketing.'"[1]

Experiential marketing can be used beneficially in many situations including

- To turn around a declining brand
- To differentiate a product from competition
- To create an image and identity for a corporation
- To promote innovations
- To induce trial, purchase and, most important, loyal consumption

So, will experiential marketing replace traditional marketing in its entirety? Or is it an alternative approach that complements traditional marketing? Most important, is experiential marketing likely to last?

Answers to these questions depend on the product category and industry as well as the intended customer target and management. In some industries (consumer products and services) experiential marketing is likely to remain the focus for the foreseeable future, especially given the trends discussed in chapter 1. In other industries (e.g., business-to-business, industrial, and technology markets) experiential marketing enriches the offer and provides a valuable complementary approach to traditional marketing.

For the moment, let's take a look around and see where and how experiential marketing is being used. We'll start our tour with transportation vehicles (like cars, trains, and airplanes) and then move on to more unexpected places where experiential marketing is turning up, such as technology and industrial products; news and entertainment; consulting, medical, and other professional services; and financial products.

THE REALM OF TRANSPORTATION

Transportation vehicles like cars, trains, and airplanes are complex products that offer numerous opportunities to appeal to customer experiences. Relative to many other products, vehicles occupy tremendous space. Moreover, transportation (moving from one place to another) constitutes a consumption situation that extends over time, and it often occurs in the presence of others. Not surprisingly, customers treat transportation vehicles as objects of beauty, passion, and desire. They use transportation vehicles to say something about themselves as well as impress others. Finally, transportation vehicles epitomize a society's tastes, values, and aesthetic preferences.

Cars: Quintessentially Experiential Products

The automotive industry can teach us a lot of valuable lessons about connecting with customers' experiences. From the look, feel, and touch of the car to the actual driving experience, cars provide rich sensations and strong feelings. They stimulate our thinking and affect our actions, thus helping us to define ourselves. Marketers in the car industry have understood for a long time that they are not selling just a product—they are selling a whole complex of feelings and associations and experiences.

Let's take a quick look at some experiential pitches for different cars. In the case of Jaguar, we are dealing with an entirely experiential car. High performance, gorgeous design, and a brilliant tradition all add up to the ideal luxury car.

For years, Jaguar was plagued by quality concerns. Then when Ford took

Ad for Jaguar XJR

over the company in 1989, it used an experiential approach as the basis for re-tooling the rusty brand image.

Nowhere is this experiential approach better captured than in Jaguar's fulfillment video, given to customers when they purchase one of the luxury vehicles. The video tells the story of Jaguar from its beginnings in Blackpool, England, fifty years ago, through its years of glory on the racecourses of the world. The Jaguar tradition is traced right up through today, as designers and factory workers take us through a manufacturing plant in the north of England. Designers talk lovingly about the sensual lines of the car, craftsmen proudly show off the fine woods and leathers used in the interiors, and engineers demonstrate the technological advances of the engine. The connection to Jaguar history is given a personal touch, as factory workers talk about fathers and uncles who worked at the plant in the past.[2]

Jaguar's web site, designed in elegant black and white, carries through the experiential appeal. The home page features a striking photo of the classic Jaguar hood ornament, dramatically lit and almost leaping off the screen, with the slogan "Where inspiration takes shape." The "Heritage" link features an animation of great Jaguars from the past; links to "Quantum Leaps," "Evolution," and "A New Era" take us to pages featuring historical vehicles as well as design and engineering innovations through the years, right through the formation of Jaguar Sport.

Ogilvy and Mather have designed a multipronged marketing approach for Jaguar, themed "Changing your perception of Jaguar." The message across the board tells the story of the dramatic changes that took place at Jaguar since the company's takeover by Ford, including renewed engine and assembly plants and a new self-monitoring diagnostic system for the new XK8. And the campaign extends far beyond a pitch for the "new and improved" Jag—it incorporates the notion of a new breed of Jaguar owner as well. According to Ogilvy and Mather, Jaguar's brandprint explicitly repudiates "features and benefits" thinking in favor of experiential relating: "The difference between Jaguar and other cars runs deeper than sheet metal and engineering. It's about soul, passion, and originality. A Jaguar is a copy of nothing . . . just like its owners."

Jaguar's "Lifestyle/Windows" campaign links the XJ8, another new

Jaguar model, with the consumer's passion for life. A lush television ad shows a diverse group of people, ranging from a twin pair of ethereally beautiful Asian women to a fit African-American cyclist, gazing into the window of a Jag and seeing themselves reflected in the car, both literally and metaphorically. Other ads characterize Jaguar owners as people with a tremendous zest for life, the kind of people who may see themselves mastering mountain golf or kayaking through Class III rapids. Jaguar has done an exceptional job of relating its product to the feelings and aspirations of target buyers.

A rival luxury car, BMW, has launched a similarly evocative campaign billed as "Invitation to the dance." A four-color magazine spread features a shot of a manual gearshift, and on the facing page the text "the steps are even engraved for you." The image creates a strong desire to reach into the photo and grasp the rich walnut-and-leather shift knob and push it into gear. You can almost feel what it is like to be in the driver's seat. The physical appeal of the "dance" of driving, the interplay between car and driver, is palpable. The copy stresses the sensual appeal of manual shift: "In a BMW, you're an active participant in the driving experience, not just an observer. That's why we offer manual transmissions on such a wide range of models. Why sit through a drive when you can revel in it?" The sensual appeal of the print ads is echoed in the TV ad campaign: "The fun is in the curve."

Like Jaguar, BMW creates experiences not only via the medium of television and print ads. There are driver events, sponsorships, flagship showrooms, and an exciting web site featuring a test-drive in the BMW Roadster.

A recent ad for the Lincoln Town Car demonstrates just how far automotive marketing has moved away from traditional features-and-benefits advertising. Twin photos of a sleek Town Car are captioned, respectively, "A dilemma for your accountant: Is it travel? Or entertainment?"

But it's not just luxury cars that focus on experience. The popular sport utility vehicle, with its potential for travel and adventure, is a natural for experiential marketing. One ad for the Mercury Villager shows a pair of photos, one above the other. On the top is a bookshelf, with travel and adventure titles like *Westward Sojourn* and *The Compass Pointed North*. Beneath is a shot of a Mercury Villager parked on a remote seaside cliff, a misty sunset in the background. The tag line reads, "Instead of just reading about adventures, imagine

having more of your own. Imagine yourself in a Mercury." And the copy begins with an explicit reference to experience: "You could fill a few books on
the shelf with your own experiences."

Ford has put a creative experiential spin on marketing its products
through its sponsorship of the Ford Center for the Performing Arts as part of
the New York Times Square renaissance program. This beautiful new theater
is in fact a restoration of a building that housed two venerable Broadway theaters, the Lyric and the Apollo. No expense has been spared to create a world-
class performing arts center, and the beautiful lobby has been designed in
the turn-of-the-century style of the theater's first show, an adaptation of
E. L. Doctorow's novel *Ragtime.* Reproductions of early Ford advertising
posters hang framed in the lobby. The show itself traces the intertwining lives
of several fictional American families and also features real-life characters
such as J. P. Morgan, Booker T. Washington, and—not coincidentally—
Henry Ford himself. At the center of the plot is a beautiful car that rolls dramatically off the assembly line at the end of a production number set in a Ford
plant. Program notes for the play profile Ford and his innovation of the assem-
bly-line production process, while also acknowledging some of the darker
sides of Ford's character. The program itself is entirely a Ford production:
most Broadway shows distribute a magazine called *Playbill,* but because
Playbill accepts advertisements for other brands, Ford banned the publication
and created a lookalike program named *Showbill.* Needless to say, *Showbill*
features only Ford products. A focused and integrated effort has been made to
link Ford and its theater with the spirit of *Ragtime* and Broadway in general.
As Ross Roberts, a Ford vice president, writes in the program, "Ford is proud
to participate in the restoration of the . . . legendary Lyric and Apollo theatres,
which opened at about the same time the Model T came along. Ford and
Broadway have been part of the fabric of American life for virtually the entire

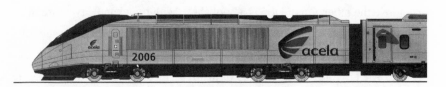

century. At Ford, we know the vitality of our company comes from being involved in the community not just economically, but culturally as well. . . . *Ragtime* looks back to the time when Broadway and Ford were in their infancies. As you enjoy the performance, I hope you'll take a moment to look around you. Imagine how much theatrical history has transpired on this site. Imagine how much more is yet to come. We're here to celebrate both."

Amtrak: A New High-Speed Train for the New Century

Trains, like cars, offer plenty of opportunities to appeal to customer experiences. Famous trains of the past, like the *Orient Express,* have become fantasy products. The long-distance train ride experience had been a luxury. Ladies dressed in hats, gloves, and suits; the men too were attired in suits. Dining, as well, was a luxurious experience. Yet if cars are now marketed to customers as the experiential products that they are, trains—at least in the United States—have until recently been viewed in purely functional and utilitarian terms.

A new comprehensive branding effort underway at the National Railroad Passenger Corporation, Amtrak, is supposed to change all that and increase market share and revenues for a corporation currently struggling for survival.[3]

"I think that it is a terrific example of experiential marketing," wrote Barbara Richardson, corporate chief of staff, in her letter in which she graciously shared with me information about Amtrak's branding efforts and the new high-speed rail service from Boston to Washington, D.C. I had met Ms. Richardson shortly before in an executive program in which I presented the concept of experiential marketing.

The Amtrak brand revitalization approach represents one of the most ambitious, comprehensive, and systematic experiential marketing approaches I

Interiors of the Amtrak trains

have ever seen. The approach was guided by a simple formula: Brand = Reputation (in the marketplace) + Promise (to the marketplace) + Experience (of customers). It encompassed market-focused business planning and a product strategy (including new product planning, service strategy development, and the development of national service standards), as well as positioning, visual identity development, marketing communications, and employee communications. Travel market trends, nationwide focus groups, anthropological studies, and brand foundation research conducted by DDB Needham pointed to an opportunity that Amtrak had thus far failed to grasp. Train travel had an appealing, distinctive image full of experiential aspects such as self-discovery, scenery, relaxation, romance, and sociability. The company, however, was seen as complacent, outdated, and old-fashioned in focus, and the typical cus-

tomer was seen as an old-fashioned "Sears/Kmart/Wal-Mart value shopper," disheveled, unkempt, and a little shabby. To change all that, Amtrak committed itself to "humanizing travel" by giving travelers more control over the quality of the travel experience. A positioning video aired at the Amtrak Board of Directors Meeting in April 1998 stated: "We are Amtrak and we take you to a place no one else can/A place where you find self-enrichment/Where your individuality is respected/Where you can discover your potential/Where you can commune and share ideas and adventures/We are Amtrak."

The new high-speed rail launched in 1999 sets new transportation standards—the highest speed in the United States (up to 150 m.p.h.), world safety standards, and interior (and exterior) design innovations focusing on the entire experience of the traveler from the initial contact throughout the journey.

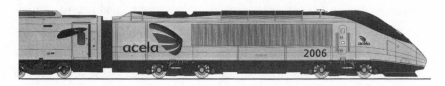

Singapore Airlines: A New Experience Takes Flight

Like trains, U.S. airlines are typically not the place of rich and rewarding customer experiences—to say the least. Lost baggage, flight delays and, most important, inattentive, rude in-flight service and often dirty aircraft have resulted in a bad reputation for the industry as a whole and have destroyed the romance of air travel.

In Asia the picture is entirely different. Many Asian airlines (such as Hong Kong–based Cathay Pacific Airways, the Japanese carriers Japan Airlines and All Nippon Airlines, Malaysian Airways, Thai Airways, Korean Air, and the Korean upstart Asiana Airlines) have become known for their superb in-flight service. But the queen of them all is Singapore Airlines, a carrier with a long and brilliant history of customer service.

Singapore Airlines' success story has been based on its attention to customer needs and marketing of its distinct identity. It was out of this idea that the "Singapore Girl" was born—the flight attendant who has become an icon of personal caring and attentiveness, attired in a distinctive batik sarong that conveys the country's culture. The Singapore Girl is more than just promotion: over the years the airline has devoted great care to selecting, training, and retaining the very best flight attendants, paying them above-average wages, and offering them promotions to senior staff positions. This attention to customer needs has paid off, making Singapore Airlines one of the ten largest and one of the most profitable airlines in the world.

I first experienced the Singapore Airlines service aboard its inaugural flight on July 2, 1992, from New York to Singapore. Like many other customers, I was stunned by the meticulous attention to detail and overall service experience. In 1998, the company outdid itself by taking its customer service to new heights and providing an even more sophisticated appeal to customer experiences.[4]

The airline put luxurious Boeing 747-400s (called "Megatop 747s" by Singapore Airlines) into service, featuring leather and wood interiors, mini-suites in first class, built-in air mattresses, feather comforters, dinnerware designed by Givenchy, and enlarged personal video screens showing over sixty entertainment options. In-flight service is complemented by improved ground

Singapore Airlines first-class cabin and first-class food

services that begin at curbside, where first-class passengers are met and personally escorted into an elegant reception lounge.

Singapore Airlines' Deputy Chairman and CEO Cheong Choong Kong explains the initiative behind Singapore Airlines' US$300 million biggest-ever product launch: "The product launch involves every dimension of the customer's experience with the airline. We looked at everything. . . . Although our current product continues to rank among the best in the industry, it was time to make a bold and exciting change. We wanted to send a very clear message to the industry: our customers expect the best of SIA, and the best is what they will get." Singapore Airlines' new experiential initiative is heralded by their web site and print advertising proclaiming, "A new air travel experience takes wing." It is supported by a new advertising campaign with the theme "Now more than ever, a great way to fly."

In sum, the realm of transportation vehicles provides a rich benchmark for experiential marketing in other industries. Therefore, among many other industries, I will feature examples from the cars and airlines industry at several other places in this book.

AUNTIE ANNE'S: CREATING AN EXPERIENCE IN A TRANSITIONAL ENVIRONMENT

Experiential marketing is not limited to transportation vehicles as such. At gas stations (e.g., Mobil in California), airports (e.g., Denver and Hong Kong), train stations (e.g., the new Grand Central in New York), and malls, experiential marketing is evident just as well.

Or, consider Auntie Anne's Soft Pretzels, a wholesome, low-fat snack from the vendor at airports and train stations.[5] Drawing on associations from the American countryside, Auntie Anne's presents an experiential marketing campaign. The campaign starts with the sensory appeal of the product itself. Baking is done on the premises, and the aroma wafting from an Auntie Anne's store is enough to trigger any passing shopper or traveler to act and buy a pretzel. All pretzels sold have been made within the past half-hour, ensuring that customers receive a warm pretzel. And the company's slogan, "Better than the best you've ever tasted," does not oversell the quality of these pretzels.

Sensory appeal is carried through in the company's signage and promotional materials. Auntie Anne's consistently uses Pantone blue 292 on a white background, a calming, simple choice evocative of the Pennsylvania Dutch associations of the product. The typeface used is old-fashioned, appearing almost handwritten, suggesting a company that is people oriented.

Customers can relate to Auntie Anne the person as well as the shop. The name is traditional, wholesome, and familiar, and pictures of Anne herself are used as a symbol for the business. Anne's signature appears on every brochure, and she is pictured making the pretzels herself. Promotional materials also use pictures of children, fairhaired, barefooted, wearing straw hats and suspenders, encouraging us to relate to simpler times and simpler pleasures.

Consumers are also encouraged to feel good about this company. Auntie Anne's donates a portion of its profits to charity, in keeping with its statement that "Auntie Anne's is not about ourselves, it is about helping others." The stores are franchises, and a family feeling pervades the relations between the company and its franchisees. One promotional piece goes so far as to say that Auntie Anne's is fighting the "breakdown of the American family unit." Regardless of its success in that area, Auntie Anne's is a booming success for experiential marketing and a wonderfully managed brand.

Let's look at some more unexpected places where experiential marketing is turning up.

TECHNOLOGY PRODUCTS: THE PALM COMPUTING PRODUCTS, CROSSWORLDS SOFTWARE, AND MICROSOFT

A good place to start our tour is technology products. Constantly innovating and improving their features and benefits, these product have nevertheless embraced an experiential approach—not just in marketing but also in product design.

Consider the cool new products the Palm III and Palm V Organizers by 3Com Palm Computing, Inc., a company which I mentioned in chapter 1. Positioned to compete with standard techno organizers by PSION or Hewlett-

Packard, the Palm Computing Products look more like Gameboys than typical organizers. They don't even have a keyboard. What's more, they can "talk" to each other, using infrared technology to "beam" data. Used to their fullest potential, the Palm III and Palm V Organizers can become the center of all your information needs: carry them with you and use them to "talk" to other Palm III and Palm V Organizers; take them to the office where, placed in their cradles, they can "talk" to your PC. You can get rid of your datebook, your business cards, your desk calendar. The Palm Computing Products set the stage for a complete reorganization and reconceptualization of your life—and they are so cool.

Now imagine you're flipping through the staid advertising pages of *The Economist.* Suddenly you come across a full-page spread of a striking-looking woman. Standing against a white background, she's wearing a low-cut black cocktail dress and diamond earrings. She's looking confidently into the camera; that is, right at you.

The shot is by fashion photographer Richard Avedon, the hair and makeup are professional, but this woman is not a model. She's Katrina Garnett, founder, president, and CEO of California-based CrossWorlds Software, and she's all business. CrossWorlds is a hot new global company that has attracted talent from Microsoft, Netscape, Allied Signal, and McKinsey. Its corporate investors include Intel and Compaq, among others, and it is the acknowledged industry leader in enterprise application integration. Garnett, CrossWorlds' thirty-six-year-old founder, is a mother of two who has installed a nursery next to her office. Featured in a *Newsweek* article and as part of a *Forbes* cover story on female business owners among other high-profile media exposures, Garnett has enough business savvy and experience to hold her own in the fastest corporate company. But her venture into fashion photography—and experiential marketing—has probably attracted more attention than any amount of corporate achievement.[6]

Even Microsoft is now running campaigns that focus on thought experiences and imagination rather than on their latest technological innovations. In print ads, Microsoft asks, "Where do you want to go next?" The campaign is about potential and about dreams, decidedly *not* about features and benefits. I will discuss that campaign in more detail in the next chapter.

CrossWorlds ad featuring founder and CEO Katrina Garnett

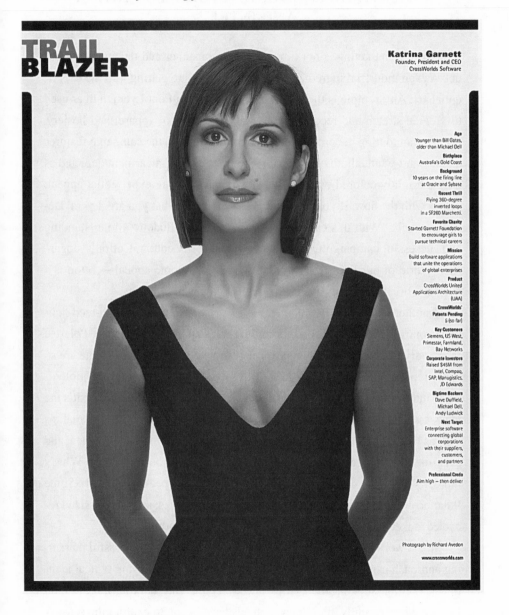

INDUSTRIAL PRODUCTS: LYCRA, POLARTEC, AND INTEL

Experiential marketing is not limited just to consumer and technology products—even industrial ingredients and components are getting into the experiential act. An example is the recent campaign for Du Pont Lycra, a fiber used to provide stretch and recovery in a variety of types of apparel and hosiery. Rather than touting the product's durability or strength, the campaign features a black-and-white photo of a woman's body "wearing" a garment depicted as only a brightly colored outline. The slogan has a strong experiential appeal: "Goes with the flow. If you are what you wear, wear what you are. Lycra. Define yourself." With this campaign, Lycra seems to allude to a long-standing and successful campaign for another popular fabric: cotton. Cotton's slogan, "The fabric of our lives," has a comforting, down-home appeal—cotton is a natural fabric that has always been with us and always will be.

Another experiential component is Polartec, a family of high-tech "climate control fabrics" designed for cutting-edge sports performance. Polartec fabrics dry quickly and keep you warm even when they are wet. Some are so water-repellent they can be used for scuba diving. But it is not the technological features and benefits of the products that make them so appealing; it's the ideas associated with Polartec that make it a favorite for wear at the mall as well as on the mountainside. Polartec has the cachet of top performance, and even the most sluggish couch potato can wear what the pros wear. What's more, its high-tech design makes it cool (figuratively speaking, that is). Some Polartec products are even made of recycled soda bottles; an average-sized recycled jacket keeps 25 two-liter soda bottles out of landfills.[7]

In the world of computer chips, we can also see a very successful marketing approach using experiential techniques. Intel had been using typical identity marketing, sticking their chips into every PC and marking boxes "Intel Inside." More recently, their television ads have begun to explore the sensory realm, with Intel's "auditory slogan," a distinctive little four-tone jingle. Of course, for years Macintosh and Windows have used this kind of musical trademark in their characteristic start-up tones. But Intel is the first component maker that uses the same approach in their marketing.

Du Pont ad for Lycra

NEWS AND ENTERTAINMENT: OPRAH WINFREY, CNN, AND CNBC

Turn on the television and you will see an explosion of experiential programming. I'm not just talking about the obviously fictional shows that have
always run—movies, sitcoms, and the like. I mean the new breed of experien-

tial programming that has usurped traditional genres. From Oprah Winfrey to Montel Williams to Jerry Springer and so on, the genre of "talk show" has been transformed into "experience show." Even news programming is now about experience and entertainment. CNN has been masterful at spinning the news into a wide variety of soft features: *CNN and Co.,* a talk/news show pitched for women; *Crossfire,* presenting pugilistic exchanges about current events from the left- and right-wing perspectives; and the popular *Larry King Live,* an interview program that presents challenging issues in a stimulating and entertaining format. Other networks have been quick to develop experiential shows of their own, like *Hardball* on CNBC.

CONSULTING, MEDICAL, AND OTHER PROFESSIONAL SERVICES: ANDERSEN CONSULTING, CRYSTAL RUN HEALTH CARE LLP, AND KINKO'S

Management consulting firms have traditionally eschewed advertising campaigns. According to Robert Duboff of Mercer Management, "Ten years ago, if I'd suggested we advertise, I'd have been shot; five years ago I'd have been whipped."[8] The largest consulting firm in the world, with 59,000 employees at the time of writing, Andersen Consulting broke ranks in 1994 by leapfrogging traditional marketing and initiating an experiential branding campaign to establish its identity and distinct position in the consulting marketplace. Young & Rubicam was called upon to develop this campaign, communicating Andersen Consulting's unique holistic approach to management consulting, in which strategy formulation, information technology, people, and work processes are seen not separately, but as elements that should be designed to work in concert.

One of the first ads developed by Y&R to communicate this holistic approach featured a school of fish banding together and swimming in a formation resembling a shark. The fish, by themselves an easy mark for predators, can thus navigate through their environment with confidence. The reader or viewer is then asked the pivotal question: "What shape is your business in?"

Later ads similarly stressed the idea of teams accomplishing objectives

Andersen Consulting advertisement

that would be out of reach for the constituent parts individually. In the "Birds" ad launched in January 1998, for instance, five hawks dive down to the surface of a lake and together manage to pull an improbably large fish out of the water.

It would have been tempting for Andersen Consulting to go with a traditional features-and-benefits approach, reciting impressive statistics and cases of spectacular success. But research had demonstrated that viewers' eyes just glazed over at this kind of information, and it was thought that with this cynical and overexposed target audience a simple message would have the greatest impact. In the end, the ads carry almost no copy, and the appeal is entirely experiential. And in keeping with Andersen Consulting's global presence, it is an added bonus that the metaphorical language is equally comprehensible to all cultures.

Like management consulting, the medical profession traditionally has not been sensitive to experiences. In fact, professional societies like the American Medical Association prohibited their members from advertising. Once the Supreme Court ruled that the "learned professions" of law and medicine were subject to antitrust laws, these professionals were free to advertise their services and began to educate themselves about marketing.

Let me share with you the case of Crystal Run Health Care LLP, a small group medical practice that happens to be run by one of my former executive MBA students, Dr. Hal Teitelbaum, M.D. When Hal and his partner, Robert Dinsmore, first started advertising their practice, they relied on traditional, highly conservative print advertising: "Hal Teitelbaum, M.D., and Robert Dinsmore, M.D., are pleased to announce that they are now accepting new patients in the specialty of Internal Medicine. Hours by appointment. Participate in most insurance plans." The copy is factual and straightforward but gives potential patients absolutely no feeling for the doctors or their practice. It was marketing that seemed to reflect the AMA's old position that there was something unprofessional or unseemly about promoting a medical practice. What's more, it seemed entirely out of step with the powerful emotional associations that medical care evokes and that marketing can tap into.

But as the doctors' business expanded, they began to conceive of their practice in an experiential, integrated way. After all, for most of us, going to the doctor is an experience that adds up to much more than the competence of the service we receive. To be sure, we expect professional and reliable treatment. But we also want to feel that our doctors care about us (for more than just our checkbooks) and understand our lifestyles and our values. To create a new image and identity for their practice that would reflect this human and caring element, Hal and Bob turned to experiential marketing.

Their first step was to choose a name. Their goal was to find a name that would convey the essence of their practice. They were especially concerned to avoid anything that might seem cold and sterile. The name "Crystal Run" was initially suggested by the historical name of the region where their main office is located. The name has no specific meaning, but the doctors liked it because it suggested calmness, pureness, and clarity—all values they felt represented their consumer-focused health care practice.

The next step was designing a logo. With the help of a graphic designer, they created a logo with curved edges and three gently waving lines on a blue background, suggesting the clear path of a stream. The doctors felt the use of curved elements in the logo suggested a softer, more personal identity in a field that is becoming increasingly high-tech and impersonal. The image of the flowing stream reinforced the soothing, calming message conveyed in the name of the practice.

Their print advertising changed as well. One ad displayed their new logo with the headline "Return of the family doctor." In this simple phrase, the ad harks back to a time when a visit to the doctor was not a trip down an assembly line but a consultation with an old and trusted friend. Later ads featured pictures of the practice doctors themselves, literally putting a human face on the sometimes frighteningly impersonal world of medical care.

Even a relatively small business, in an industry not traditionally attuned to marketing, can reap the benefits of experiential marketing techniques.

And experiential marketing will be increasingly important for larger health care providers such as HMOs as health care becomes more business- and finance-driven. Customers will continue to expect the human touch in medical care and will look for an experience they can relate to. As health care becomes more of a commodity, and as the industry becomes more competitive, providers can differentiate themselves from their competitors through the experiences they offer consumers, not just in the office but in promotional materials as well.

Kinko's, the national chain of photocopying and office-services outlets, uses an experiential approach that relates to the lifestyles of people running their own businesses. Kinko's is styling itself "The new place to office," and its web site offers the derivation of this new verb: "How a noun became a verb. The office isn't what it used to be. That's because the way we think of the office is changing. (*Uh, roger, Houston, we've got a paradigm shift.*) More and more, the term office defines a state of activity rather than a place. Instead of adapting our lives to it, the office is becoming what we need it to be. This is a good thing. As long as the tools and the knowledge are available to make it work. And they are. At Kinko's. We have the equipment and expertise to help companies and individuals do a better job creating and producing documents. . . . With Kinko's, you have an office (*noun*) but only when you need to office (*verb*). That's why we're the new way to office." The copy is peppered with trendy expressions—its message is that Kinko's speaks your language and understands your needs. Print ads feature little quotations representing the thoughts of small business operators: "Do I really need an office?" "I'm getting more done. So is the rest of the world." "With Kinko's, I'll office whenever I need to." By tapping into the experiences of its target customers, Kinko's is able to style itself as a part of their lifestyles.

FINANCIAL PRODUCTS

Financial products, perhaps the best example of rational-marketing products, have also discovered the virtues of an experiential approach to marketing. Over the last couple of years, I have seen more and more mutual funds use experiential metaphors: rock climbers to illustrate the challenge of investing; Brahms' "*Guten Abend, gute Nacht*" to say "Don't worry"; a fogged front mirror in a car to illustrate "clear strategy, clear vision." Marketers have realized that people have feelings about financial products—indeed, some of our strongest feelings are connected to the ideas of well-being and security associated with financial success. With experiential marketing, financial products can tap into these intense feelings without sacrificing the message of conser-

PEOPLE AS EXPERIENTIAL BRANDS

It's not just products and companies that are branded today; individuals as diverse as artists, businessmen, and sports celebrities are perfecting the art of experiential branding.

Consider the image and the subsequent (at times involuntary) branding of the actress Gwyneth Paltrow. She appeals to everybody at all times at all levels. In *Shakespeare in Love* she is an independent thinker, a free spirit, a modern woman in period dress, and even a man. She is present on hundreds of web sites, newsgroups and chat rooms worldwide. Her face and character have assumed an iconic and mythical quality. She is the modern Helena of Goethe's Faust II.

With Andy Warhol artwork fetching top dollar around the world, his instantly recognizable style identifies not just the art but the artist himself as a brand. And now, according to *The Economist,* aspiring artists, seeing by the success of the lucrative Warhol brand, are increasingly treating themselves as products: "They want to make themselves into brands so that their mere names conjure up a host of assorted values which (they hope) will lure consumers into buying their output."[9]

An example from Asia is David Tang, the Hong Kong millionaire and owner of China Clubs in Hong Kong and Beijing, who is making the name Shanghai Tang known to the fashion world. Shanghai Tang boutiques feature elegant designs with a traditional Chinese touch. His trademark "Tang suit" features a Mandarin jacket over billowing silk pants. The traditional cheongsam is restyled as cutting-edge fashion. Tang has also taken the drab Mao jacket, run it up in lime green, and created a fashion hit. But Tang isn't just a designer: trained as an attorney, he has spun a series of business ventures and has also promoted himself as quite an unusual business person. In 1998, Mr. Tang was featured on CBS's *60 Minutes.*

Later on, we'll take a close look at Michael Jordan's foray into the fragrance business. In 1998, before Jordan retired, *Fortune* magazine estimated his impact on the economy as a staggering $10 billion. From product endorsements to movie appearances to sneaker designs, Jordan has become an empire unto himself, shaping our perceptions not just of products but also of sports and athletes in general. In the words of Bill Schmidt, vice president of worldwide sports marketing at Gatorade, Michael Jordan is "a property much like the NBA, NFL, or any other property. We manage him as if he were a brand"[10] vatism and responsibility traditionally associated with the marketing of these products.

In summary, a growing number of successful companies are learning that it pays to market their products and services by tapping into consumers' experiences. Experiential marketing is all around us—the more you look, the more you see. It is being used by major global conglomerates and small local brands alike. From cars to industrial ingredients to professional and financial services and beyond, more and more businesses are using experiential marketing to forge strong connections with customers.

HOW DO TRADITIONAL MARKETERS VIEW EXPERIENTIAL MARKETING?

Traditional marketers are surprised by these trends and are unable to comprehend them within the customary F&B approach. For them, experiential aspects of products are "irrelevant attributes" and "meaningless differentiation" that fool naïve customers.

In a much-quoted article from the prestigious *Journal of Marketing Research* entitled "Meaningful Brands from Meaningless Differentiation: The Dependence on Irrelevant Attributes," professors Gregory Carpenter of Northwestern University, Rashi Glazer of the University of California at Berkeley, and Kent Nakamoto of the University of Colorado write:

"[Michael] Porter describes differentiation as developing a unique position on an attribute that is 'widely valued by buyers' (Porter 1985, p. 14). However, many brands also successfully differentiate on an attribute that *appears* [emphasis by the authors] valuable but, on closer examination, is irrelevant to creating the implied benefit. For example, Procter & Gamble differentiates instant Folger's coffee by its 'flaked coffee crystals' created through a 'unique, patented process,' implying (but not stating) in its advertising that flaked coffee crystals improve the taste of coffee. In fact, the shape of the coffee particle is relevant for ground coffee (greater surface area exposed during brewing extracts more flavor), but it is irrelevant for instant coffee: the crystal simply dissolves, so its surface area does not affect flavor. Similarly, Alberto Culver differentiates its Alberto Natural Silk shampoo by including silk in the shampoo, and advertising it with the slogan 'We put silk in a bottle' to suggest a user's hair will be silky. However, a company spokesman conceded that silk 'doesn't really do anything for hair' (*Adweek,* 1986). Consumers apparently value these differentiating attributes even though they are, in one sense, irrelevant."[11]

After investigating the phenomenon further through experimental studies, the authors are surprised when they find that this "meaningless differentiation" is sustainable and that increasing price increases demand. "Our results show that meaningless differentiation is valued by consumers in a surprising number of situations. For example, meaningless differentiation is valued even if the differentiated brand is priced above all others, and, more surprisingly, in some cases increasing price actually can increase preference for the differentiated brand. Furthermore, the competitive advantage created by adding an irrelevant attribute can be sustained even if consumers acknowledge that the differentiating attribute is irrelevant."

I have no problem whatsoever with any of the findings. I do not question them for a minute. What boggles my mind is the terminology and interpretation of "irrelevant" and "meaningless." These attributes are only irrelevant and meaningless from a traditional F&B perspective, just as many natural phenomena made no sense as long as people assumed that the world was flat. From an experiential marketing perspective, there is nothing surprising here. Flaked coffee crystals, silk in a shampoo bottle—as well as some of the other brand attributes these authors used in their experiments, such as authentic Milanese-style pasta, Alpine-class down-filled jackets, and studio-designed signal processing systems for compact disc players—provide sensory, affective, and creative associations. They generate experiences through language and symbolism and thus enrich a brand. Today's consumers are simply not what the rational model of marketing wants them to be.

AN OVERVIEW OF THE REMAINDER OF THE BOOK

Experiential marketing is everywhere, but the question remains, What exactly is an experience? Why are experiences important? Are there different types of experiences? And how can marketers tap into these customer experiences?

Finally, how can we manage experiences strategically, and what type of organization is needed for doing the job well?

The remainder of the book addresses these questions. Chapter 3 defines the term "experience" and provides a conceptual framework for managing customer experiences, distinguishing five types of experiences and different ways of providing these customer experiences. In chapters 4 through 8, I will describe each type of experience and show how marketers can create and manage it. In the remaining chapters, I will discuss broader issues of experiential marketing. Chapter 9 addresses structural issues. I will show how marketers can build experiential hybrids and accomplish the ultimate goal of experiential marketing: holistically integrated experiences. Chapter 10 discusses a variety of strategic issues. Chapter 11 concludes with a discussion of organizational issues of experiential marketing.

And at the end of each chapter, you will make contact with the critical voice of LAURA BROWN.

3

A FRAMEWORK FOR MANAGING CUSTOMER EXPERIENCES

In chapter 1, I argued that it is increasingly necessary to appeal to customer experiences because of three converging trends occurring at the turn of the new century. In chapter 2, I have provided numerous applications of successful experiential marketing in a variety of industries. There is, however, a more fundamental reason why any marketer should consider experiences and not only functional features and benefits.

For centuries, philosophers from Aristotle to Kant, psychologists from William James to Carl Rogers, and other more popular thinkers from Steve Covey to Woody Allen, have repeatedly asked the question: What motivates people? What makes life worth living? What is a good life?

And the (admittedly vague but important) consensus is: something beyond mere need satisfaction; something beyond the constraints of "stimulus-response" reactions; something that somehow transcends our lives. Mihaly Csikszentmihalyi, a professor and former chairman of the Psychology Department at the University of Chicago, calls this something "Flow." For Csikszentmihalyi, flow is about optimal experiences and enjoyment in life: "flow through the senses," "the flow of thought," "the body in flow," "other people as flow," and (yes!) "enjoying work as flow." Flow is in the mind, it is about "the making of meaning"; the ultimate goal is "turning all life into a unified

59

flow experience."[1] Interestingly enough, the German word for experience, *Erlebnis,* is etymologically related to the verb "to live" (*leben*).

Don't let the "flower power"/"new age" terminology disturb you. You can change the terms. The bottom line for you as a manager remains: you have to somehow enrich people's lives and provide enjoyment for your customers. To define the purpose of marketing in terms of need satisfaction, problem solution, or benefit delivery is too narrow. The ultimate—if you will, humanistic—goal of marketing is providing customers with valuable (i.e., optimal) experiences.

Peter Drucker wrote: "There is only one valid definition of business purpose: to create a customer."[2] Similarly, there is only one valid definition of the purpose of marketing: to create a valuable customer experience. And it is good business: your customers will thank you for it, stay loyal to your business, and pay a premium for it.

In this chapter, I provide a conceptual framework for managing customer experiences.[3] The framework focuses on two key concepts: strategic experiential modules (SEMs), which constitute different types of experiences with their own distinct structures and principles, and experience providers (ExPros) through which the SEMs are created. However, before I discuss the framework, let us first briefly focus on philosophical and definitional issues.

WHAT EXACTLY IS AN EXPERIENCE?

Experiences are private events that occur in response to some stimulation (e.g., as provided by marketing efforts before and after purchase). Experiences involve the entire living being. They often result from direct observation and/or participation in events—whether they are real, dreamlike, or virtual. As philosopher Merleau-Ponty put it in his well-known book *Phenomenology of Perception,* "The world is not an object such that I have in my possession the law of its making; it is the natural setting of, and field for, all my thoughts and all my explicit perceptions."[4] In other words, as a marketer you need to provide the right environment and setting for the desired customer experiences to emerge.

Experiences are usually not self-generated but induced. Or, as philosophers and psychologists in the phenomenological tradition have called it, experiences are "of" or "about" something; they have reference and intentionality.[5] This basic fact of experiences is clearly reflected in language. As psycholinguists Roger Brown and Deborah Fish have demonstrated, verbs that describe experiences (such as "like," "admire," "hate," "attract") typically describe the stimulus that produces the experience as opposed to the person who has the experience.[6] To demonstrate this, they showed people simple sentences of the type "X likes Y" and asked: "Is this because X is the kind of person who generally likes other people, or is this because Y is the type of person whom other people typically like?" Brown and Fish found that people tend to assume the latter, and not only for "like" but for most other experience verbs (such as "admire," "hate," "attract," etc.). Indeed, language reflects this assumption: derivatives of these experience words such as "likeable," "admirable," "hateful," and attractive" all refer to the stimulus—not to the person who has the experience. This is true not only for English but also many other languages psycholinguists have researched.

As a marketer, you provide stimuli that result in customer experiences: you select the "experience providers." You are in charge. Depending on what you do and how you do it, your company and brand are seen as more or less likeable, admirable, or attractive. This does not mean that the consumer is passive. It means that you have to take the first action. This is how the world works, and it has been incorporated as a general experience schema into our languages.

One last point about experiences. Experiences may be viewed as complex, emerging structures.[7] Emerging structures in the physical world display what is called "perpetual novelty." That is, no two experiences are exactly alike. But, as we will see, they may nonetheless be categorized in terms of their generic emerging properties into different types of experiences. Therefore, as a manager, rather than being concerned with any particular individual experience, you need to ask yourself the more important strategic question of what types of experiences you want to provide and how you can provide them with perpetually fresh appeal.

EXPERIENCES AS TYPOLOGIES OF THE MIND

To use experiences as part of marketing strategy and practice, it is essential to discuss some key neurobiological and psychological facts regarding experiences. The idea that there are distinct functional areas in the brain that correspond with distinct experiences has been called the "modular view of the mind."

"The word 'module' brings to mind detachable, snap-in components, and that is misleading. Mental modules are not likely to be visible to the naked eye as circumscribed territories on the surface of the brain, like the flank steak and the rump roast on the supermarket cow display. [. . .] Modules are defined by the special things they do with information available to them, not necessarily by the kinds of information they have available."[8]

In other words, the physical substrate is always identical, no matter what and how you experience it: it is always a matter of nerve cells forming connections among information by relaying chemical and electric impulses. However, in terms of the phenomenology of experience, there are several distinct functional areas.[9]

First, there is a perceptual or sensory system located in the thalamus. This system processes the sensory input in the form of light waves, sound waves, haptic and textile information that reaches the retina, the ear, and other sensors. Then there is an affective system, which is housed in two separate locations: first, in the limbic system and a nearby region called the amygdala, as well as in the neocortex. The "lower systems" of the limbic system and the amygdala produce a fast "gut" affective response without much thought and analysis, whereas the neocortex can produce more complex emotions. Finally, there are other parts of the neocortex which are the seats of elaborate cognition, thinking, and creativity.[10]

Think of it this way. Pick up a knife and have a look at it. It is impossible for you to look at the knife and see it suddenly bending or turning blue or red (even if you are color-blind). You can try as hard as you like; it won't work. So your perception is constrained by your perceptual system and is not really under your voluntary control: Light waves hit your retina and produce a certain impression that you cannot control. Of course, you can imagine the knife flying up and out the window and describe to others how it may land on people who walk by it. But that is cognition, i.e., a thought process of your creative imagination. It is not sensory perception. And, if a mugger ever broke into your house and tried to stab you with this knife, you may still have a weird response in your stomach each time you see it—you can't help it. That is affect, and you can see how affect, like sensation, is partly independent from cognition. In other words, these three systems—sensation, cognition, and affect—have their own structures and principles although they interact to produce one coherent sensory perception, feeling, and thought. Consequently, as we will see later, if our goal as marketers is to appeal to the senses, we need to employ different strategies than if we target feelings or creative thinking.

In addition to sensation, cognition, and affect, psychologists and sociologists often add two more experiential components: first, the individual's actions extended over time (ranging from physical experiences to broader patterns of behavior and lifestyles), and, second, a relational experience, i.e., the individual's experience of belonging to a group, society, or culture.

These philosophical insights as well as neurobiological, psychological, and sociological models provide a solid foundation for developing a conceptual framework for managing customer experiences. Unlike F&B marketing, which lacks a fundamental basis and insightful understanding of customers, experiential marketing is grounded on psychological, yet practical, theory of the individual customer and his/her social behavior. The framework has two aspects: strategic experiential models (SEMs), which form the strategic underpinning of experiential marketing, and experience providers (ExPros), which are the tactical tools of experiential marketing.

THE STRATEGIC UNDERPINNINGS OF EXPERIENTIAL MARKETING: SEMS

Modularity of the mind, i.e., the view that the mind is composed of specialized functional parts, provides a wonderful metaphor and practical lesson for experiential marketing: Experiences may be dissected into different types, each with their own inherent structures and processes. As a manager you may view these different types of experiences as strategic experiential modules (SEMs) that constitute the objectives and strategies of your marketing efforts.

Let me provide a brief description of the five types of customer experiences that form the basis of the Experiential Marketing Framework (see Figure 3.1).

SENSE

SENSE marketing appeals to the senses with the objective of creating sensory experiences through sight, sound, touch, taste, and smell. SENSE marketing may be used to differentiate companies and products, to motivate customers, and to add value to products. As we will see, SENSE marketing requires an understanding of how to achieve sensory impact.

Richart, a maker of luxury chocolates, employs an integrated SENSE marketing approach that fully exploits the experiential nature of chocolate purchase and consumption.[11] This approach starts with the name of the company itself: Richart Design et Chocolat. Richart bills itself as a design company first, a chocolate company second. Attention to design is carried through all the marketing and packaging materials and into the products themselves. The

FIGURE 3.1

Strategic Experiential Modules (SEMs)

SENSE

FEEL

THINK

ACT

RELATE

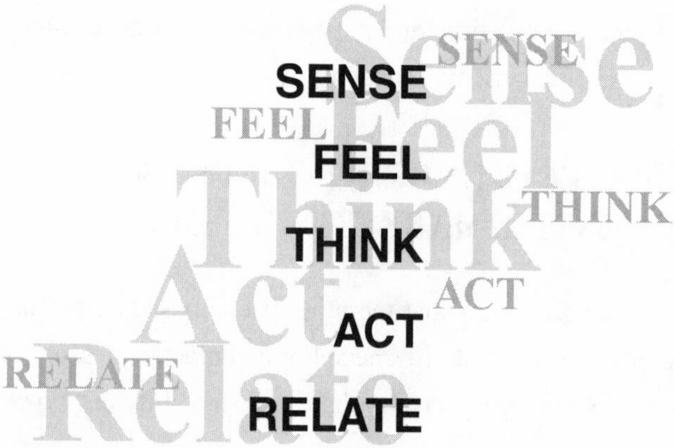

Richart logo is done in an art deco typeface with a distinctive leaning "A" that graphically demarcates the words "rich" and "art." Richart chocolates are sold in a showroom that resembles that of a fine jeweler, with items displayed in glass cases on a spacious, brightly lit sales floor. They are also available through a catalog reminiscent of that of an up-market clothing or jewelry designer, labeled "Collection 97/98." Products are lit and photographed in the catalog as if they were fine pieces of art or jewelry. Headlines in the catalog are in French and English. Promotional materials are printed on smooth, heavy papers.

The packaging is no less elegant. Chocolate boxes are pure glossy white, with gold or silver embossed lettering. Red cloth ribbons seal the packages. Box liners are segmented so that each work of chocolate art is displayed in its own compartment.

The chocolates themselves are a feast for the visual sense. They are beautifully shaped and decorated with different patterns and colors of ornamenta-

Chocolate design for Richart Classics

Gourmande Ballotin
5-drawer ballotin
Petits Richart, Bonbons,
Ultra Fines,
"Children's Design"
and Mendiants
$155 (item GM5)

tions (a special line displays a charming set of children's drawings). Special chocolate plaques can be made to customers' specifications. So precious are these chocolates that Richart even sells a burlwood chocolate vault with temperature and humidity gauges, like a humidor, for $650. And British *Vogue* magazine called Richart Chocolates "the most beautiful chocolates in the world."

Sensory experiences were the subject of the book *Marketing Aesthetics,* which I coauthored in 1997.[12] In it, my coauthor and I coined the term "marketing aesthetics" to refer to "the marketing of sensory experiences in corporate or brand output that contributes to the organization's or brand's identity."[13] In chapter 4, on SENSE, I will review and update some of the material presented in the earlier book. At the same time, I will broaden the focus from identity to marketing efforts that affect pre-purchase, purchase, and consumption processes. Moreover, I will present the S(stimuli)-P(process)-C(consequences) model for achieving SENSE impact.

More examples of SENSE marketing, including Nokia, Tiffany, and British Airways, will appear in chapter 4.

FEEL

FEEL marketing appeals to customers' inner feelings and emotions, with the objective of creating affective experiences that range from mildly positive moods linked to a brand (e.g., for a noninvolving, nondurable grocery brand or service or industrial product) to strong emotions of joy and pride (e.g., for a consumer durable, technology, or social marketing campaign). As we will see, most affect occurs during consumption. Therefore standard emotional advertising is often inappropriate because it does not target feelings during consumption. What is needed for FEEL marketing to work is a close understanding of what stimuli can trigger certain emotions as well as the willingness of the consumer to engage in perspective taking and empathy.

An example of FEEL marketing is Clinique's first new fragrance in seven years, called "Happy." Videos at the point of purchase reinforce the name's message, reflecting the product's sunny orange packaging, showing the jumping, joyfully smiling figure of model Kylie Bax. Television ads incorporate movement and music with lively camera work. In mounting the "Happy" campaign, Clinique is riding a growing antigrunge wave that is sparking a trend toward more cheerful fashions. As a tie-in, Clinique has produced a limited-edition CD of "happy" songs, including Judy Garland's "Get Happy" and the Turtles' "Happy Together."[14] "Happy" makes you feel happy.

More examples of FEEL marketing, such as Häagen-Dazs Cafés in Europe and Asia, Campbell's Soup, and the approach used by Victoria Gallegos, one of the highest-selling salespeople in New York City, will appear in chapter 5.

THINK

THINK marketing appeals to the intellect with the objective of creating cognitive, problem-solving experiences that engage customers creatively. THINK appeals to engage customers' convergent and divergent thinking through surprise, intrigue, and provocation. THINK campaigns are common for new technology products. But THINK marketing is not restricted only to high-tech products. THINK marketing has also been used in product design, retailing, and in communications in many other industries.

A good example is Microsoft's new multimillion-dollar campaign, "Where Do You Want to Go Today," created by Widen & Kennedy, the ad agency best known for its "Just do it" campaign for Nike. As a symbol for the campaign, the slogan does a brilliant job of encompassing all of Microsoft's many ventures and activities. Microsoft is closely associated in consumers' minds with the explosion in computers and the feeling today that with technology anything is possible. With this slogan, Microsoft positions itself as the company responsible for these infinite possibilities—it's just a matter of naming your destination, and Microsoft will get you there. Indeed, the objective of the approach was "to creatively understand what it means for people to use computers . . . in the 90s." The spatial metaphor links well with the geographical metaphors of the Internet—web pages are spoken of as "sites" that can be "visited"—and Microsoft's products for the net. The question "Where do you want to go today?" can be taken literally for Microsoft's Expedia, the travel services web site, or its Sidewalk, the city site guide.[15]

More THINK marketing cases, such as Genesis ElderCare, Apple Computers, Siemens, RCN, and Finlandia vodka, will appear in chapter 6.

ACT

ACT marketing aims to affect bodily experiences, lifestyles, and interactions. ACT marketing enriches customers' lives by enhancing their physical experiences, showing them alternative ways of doing things (e.g., in business-to-business and industrial markets), alternative lifestyles, and interactions. As I will show, analytical, rational approaches to behavior change are only one of many behavioral change options. Changes in lifestyles are often more motivational, inspirational, and spontaneous in nature and brought about by role models (e.g., movie stars or famous athletes).

Nike sells more than 160 million pairs of shoes a year—almost one of every two pairs sold in the United States. One major part of the success of the company has been the brilliant "Just do it" campaign. Frequently depicting famous athletes in action, it is a classic of ACT marketing, transforming the experience of physical exercise.[16]

More ACT marketing examples, such as the Gillette Mach3, the Milk Mustache campaign, and Martha Stewart Living will appear in chapter 7.

RELATE

RELATE marketing contains aspects of SENSE, FEEL, THINK, and ACT marketing. However, RELATE marketing expands beyond the individual's personal, private feelings, thus adding to "individual experiences" and relating the individual to his or her ideal self, other people, or cultures.

RELATE campaigns appeal to the individual's desire for self-improvement (e.g., a future "ideal self" that he or she wants to relate to). They appeal to the need to be perceived positively by individual others (e.g., one's peers, girlfriend, boyfriend, or spouse; family and colleagues). They relate the person to a broader social system (a subculture, a country, etc.), thus establishing strong brand relations and brand communities.

RELATE campaigns have been used in a variety of industries, ranging from cosmetics, personal care, and lingerie (to create fantasies about the other sex) to national image improvement programs. The American motorcycle Harley-Davidson is a RELATE brand par excellence. Harley is a way of life. From the bikes themselves to Harley-related merchandise to Harley-Davidson tattoos on the bodies of enthusiasts (who cut across all social groups), consumers see Harley as a part of their identity. The Harley web page gets to the heart of the matter: "Suppose time takes a picture—one picture that represents your entire life here on earth. You have to ask yourself how you'd rather be remembered. As a pasty, web-wired computer wiz, strapped to an office chair? Or as a leather-clad adventurer who lived life to the fullest astride a Harley-Davidson? You can decide which it is, but think quickly. Time is framing up that picture, and it's got a pretty itchy shutter finger."

More on Harley-Davidson, plus many more examples of RELATE marketing campaigns, such as Tommy Hilfiger, the Wonderbra, and Michael Jordan fragrance, will appear in chapter 8.

EXPERIENTIAL HYBRIDS AND HOLISTIC EXPERIENCES

Chapters 4 through 8 will provide in-depth descriptions of the SEMs and how they need to be managed. Each chapter will review the latest concepts and models as well as methodological tools and strategies regarding each type of SEM.

However, experiential appeals rarely result in only one type of experience. Many successful corporations employ experiential hybrids that combine two or more SEMs in order to broaden the experiential appeal.

An automotive hybrid is the new Volvo C70 coupe. Traditionally, Volvo cars have been built—and marketed—based on their solid reputation for safety. In 1997, when I spoke to a group of Volvo executives on their branding approach, they told me that safety alone was no longer enough: consumers rated key competitors' cars (Mercedes, BMW, Lexus) just as safe. As a result, Volvo has been restyling itself to incorporate a sexier, more sensual image, while not giving up the claim as one of the safest cars on the planet. The new C70 coupe shows off its sleek and beautiful lines on a series of outdoor installations, with the advertising neatly and wittily encompassing various experiential appeals: "for those who combine a passion for living, with a passion for living"; "a surge of adrenaline, then a surge of peace-of-mind"; "ah, the sun, the moon, the side impact protection system . . . "; "the new Volvo C70 convertible: Ingenious new hair dryer from Sweden"; "protect the body, ignite the soul." The hybrid appeal is explicitly spelled out in corporate promotions: "Call it a race car for the rational. Or the blissful marriage of safety and sensually sculpted beauty. Either way, the new Volvo C70 will move you ways Volvo never has."

Ideally, marketers should strive strategically for creating holistically integrated experiences that possess, at the same time, SENSE, FEEL, THINK, ACT, and RELATE qualities (see Figure 3.2). Do you remember Singapore Airlines, which we discussed in chapter 2? The goals of the company are entirely holistic: to be a visually appealing and elegant airline (SENSE), a kind and hospitable airline (FEEL), innovative and creative (THINK), service- and action-oriented (ACT), and international and Singaporean at the same time (RELATE).

Volvo ad for C70

FIGURE 3.2

The Ultimate Goal of Experiential Marketing

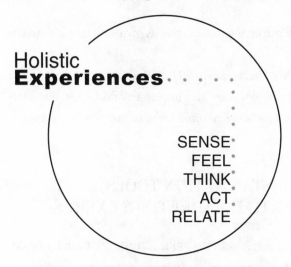

Experiential hybrids and holistic experiences as well as strategic issues surrounding them, will be addressed in chapters 9 and 10.

THE INTERNAL STRUCTURE OF SEMS

I consider the five types of SEMs as modules. Like mental modules, they have their inherent structures and principles. Let me illustrate my point with advertising.

SENSE TV ad campaigns typically dazzle viewers' senses with fast-paced, fast-cut images and music. They are dynamic and attention-getting and may leave a strong impression after just fifteen seconds.

FEEL TV ads, in contrast, are often slice-of-life ads that take time to draw the viewer in, building emotion gradually. Successful Hallmark ads, the prototypical FEEL spots, all last for more than a minute.

THINK campaigns are often sedate. They begin with a voiceover, then move to text on the screen, in order to be thought-provoking.

ACT campaigns show behavioral outcomes or lifestyles.

RELATE campaigns typically show the referent person or group that the customer is supposed to relate to.

In sum, each strategic marketing module has its own structure and executional principles.

But how are the SEMs "instantiated?" How do marketers create these experiences? In other words, what are the implementation tools that marketers can use to achieve their strategic objectives of creating these experiences?

THE INSTANTIATION TOOLS
OF EXPERIENTIAL MARKETING: EXPROS

The instantiation of the strategic SENSE, FEEL, THINK, ACT, and RELATE modules occurs by means of what I call "experience providers," or ExPros. ExPros are tactical implementation components at the disposal of the marketer for creating a SENSE, FEEL, THINK, ACT, or RELATE campaign. They include communications, visual and verbal identity, product presence, co-branding, spatial environments, electronic media, and people (see Figure 3.3).

With the SEMs and ExPros we can construct the Experiential Grid, which is the key strategic planning tool of experiential marketing, as shown in Figure 3.4. That is, as a manager, you need to decide which ExPros should be used to create which SEM in order to define the experiential image of your organization and/or brand appropriately. We will return to this point in chapter 10. For now, let's examine the ExPros further.

Communications

Communications ExPros include advertising, external and internal company communications (such as magalogs, brochures and newsletters, annual reports, etc.) as well branded public relations campaigns. I will first discuss advertising—one of the most important communications ExPros for many companies—and then turn to two more unusual communication ExPros: magalogs and annual reports.

FIGURE 3.3

Key Experiential Providers (ExPros)

Advertising

Like other ExPros, advertising can create any of the five different strategic modules of SENSE, FEEL, THINK, ACT, and RELATE. Let us look at an example of an advertising campaign for each one of the SEMs.

SENSE. A powerful SENSE advertising campaign is paving the way for the renaissance of a once-popular brand: Clairol Herbal Essences shampoo.[17] Clairol Herbal Essences was the first natural botanical shampoo in the U.S. market. After a strong showing in the 1970s, when it attained an 8 percent market share, by 1994 it had slipped to about 2 percent of the market. Surveys found, though, that 80 percent of American women retained fond memories of the product, and Clairol decided to re-launch the line of naturally based shampoos.

Wells Rich Greene BDDP launched a tremendously successful SENSE campaign for Herbal Essences. Rather than making the conventional claim

FIGURE 3.4

The Experiential Grid

that the product would promote beautiful, shiny hair, they marketed the experience of using the product with the tag line "a totally organic experience." The campaign featured a TV spot that imitated a scene from the film *When Harry Met Sally,* in which Meg Ryan simulates an orgasm. In the commercial, a woman steps into the shower and begins to shampoo her hair. The shampoo smells great, and she responds with gasps of enthusiastic pleasure. The ad then cuts to a bored couple watching this scene on television, and the wife comments, "I wanna get the shampoo she's using."

Print ads echo the experiential message. Colorful layouts show a bottle of Herbal Essences, with wildflowers and herbs bursting out of it, with the headline, "When was the last time you had a totally organic experience?"

FEEL. A compelling print advertising example for FEEL is the advertising for the luxury watchmaker Patek Philippe. Patek Philippe is one of the world's oldest and most expensive watches—a luxury and status brand known the world over, and a significant investment. In recent ads created by London ad agency Leagas Delaney, an attractive and well-groomed young woman, dressed in a casual leather jacket, is sitting on a bench. Climbing up behind her is a little girl, perhaps five years old, dressed in a plaid jumper, covering the woman's eyes in a happy game of "guess who?" Mother and daughter are both smiling and laughing. The picture is one of relaxed affluence. The young mother is wearing a simple gold wedding band—and no visible watch. The ad headline reads, "You never actually own a Patek Philippe. You merely look after it for the next generation. Begin your own tradition." The message is twofold: a sense of present happiness combined with the notion that a Patek Philippe is an heirloom to be passed from mother to daughter, an enduring emblem of family happiness and security. The ad combines a strong traditional feeling with a contemporary one, ringing changes on the notion that fine watches are passed down from father to son.[18]

Patek Philippe ad

THINK. A three-year THINK advertising campaign was launched by the Newspaper Association of America, with the help of Jerry Della Femina and his team at Jerry & Ketchum.[19]

The purpose of the campaign is to promote literacy and encourage readership by showcasing newspapers as a vibrant and relevant medium. The campaign's main theme is the important role that newspapers can play in learning by young people. The ads show celebrities reading a newspaper with the lines "Encourage your children to read every day," and "It all starts with newspapers."

The campaign has broad appeal through its use of a wide variety of spokespersons, who encourage us to think of newspapers and daily reading as an integral part of life. These include former presidents George Bush and Jimmy Carter, retired general Norman Schwarzkopf, MTV journalist Tabitha Soren, Super Bowl quarterback John Elway, and rapper LL Cool J. Publishers are also encouraged to give the campaign local flavor through use of local celebrities.

ACT. "Gentlemen, start your follicles." This one-line tag appears in a recent print advertisement for Rogaine, the medication designed to stimulate the growth of thinning hair. The key word in this ACT marketing campaign is "start." Consumers get a "starter kit," which includes a video called "Getting Started." The slogan is a powerful allusion to the masculine world of auto racing, and the thrilling words that traditionally begin the Indianapolis 500: "Gentlemen, start your engines." The campaign appeals to male consumers who may be feeling inadequate because of hair loss, and empower them to ACT by evoking the manly sport of auto racing.

RELATE. Rather than arguing for the health benefits of orange juice, Tropicana Pure Premium Orange Juice is running a series of RELATE print ads relating the brand to lifestyle roles. One ad that appeared in *Golf Digest* shows an athletic-looking man in workout clothes sitting on an apartment terrace with a city skyline in the background. He is surrounded by exercise equipment, taking a break from his morning workout to have some oj. The photo is in black and white, except for the bright orange juice. Superimposed over this shot are floating slices of juicy orange, and across the bottom of the spread a rich ocean of orange juice. The tag line reads, "Morning without Tropicana Pure Premium? Not an option."

Magalogs

Another form of communications ExPro is the magalog. As its name suggests, the magalog is a cross between a magazine and a catalog. Magalogs typically offer a mix of features ranging from cataloglike spreads of products and prices to evocative art photography to articles about lifestyle and image issues. The premier issue of Abercrombie & Fitch's magalog, *A&F Quarterly,* included features on choosing the right dog ("Must-have mongrels," which offered the advice "Similar to the golden rules of human courtship, never pick a dog that's too desperate or too eager"), cool cars and trucks (including the New Beetle and Mercedes' new SUV), the coolest beers and wines, and a travel note called "Sun, Surf, Sex, and Sydney." In sum, the magalog is part of the company's ACT and lifestyle branding.[20]

A distinctly different lifestyle is targeted by the Hermès magalog, *Le Monde D'Hermès.* The Spring-Summer 1998 issue honors trees, and the magalog is prefaced by an experiential message from Hermès president Jean Louis Dumas-Hermès: "Where would we be without trees? Hermès is celebrating the tree all through 1998. This issue of *Le Monde D'Hermès* is dedicated to it. A haiku tells us to 'look at a tree and become that tree,' so let us encourage our young shoots, draw up the sap from our living roots, raise our eyes toward the distant horizons that beckon from the high boughs. And may our actions bear rich fruit! Hermès: fine tree of rare yet simple descent seeks connoisseurs for fruitful and pleasant relationship." The rest of the magalog does indeed resemble a magazine for the connoisseur, sort of an upscale *Smithsonian.* Printed on glossy stock with copious color photography, it includes features on bronze and pottery horses from the Han and Tang dynasties, mythologies of the tree, and the Gregoire Technical Training Center, where young people learn the art of saddlery and leatherworking. Hermès products are featured in lavish and beautiful fashion-photography spreads that carry through the "tree" theme, and beautiful photos of ancient trees appear throughout the publication. Even the advertising from other retailers included in the magalog echos the theme: an ad from the Discount Bank and Trust

Company shows two little boys walking along a forest path; another, from Louis Roederer champagne, features decorative trees around a piazza at the Villa Medicis in Rome.

Magalogs are an increasingly popular way for retailers to establish experiential connections between themselves and targeted consumers, and even traditional mail-order marketers like Williams-Sonoma and Land's End are beginning to incorporate more editorial materials—like recipes and fiction—into their catalogs.

Annual Reports

Even the stodgiest of corporate communications, the annual report, is becoming an experiential tool. Victor Rivera, creative director of Addison, highlighted a few of his favorites in the 1997 issue of *Addison Magazine.* In an early example, in 1984 H. J. Heinz Company marked twenty consecutive years of financial growth by issuing an annual report celebrating the tomato. The firm commissioned eleven famous artists, including Red Grooms, to contribute their own visions of the tomato. According to Rivera, the result is an annual report that is a work of art and a tribute to the mainstay of over five hundred Heinz products. Another is Duracell's 1994 report that positions the firm as a true global player by styling the entire report as a passport, complete with stamps, pictures from different countries, and employee photos taken at picture booths around the world.

Visual/Verbal Identity

Like communications and other ExPros, visual/verbal identity can be used to create SENSE, FEEL, THINK, ACT, and RELATE brands. The set of identity ExPros consists of names, logos, and signage. Visual/verbal identity is the prime domain of so-called corporate identity consultants.

Names

There are numerous experiential brand names for products, such as Sunkist (citrus fruits), Skin-So-Soft (an Avon product), Silverstone (a Du Pont non-stick cooking surface), Tide and Cheer (detergents), and Jolt (a high-caffeine cola). Experiential names are less common for industrial companies, which often prefer the names of the initial owner, acronyms, or descriptive, functional names. However, there are a few examples, especially in the high-tech industry. In a special report on information technology, *Fortune* magazine listed the following "cool companies 1998": Teligent, Reality Fusion, Autonomy, Check Point Software, Efusion, Dragon Systems, and E Ink.[21]

Logos and Signage

Ciba Chemicals, a spinoff from the giant Ciba Geigy, took an experiential approach to its logo and visual identity from its inception. The logo is shaped like a butterfly, used as a symbol for Ciba's transformation and appropriate to represent the company's continued development into the future. The butterfly itself is made up of a collection of colored pixels of various sizes, each color representing a different division of Ciba's business: blue representing Additives, aqua representing Consumer Care Chemicals, green representing Textile Dyes, etc. The overall corporate color, violet, was chosen to represent nobility and strength.[22]

Another unusual and creative use of experiential logos and signage comes from Nickelodeon, the children's cable network. "Nick" has set a few guidelines for logo design: all logos are to be in Pantone 021 orange with white lettering, the font is always Balloon Bold in all caps, and the lettering of the word "Nickelodeon" is always the same. Beyond that, designers have free rein to create different shapes and designs for the Nick logo, ranging from animal shapes to footprints to spaceships to exploding firecrackers and on and on. The creativity in the logo design policy mirrors the company's connection with kids and their imaginative energy—kids can even design their own Nick logos!

Product Presence

Like communications and visual/verbal identity, product presence can also be used to instantiate an experience. Product-presence ExPros include product design, packaging and product display, and brand characters that are used as part of packaging and point-of-sale materials.

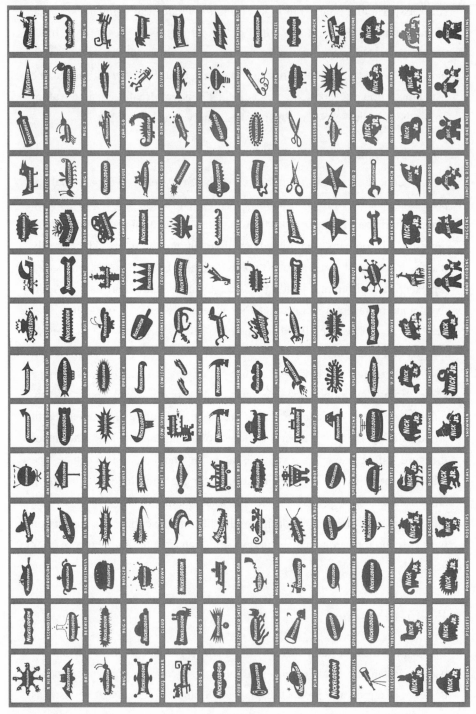

Nickelodeon logos

Today, there is no predominant style in product design. "There's just more and more stuff that has been styled, molded, carved, folded, patterned, cut-and-pasted, prototyped, mocked up, punched up, laid out, recycled and shrink-wrapped . . . Today, the most powerful laws governing design are dictated by the marketplace. Catch the eye. Stimulate desire. Move the merchandise," writes Herbert Muschamp, the architecture critic of the *New York Times*. Leading architect Rem Koolhaas has argued similarly for architecture, "our style of building is less and less permanent and more and more frivolous and flimsy."[23] In addition to the core product design there are the product designs of the after-sales market. For example, the after-sales market for the Corvette includes T-shirts, mailboxes, car covers, and Corvette-shaped cookies—a $30 million business in 1998 for Midamerica Design, the company that provides these items.[24] In this market-driven environment, the right planning of the experience to attract eyes and feelings is key.

Product Design

An excellent example of experiential product design comes from a new Philips product, the Satinelle epilator. Created for women, the product design conveys femininity on a number of levels: the overall shape is suggestive of female anatomy, and the subtle shading of colors suggests the petals of a tulip. The feminine RELATE appeal is carried through in the product name, Satinelle, and the descriptor, "sensitive," printed beneath the name.

Packaging

Another obvious place to look for experiential executions is in packaging. Indeed, consumers have become increasingly attentive to packaging and have higher and higher expectations of it. According to Paul Lukas, writing in *Fortune* magazine, "on merchandise ranging from chocolate-covered raisins to toilet paper, more and more packages are now explicitly calling attention to themselves, as if to suggest that consumers are more interested in the packaging than in the product itself."[25]

Consider packaging for beverages. The beverage formulation certainly matters, and beverage manufacturers are constantly inventing new formulas and trends (the "fruit smoothie" rage being one of the latest). But, asks Ken

Brochure for Philips Satinelle brand

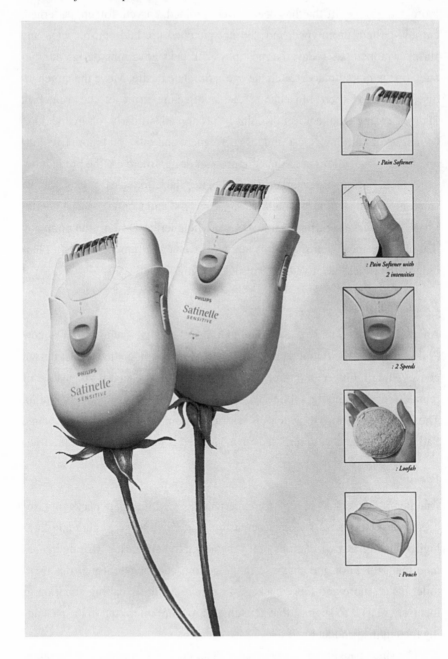

Miller, vice president of IDI, a packaging innovation consultancy that designed the new Whipper Snapple bottle (Snapple's entry into the smoothie category; see chapter 7), "what is it that makes these and the tried-and-true beverages really sing? Packaging . . . It [the packaging] has become worthy of serious investment because major players have found it pays off big."[26]

Wallace Church, a New York City–based design consultancy and a leader in experiential packaging, claims that 70 percent of all grocery purchase decisions are made at the shelf. The company redesigned the product identity of Jack & Jill ice cream to evoke the "ice cream man" that many of us remember from childhood. The new brand logo resembles an embroidered emblem that might have been on the ice cream man's uniform. The background illustration on the packaging depicts a nostalgic neighborhood scene of children eagerly waiting for a treat next to an old-time ice cream truck. The shape of the packaging was also redesigned, creating a distinctive oval half-gallon that suggests a traditional hand-packed tub. In this integrated revamping of the brand, Wallace Church recaptured the emotion rooted in the brand's history, from an era when the product was originally sold by the ice cream man. If handled correctly, nostalgia is a powerful emotion-building tool, and we will see it used in a variety of FEEL campaigns in chapter 5.[27]

Brand Characters

Wallace Church was also quick to see the FEEL value in the Pillsbury doughboy when it inherited this venerable spokescharacter. The doughboy has been slimmed down and given a more dynamic expression; his engaging persona "celebrates anew the essence of family fun that is central to the brand's congenial personality."[28]

Wallace Church has revamped several other old-fashioned brand characters with a new experiential feel. To celebrate Cracker Jack's 100th anniversary, for example, Sailor Jack was transformed from a sailor to a Little Leaguer wearing a sailor hat; the redesign echoes the product's baseball connections and has a strong RELATE appeal for kids of all ages. Even the Kool-Aid pitcherman has been streamlined and turned into an ACT marketing tool—he can now be seen playing tennis, spilling a bit of Kool-Aid as he returns a serve.

The Pillsbury doughboy

Point-of-sale product displays often tie into movie characters. For example, videos of the recently re-released *Star Wars* trilogy were displayed in a life-size cardboard Darth Vader display. (So realistic was the display that the thrill of experiencing the Dark Lord up close was a bit too much for one small child, who was seen crying and hiding behind his mom in a video store!)

Co-branding

Like other ExPros, co-branding can be used to develop any of the five strategic experiential modules. Co-branding ExPros include event marketing and sponsorship, alliances and partnerships, licensing, product placements in movies, and co-op campaigns and other types of cooperative arrangements. Let me discuss two of the co-branding techniques, event marketing and sponsorships and product placement, in more detail.

Event Marketing and Sponsorships

As Mava Heffler, MasterCard's senior vice president of global promotions and sponsorships, put it, "It is not enough for a brand to be seen or heard, it has to be experienced. Sponsorships are an important catalyst and component of that experiential marketing."[29]

To celebrate its 125th anniversary in 1998, Zurich Insurance Company created a special brochure (designed by Wirz AG, a Zurich-based identity firm) and sponsored a series of events, including a fireworks display over Zurich's famous lake, a series of cultural workshops in conjunction with UNICEF, a series of internal events for employees and management, and the opening of new outdoor fitness trails.

The purpose of event marketing, according to Mark Dowley, CEO of Momentum Experiential Marketing Group, is "forging an emotional and memorable connection with consumers where they live, work, and play."[30] Event marketing requires a qualitative understanding of the appropriateness of a particular event as well as quantitative research to demonstrate its effectiveness in reach (e.g., in terms of cost per thousand) and frequency. In general, special events tend to be more effective and less costly than media advertising. Media advertising is often characterized by huge clutter. Also, it may get awareness up—but rarely results in purchase intention or purchase. Therefore, to supplement media advertising, more and more marketers are turning to event marketing to create impact. Guinness uses the Guinness Fleadh (pronounced "flah") events in New York, San Francisco, and Chicago to create an "Irish Village" theme with pre-event point-of-purchase efforts to retailers and promotions and lots of beer sampling during the events.[31] BMW uses event marketing to get customers to buy its cars by traveling to six cities with its Ultimate Driving Experience.

Or consider the Olympic Games, according to Mark Dowley, "the greatest marketing orgy of all times." During the Atlanta Olympics about 3,800

Brochure for Zurich's 125-year anniversary

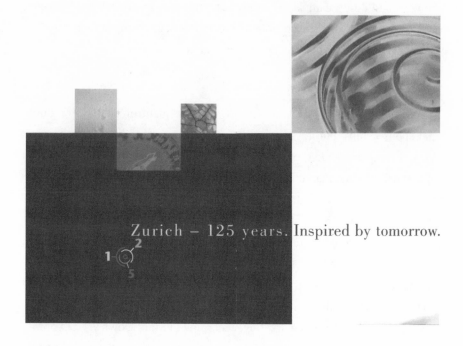

Zurich – 125 years. Inspired by tomorrow.

spots were shown by some of the best marketers in the world. Out of these 3,800 spots, a major sponsor like GE may get 100 to 125 only for a hefty price tag of $20 million. Instead of media advertising, sponsoring the torch relay may be more effective. During the Atlanta Olympics, Coca-Cola provided a strong FEEL appeal by sponsoring the Coca-Cola 1996 Olympic Torch Relay. The objective here was to "share the Olympic Games with America," and the sponsorship included a 15,000-mile rolling street party along the path of the Olympic Torch runners. As a result, over 3 million Cokes were sold along the Torch Relay, and an estimated 500 million media impressions were made. It was the largest event ever sponsored by Coca-Cola.

Product Placement

Product placement in movies is becoming an increasingly rich source of co-branding. According to *The Hollywood Reporter,* "Even before paid advertising began appearing . . . for the holiday release of *Tomorrow Never Dies,* the image of actor Pierce Brosnan as James Bond was being seen in commercials. There was 007 dashing around in this BMW, wearing his Omega watch and using his Ericsson cell phone. The Bond movie was also featured in ads for Visa International, Smirnoff Vodka, and many others. Those commercials signaled a breakthrough; never before had a studio been so accommodating in sharing movie images and properties."[32]

Tie-ins have been a staple of studios like Disney and partners like McDonald's for many years. But the growth of "event" movies has lured more and more new promotional partners to Hollywood, including Reebok, Sony, Casio, and Shell. And promotional tie-ins are no longer limited to children's movies; new partnerships have included Tanqueray gin and *Volcano,* Holland America and *Out to Sea,* Gulden's mustard and *Picture Perfect,* and Apple Computer and *Mission Impossible.* Ray-Ban tripled sales of its Predator 2 line of dark glasses through its tie-in with *Men in Black.* Even R-rated movies, traditionally harder to sell, are getting in on the act, although six airlines and Bekins Moving passed on the noir hit *L.A. Confidential.* Microsoft, Packard-Bell, and the Sci-Fi Network were apparently made of stronger stuff and forged partnerships with the dark and gory *Starship Troopers.*

Spatial Environments

Spatial environments include buildings, offices, and factory spaces, retail and public spaces, and trade booths.

Experiential environments are often the most comprehensive expression of what John Bowen, the chairman of Bowen Consulting, calls "brand culture," the values and behaviors of the managers behind a brand.[33] IBM's new corporate headquarters in Armonk, New York, expresses through architecture and landscaping the way the company perceives itself and the experience it wants to create for its customers and employees.[34] Situated on the site of its old, shoeboxlike headquarters, the new building lies close to the ground, following the configurations of the landscape. An example of corporate downsizing, the building is 120,000 square feet smaller than the old headquarters, housing a third fewer employees. The new site represents 1990s' ideas about corporate hierarchy, with fewer office doors that close, and more cubicles with windows that overlook the surrounding woodlands. Among the cubicles are loose arrangements of chairs used for brainstorming. Parking lots are hidden from view, and a jogging trail rings the grounds. Both exterior and interior convey IBM's new vision of itself. The design, by the Manhattan firm Kohn Pedersen Fox Associates PC, is close to the ground, close to nature, compatible with its natural surroundings; the interiors, by Swanke Hayden Connell Architects, are simple, adaptable, and unstructured.

Experiential marketing is also becoming common in retail spaces. Just think about Pottery Barn, Starbucks, Niketown, and theme stores and restaurants (such as Coca-Cola Disney, Warner Brothers, NFL, Planet Hollywood, Harley-Davidson Café), as well as numerous designer boutiques and department stores. The challenge for experiential marketers using retail branding is to make sure that each store follows the experiential marketing approach. This task can easily be overwhelming when you are dealing with several thousand store owners as part of a franchise system.

"Traditionally, retail management has said 'Quality, Service, Style, Selection—if we do those things right and get the pricing right, we will be fine,'" states Gerald Lewis, chairman of New York–based CDI Group Inc. "But the customer says, 'I want an experience.'"[35] "In a store or restaurant, the customer's experience is vital: One bad encounter, and you've lost a customer for life," write Howard Schultz, CEO of Starbucks Coffee, and Dori Jones Yang.[36]

The experience is also a critical component of the Sephora cosmetics stores in New York City, Orange County in California, and Coconut Grove in Florida. Owned by French luxury goods company LVMH, Sephora features high-end cosmetics displayed alphabetically in free-standing racks. Sephora provides an environment that customers can enjoy and where they are not disturbed by intrusive or snobbish salespeople.

As retail spaces become more experiential, product displays become more important ExPros. Home furnishings stores like Pottery Barn have created comfortable, homelike atmospheres where products are displayed as they might appear in your home. More relaxed than traditional furniture show-rooms, these sales spaces allow customers to plop down on sofas and take their time making decisions. Smaller products, like clocks and glassware, are integrated into these environments, making the whole retail space a kind of mega product display. And Pottery Barn's experiential space doubles as a De-sign Studio, where the look and products you like can immediately be tailored to your own home environment.

Trade booths at conventions and trade shows are also becoming increas-ingly experiential. Examples include trade designs that appeal to our senses and feelings, those that bombard us with "Think" messages and slogans, and trade booths that invite us to experience the products in virtual-reality set-tings.

As described in chapter 2, mass transportation vehicles, from passenger trains to airplanes, are becoming vehicles for total immersion and experience creation. For example, in the mid-nineties, the advertising space in New York subway cars was allocated in a new way and priced higher. For most subway cars, advertisers were required to buy ad space for the entire car. This change in policy attracted national advertisers, who were now able to install experien-tial spaces for their brands in a setting where it is easy to catch consumers' at-tention. The new policy increased revenues tremendously, because these national advertisers are able to pay higher rates than the old subway advertis-ers—mainly small businesses advertising their mousetrap and tattoo-removal services.

In the spring of 1998, on a flight from New York to Rome, I saw the same approach being used in a co-op promotion by Alitalia and Baci chocolates. The "Baci dall'Italia" (With Baci to Italy) plane had been painted in the blue-and-white color scheme of Perugina's famous Baci chocolate wrappers. Baci chocolates were handed out to passengers onboard. And romantic, touchy-feely Baci slogans were posted in English and Italian all over the interior of the plane.

Baci dall'Italia plane

Web Sites and Electronic Media

The Internet's interactive capabilities provide an ideal forum for many companies to create experiences for customers. The Internet can also entirely change a hitherto familiar communication, interaction, or transaction experience; think about banner ads, chat rooms, and buying books on one of the book sites or auctioning artworks. Unfortunately, many companies still use their web site mainly as an information-posting device rather than an opportunity to entertain or otherwise relate to customers through experiential marketing.

When I myself first began developing web sites, they started off as largely functional devices for conveying information. Over the last two years, however, I have gradually added more and more experiential elements. My latest site includes music, animations, audio and video clips, links to other web sites and chat rooms—it is rich in information and experience.

In some industries, electronic media are in the process of replacing live experiences and creating new ones. Electronic media have been used for sales transactions (instead of real salespeople); also for chat rooms (instead of face-

Experiential Marketing's web site: www.exmarketing.com

to-face or spoken phone conversations); and for running a pre-recorded fashion show (instead of a real one).[37]

Club Med's experiential web site, whose slogan is "Do it your way," focuses on providing a customized holistic experience for each person. Visitors to the web site are asked to select the location they're interested in, and to click on jaunty cartoon figures indicating whether they plan to travel as a family, a single, or a couple. The site takes it from there. The page "Village Vibes" links to virtual villages that readers can experience before they actually book their vacations. "Visions of a Club Med Vacation" leads you on a guided fantasy about your ideal vacation: "Close your eyes and picture your dream vacation! Where do you see yourself? On a sunny island in a clear blue tropical sea? Exploring pristine countryside, mountains, and valleys? Let's take a short trip together to some of our interactive villages. We've grouped them according to setting and climate. You'll have fun and you can get an idea of what a vacation at a real Club Med village is like!" Clicking on the "Mediterrean Village" leads you to a screen where you can choose from tennis, snorkeling, boating, dancing, children's activities, fitness, horseback riding, or waterskiing. Links take you to a map of the site or show you schedules for daytime and nighttime activities. Each page is lavishly illustrated by color photos and bright cartoons. The site offers a huge amount of information, easily accessible by village or by activity, including special packages and weather information, and readers can make reservations and book flights on line. Visiting the Club Med web site is like a little vacation all its own, the essence of experiential marketing.[38]

Another brilliant experiential travel web site—though purely virtual—is Discovery Channel's Planet Explorer, designed by frogdesign, located in Silicon Valley. The site promotes virtual travel to exotic places using visual design, sound, scriptwriting, voice-over acting, and Java, Shockwave, Quick Time VR, and GIF animations to provide unprecedented interactivity and an enthralling experience.

Delivering the right experience is key for e-commerce. As Bill Gates observed, "The merchants who treat e-commerce as more than a digital cash register will do the best. Sales are the ultimate goal, of course, but the sale itself is only part of the online customer experience."[39]

People

The final ExPro, people, can be a powerful provider of experience for all five SEMs. People include salespeople, company representatives, service providers, customer service providers, and anybody else who can be associated with a company or a brand.

As we shall see in more detail in chapter 5, high-end retailers best understand the power of salespeople in creating customer experiences. Not long ago, I had a firsthand taste of how a salesperson can turn a simple transaction into a holistically satisfying experience. During a trip to Los Angeles, I wandered into a Rodeo Drive boutique called Sulka. I was approached by a very friendly, well-dressed, and attentive sales associate, Sheila. After greeting me, Sheila brought me a cup of delicious coffee, just the pickup I needed after window-shopping for a few hours. While enjoying the coffee, I mentioned I might be interested in a tie and a couple of shirts. Sheila lavished me with attention and took great care in helping me find just the right things. She even got me to think a bit beyond my usual sense of style, showing me how a striped tie could be made to work with a striped shirt—a combination I had previously thought forbidden. Even this relatively modest contact with the world of designer boutiques made me feel like I was part of a different world. Suddenly I could relate to the crowd who haunts Rodeo Drive, Madison Avenue, Via Napoleone, Faubourg Saint Honoré, Königsallee, Saville Row, Ometesando (direction Aoyama *not* Meiji Shrine)!

Shortly after I returned to New York, this handwritten note, on Sulka letterhead, arrived in the mail:

Dear Mr. Schmitt:

I hope this note finds you in the best of health and spirits. I would like to take this opportunity to thank you for your patronage at Sulka and also for giving me the privilege of being of service to you. I hope you are enjoying your new shirts and tie. It was a real pleasure to meet you, and please feel free to call if I can be of any assistance in the future.

I hope the star of happiness always shines upon your days.

Most sincerely,

Sheila

P.S. I found the tie that you saw in our catalog; if you are interested, please call me and I will send it to you!

SUMMARY

In this chapter, I have presented a framework for managing experiences. With this framework in mind, let me now give you a more detailed overview of the remainder of the book.

As described in this chapter, the framework is based on the idea of different types of experiences, or experiential modules SEM. Each module has its own structures and processes. To target a particular module, each experiential marketing campaign must have an objective as well as a strategy that is consistent with each module's principal structure and process. As a manager, you need to become familiar with the unique structures and principles of each module in order to create successful experiential marketing. How does each module work? How does it differ from the others? In Part Two entitled "Types of Experiences," I will discuss SEMs in more detail.

As I will show, the purpose of SENSE marketing is to incorporate sensory components (e.g., primary attributes, styles, and themes) as part of SENSE strategies (e.g., cognitive consistency/sensory variety) to appeal to customers' sense of beauty or excitement. More on SENSE marketing in chapter 4.

The purpose of FEEL marketing is to employ emotional stimuli (events, agents, and objects) as part of FEEL strategies (at the point of consumption or in communications) to affect moods and emotions. How FEEL marketing works in detail, you can read in chapter 5.

The purpose of THINK marketing is to utilize directional and associative THINK approaches that mix surprise, intrigue, and provocation to appeal to customers' creative thinking. More on THINK in chapter 6.

The purpose of ACT marketing is to enhance physical experiences, suggest alternative patterns of behaviors and lifestyles, and to enrich social interactions through experiential marketing strategies. ACT marketing is the topic of chapter 7.

The purpose of RELATE marketing is to connect the individual self of customers to broader social and cultural contexts reflected in a brand, thus creating a social identity for the customer. RELATE marketing will be discussed in detail in chapter 8.

The implementation of experiential marketing occurs via the experience providers, or ExPros. As I showed earlier, ExPro executions differ from each other depending on which module they are designed for. Advertising for the SENSE module is different from advertising targeting the FEEL module; or web sites for the FEEL modules are different from web sites for the THINK module, etc. The same principle applies to all the other ExPros (visual/verbal identity, product presence, co-branding, spatial environments, and people).

Experiential marketers must plan and implement not only strategies for individual SEMs but they also face the higher-order tasks of building experiential hybrids and holistic experiences. A tool for achieving hybrids and holistic experiences is presented in chapter 9.

Moreover, the Experiential Grid presented earlier in this chapter raises a range of broader strategic issues. These issues in conjunction with experiential brand, extensions and global experiences will be discussed further in chapter 10.

Finally, I will discuss organizational issues related to experiential marketing in terms of building the experience-oriented organization in chapter 11.

An afterthought from LAURA BROWN: Is Sheila sincere? Or a perfect fake? Isn't she just after the commission she makes on her sales? Does it matter?

PART TWO

TYPES OF EXPERIENCES

4

SENSE

S ENSE marketing appeals to the five senses—sight, sound, scent, taste, and touch. The overall purpose of SENSE marketing campaigns is to provide aesthetic pleasure, excitement, beauty, and satisfaction through sensory stimulation. As one Hyatt slogan put it: "We believe the five senses should not only be stimulated but delighted."

MARKETING AESTHETICS REDUX

Sensory experiences were the prime topic of my prior book *Marketing Aesthetics: The Strategic Management of Brands, Identity, and Image* (with Alex Simonson).[1] In *Marketing Aesthetics,* we defined the term "marketing aesthetics" as "the marketing of sensory experiences in corporate or brand output that contribute to the organization's or brand's identity."

Marketing Aesthetics paved the way for incorporating sensory experiences into marketing strategy. The book provided frameworks, concepts, and methodological tools for managing sensory experiences to create corporate and brand identities. A corporation's or brand's visual identity is often the most important component for invoking attitudes, associations, and customer responses, a phenomenon that Louis Cheskin called "sensation transfer." So, it is often the sensory experience that attracts a customer to a corporation or brand and that needs to be considered in strategic decisions.[2] Indeed, most companies and products featured in *Marketing Aesthetics*—Absolut vodka, The Gap, Starbucks, the Four Seasons hotels, and Lucent Technologies— have differentiated themselves in the marketplace to a large degree by means of their visual identities. And they continue on their paths of success.

The fortunes of some companies that have used sensory appeals in the past, however, have recently turned sour. One problem is overshooting, a good example of which is Nike. In *Marketing Aesthetics,* we had warned that Nike, despite its impressive past success with its Air shoes and Niketown, might be in danger of overdoing it by pursuing an all-out aesthetic totalitarianism. By the end of 1997, the bad news was in the newspapers: Nike's identity was seen as too loud and too aggressive.

Another problem is a half-cooked campaign. Medium rare may be fine for steaks, but it is not for a sensory marketing campaign. Cathay Pacific Airways, the Hong Kong airline featured in *Marketing Aesthetics,* had a wonderful sensory-based identity campaign designed by Landor Associates, but fell short of implementing it properly on its planes. When this book went to print, the airline still had numerous planes with the old logo and identity on them, doubtlessly as a result of the Asian financial crisis.

How exactly does SENSE marketing work? Let's look at an example. One of the unexpected places in which SENSE has recently surfaced is the traditional bastion of F&B marketing: P&G.

THE SENSE OF TIDE

Procter & Gamble's Tide, the nation's leading laundry detergent, has been promoted for years on the basis of features and benefits as a more effective cleaner than other brands. Tide's ads have been a staple of American TV viewing for years: on the left side of your TV screen was a striped shirt with a tough stain that the other brand failed to get out; on the right was the same fabric, washed brilliantly clean by Tide. The drill has been fundamentally the same for all of Tide's various incarnations: traditional Tide, Tide with bleach, perfume-free Tide. In February 1998, after I gave a presentation on experiential marketing organized by the Design Management Institute, Ms. Claudia Kotchka, vice president at Procter & Gamble, told me: "We'd need more of experiential marketing for our products including Tide."

Tide's new campaign, "Tide Mountain Fresh," has a direct sensory appeal, and P&G's marketing of the product is designed to exploit and expand this appeal. The advertising displays images of snow-capped mountains, hills covered with fragrant evergreens, and meadows full of wildflowers; the colors are cool, vivid, and refreshing. The language is equally evocative of the outdoor experience: "crisp mountain air; bright sunshine and cool breezes; fresh wildflowers; clear spring water; clean mountain snow." The copy goes on to promise, "now you can bring the fresh clean scent of the great outdoors inside with New Mountain Spring Tide." P&G has even incorporated a scratch-and-sniff feature in their print advertising to introduce the scent and allow consumers to experience it before purchasing the product. P&G has made a coherent effort to create the strong sensory experience of a cool morning on a mountaintop. What's more, they have taken a decisive step in the direction of experiential marketing. The tag line for their ads—"There's something new in the air"—heralds something more than just a new product scent! In sum, the SENSE campaign for Tide results in multiple sensory experiences.

CONCEPTS AND PLANNING TOOLS FOR SENSORY MARKETING

Some key planning tools and concepts for managing sensory experiences were presented in *Marketing Aesthetics*. As shown in Figure 4.1, corporate expressions (the public face of the organization) are projected to customers and other constituents of the organization (such as suppliers, investors, and the public at large) via primary elements, styles, and themes that result in certain customer impressions (individual representations of the organization and its brand's identity).

FIGURE 4.1

Key Concepts of Marketing Aesthetics

Customer
Impressions

Styles
Themes

Corporate
Expressions

Corporate Expressions and Identity Elements

Corporate or brand expressions manifest themselves through certain identity elements. At the highest level of abstraction, there are the Four P's of visual (or sensory) identity elements: Properties, Products, Presentations, and Publications.

Properties include, for example, buildings, plants, offices, and company vehicles. *Products* include the sensory aspects of the physical product and the sensory aspects of the core of a service. *Presentations* include packaging, shopping bags, service uniforms, and anything else that surrounds the product or service directly. *Publications* include brochures, business cards, promotional material, and advertising.

Identity elements need to be used consistently to create a visual identity for an organization or brand; otherwise an organization's constituents (customers, suppliers, employees, and investors) will be confused. In the mid-nineties, ITT Industries conducted a study in the financial community and found out that people were not certain what their key products were. Two out of three respondents listed hotels, casinos, or telephone equipment. The confusion stemmed in part from the "other ITT," ITT Corporation, which at the time was fighting off a hostile takeover by Hilton. But it also stemmed from the use of an acronym that spanned corporations, subsidiaries, divisions, and products and was used in an inconsistent manner. To remedy the situation,

Landor Associates, one of the leading brand consultancies, created a new logo and tag line and a new brand architecture, emphasizing the company's core reputation for precision-engineered products. With the tag line "Engineered for life," ITT Industries is now seen as a global company focused on superior engineering to meet human needs.[3]

Primary Elements, Styles, and Themes

A corporate or brand expression is created through primary elements, styles, and themes. Primary elements relate to the five senses—e.g., color, shape, and typeface (for sight); loudness, pitch, and meter (for sound); material and texture (for touch), etc. Primary elements are the building blocks of styles. Style refers to the distinctive, constant, and consistent quality of sensory expression. Themes add meaning and content to styles and serve as mental anchors and reference points. Let me illustrate each concept in turn.

Primary Elements

The most important primary element is color. Stolichnaya vodka uses a rich sensory approach to market its lemon-flavored Limonaya vodka. Colorful print ads, painted in the style of the Russian Constructivists in deep greens, blues, and purples, feature a lemon wedge and twist styled as an umbrella. Under the "umbrella," a "Stoli" bottle is showered with droplets of lemon juice. The yellow lemon and bottle contrast brightly with the cool, dark background, like a yellow slicker in the rain.

Interestingly enough, background color on web sites, termed "wallpaper," can affect information search and the effectiveness of electronic commerce.[4] And the color of real wallpaper in hotels can soothe you or drive you crazy.

Music can be another valuable primary element to create or enhance sensory experiences. This requires, however, that it be used strategically and in a meaningful way, not merely as background music. And even when it is used as background, the right music must be picked. When I once traveled with a group of senior executives through China, we experienced a hilarious example of a music blunder. We visited the high-tech plant of Alcatel in Pudong,

THE POPULARITY OF BLUE

Exploring the importance of color in marketing, KLM devoted the March 1998 issue of *Holland Herald,* its in-flight magazine, to the color blue. Billed as a "tribute to the color of KLM," the issue included features on the use of blue in art, architecture, and popular culture. Another article discussed independent psychological and marketing studies that found the popularity of blue on the rise. A special page offered stickers with logos of five companies that use blue as their corporate color: Cap Gemini, Volvo, Spa, Diners Club, and of course KLM. Stickers of KLM's blue planes against the blue sky were also offered. Blue in

Tiffany ad for diamond engagement ring

SOME DAYS MATTER. *Tiffany diamond engagement ring in the classic Tiffany six-prong platinum setting.*

TIFFANY & CO.

fashion and nature was explored, and a special article looked at "Eric Clapton, performer of the blues."

Color is a central part of Tiffany & Co.'s marketing approach, both to create an identification and memory as well as sensory appeal for Tiffany products. The trademark turquoise box, tied with a white ribbon, unmistakably conveys "Tiffany." The retail stores and catalog even sell porcelain versions of the Tiffany "blue box" with bow. It's happened more than once that someone has put a gift, bought elsewhere, into a Tiffany box in order to enhance its value. And this color scheme is carried through the rest of their marketing. Their turquoise shopping bags, well made and infinitely reusable, are eye-catching and instantly identifiable with Tiffany, no matter what they're being used for. Even their catalogs are mailed in the same distinctive turquoise envelopes, which instantly distinguish them from other catalogs and junk mail. A flash of turquoise bag immediately raises interest—"Someone got something from Tiffany." Tiffany's trademark color is inseparably linked to the ageless elegance and quality that define the Tiffany brand.

Tiffany's advertising also plays on the power of the "blue box." A recent print ad for Tiffany shows a well-dressed man's hands holding a small Tiffany box behind his back. Beneath the photo is a shot of a simple solitaire diamond ring in a platinum setting. The ad's tag line, "Some days matter," is so small the reader has to look for it. In fact, the tag isn't necessary. The image of the small blue box being held behind the back conveys it all—someone is getting an engagement ring from Tiffany.

the prime industrial developing zone of Shanghai, and were shown a film of the switch-gear assembly plant. The background music of the tape was "*Je t'aime, moi non plus,*" a popular and highly erotic French pop song from the seventies (ostensibly recorded by actress Jane Birkin and singer Serge Gainsbourg while making love)—a quite inappropriate accompaniment even in its orchestral version.

Nokia mobile phones, manufactured by Finland-based Nokia Group, which surpassed Motorola in 1999 as the world's dominant mobile phone manufacturer, appeal to several senses through multiple primary elements in the design of its successful mobile phones. As Johan Carlstroem, an analyst at Fischer Partners in Stockholm, put it, "Nokia has better phones, snappier colors and design."[5] Moreover, the goal is to make the phones user-friendly and chic and to give each product a personality and soul. "Technology itself is rather cold," says Frank Nuovo, VP for design at Nokia. "But if you know how to use it, then it will be intuitive and more human. And when you look at a product more as a person, instead of as an object, and you actually start to interact with it as such, it starts to take on its own personality."

How does Nokia create this human face through design? One element is the large display (described by the designers as "the eye into the soul of the product"). Another one is the revolutionary interface design with its easy-to-use soft-key interface. Nokia designers also pay special attention to shapes and forms, creating curved phones that feel good in the hand. Another aspect is color. The new 5100 series digital phones have fashionable faceplates that snap on and off for a quick color change. No wonder Nokia has been very successful in taking on Motorola, whose phones are still largely products of an F&B approach. Nokia phones, by contrast, have become, as an article in the *Singapore Times* put it, "synonymous with user-friendliness, simplicity, elegance and style."[6]

Nokia mobile phone

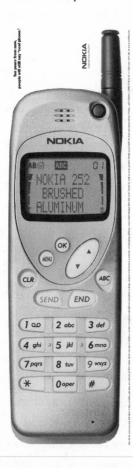

Styles

Primary elements combined constitute a style, which may be analyzed according to several style dimensions such as complexity (minimalism *vs.* ornamentalism); representation (realism *vs.* abstraction); movement (dynamic *vs.* static) and potency (loud/strong *vs.* soft/weak).

Sears, the traditional middle-of-the-road American retailer, is trying soft, minimalist styling for its new stores, The Great Indoors. Riding the home design and renovation wave, the store aims to provide everything for the home—furniture, kitchen and bath products, consumer electronics, and home improvement items. The store's styling is about as far from a conventional Sears outlet as can be imagined. The 156,000-square-foot store near Denver features a European coffee bar and restaurant, a library, a bank, and on-site floral arranging. According to vice president Bob Rodgers, the space is "very open. When you walk through the front door, you can see the entire store because there is no high racking. There are high ceilings, but the soft, bright lights produce a warm, rather than stark, lighting." Carpeting and tiles replace the cold, hard cement of most do-it-yourself stores. The Great Indoors is designed to be easy to maneuver in, not overwhelming.[7]

Themes

Themes refer to the messages that communicate content and meaning about the corporation and its brands. Themes provide mental anchors, reference points, and memory cues. They appear in the form of corporate and brand names, visual symbols, verbal slogans, jingles, general concepts, or in a combination of these theme elements to evoke sensory imagery.

Hennessy cognac has launched a striking SENSE campaign in international markets, playing on the themes of bullfighting. A bottle of Hennessy is pictured on the right of the spread, richly lit and glowing with red and amber highlights. Behind the bottle, leaning in toward it, is a beautiful dark-haired woman in a black silk suit, looking pensively downward. The graceful curve of her hip echoes exactly the lovely curve of the bottle, a sensual touch that conveys gentle swaying movement. Behind her is a bullring, bright and warm in the sun, against the backdrop of a brilliant blue sky. On the sand is another shot of the same woman, this time in a long black dress, turning dramatically toward the camera, her black lace mantilla held out behind her and lifted by the energy of her movement. In her dance, a look of intensity on her face, she becomes both bull and matador, conveying the passion of the bullring. The allure of the theme is sensual, passionate, and exotic.

Overall Impressions

Styles and themes create overall customer impressions. In the business world, certain overall impressions occur repeatedly: impressions related to time (traditional, contemporary, futuristic); time movement (retro, avant-garde, classic/timeless); space (city/country, East/West, or North/South); technology (high-tech, natural, artificial); authenticity (original, imitative); and sophistication (cheap, refined, mass appeal, exclusive).

There are cross-cultural differences in customer preferences for overall impressions as well as the primary elements, styles, and themes of which they are composed. For example, Asian consumers like naturalism, especially for grocery products. Canned fruit drinks, coffees, and sodas in Asian markets offer a visual delight to customers, depicting in excruciating detail the freshness of the ingredients (red-golden apples with drops of water on them; the vulnerable skin of a fresh peach; the dark brown-black of coffee beans). Therefore, foreign firms often need to adjust their communications, packaging, and even the products themselves. When Gatorade launched its "peach cooler" product in South Korea, the packaging did contain the aggressive red arrow but in a more subdued and smaller display. The imagery used on the packaging was that of a beautifully displayed peach with the stem intact, shown against a pink background.

GOING BEYOND *MARKETING AESTHETICS*

Marketing Aesthetics has helped managers to deal with sensory experiences and aesthetics in a structured fashion. However, from the broader perspective of experiential marketing advocated here, *Marketing Aesthetics* had several significant limitations, which will be addressed here and in later chapters.

1. *Marketing Aesthetics* practically equated "experiential needs" with "aesthetic needs." To point to sensory experiences is certainly important. Yet sensory experiences are but one type of experience and not the end of all experiential marketing. Other types of experiential marketing and, as we will see, entire holistic experiences must be part of strategic planning as well.

2. The objective of sensory experiences was defined as creating a corporate or brand identity. The experience providers (ExPros) of sensory experiences were called "identity elements." But, as shown in the previous ex-

amples, sensory experiences are used not only for identity management and image projection. Sensory marketing can be a powerful strategic and tactical tool for motivating customers directly, for adding value to customers, and for differentiating the product (internally and externally), even in the case of a weak corporate or brand identity. As a result, these types of objectives need to be viewed as inherent goals of sensory marketing campaigns.

3. What is the best way of executing a sensory experience campaign? Is there an executable principle that works in most cases? *Marketing Aesthetics* mentioned various strategic issues in style creation and theme selection but failed to identify a proven marketing principle for managing sensory experiences.

SENSE MARKETING

The experiential marketing framework presented in this book aims to overcome the major limitations of *Marketing Aesthetics*.[8] First, this book as a whole puts sensory experiences in perspective by presenting a comprehensive framework including several types of experiences, not only sensory ones. Moreover, the present chapter, which focuses on SENSE marketing, presents the objectives of sensory campaigns more clearly by focusing on the strategic objectives of sensory campaigns and key management principles.

SENSE STRATEGIC OBJECTIVES

Suppose you have been persuaded to try a SENSE approach; what should be the strategic objectives of your SENSE campaign? Without objectives, the SENSE campaign will not have direction. Without objectives, you do not know when you have reached your goal. Without objectives, you do not know what you need to coordinate and measure.

Three key strategic objectives can motivate SENSE marketing. An organization can use SENSE marketing to differentiate itself and its products in the marketplace, motivate its customers to buy its products, and deliver value to customers (see Figure 4.2).

FIGURE 4.2

SENSE Strategic Objectives

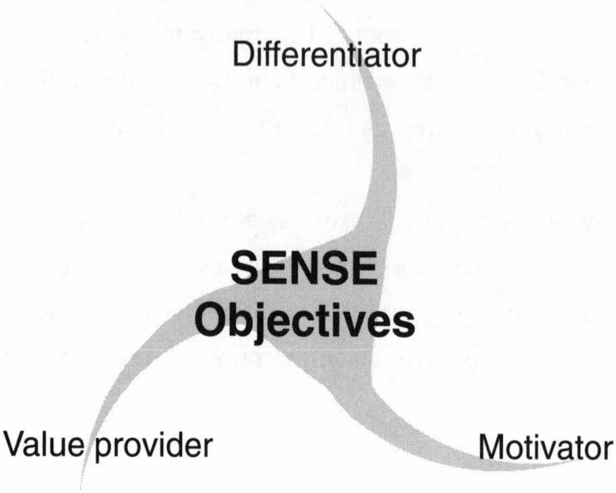

Differentiator

**SENSE
Objectives**

Value provider   Motivator

1. SENSE as Differentiator

SENSE campaigns may appeal to customers because they are executed in an unusual and special fashion. They go beyond standard executions that we are accustomed to in product design, communications, or retail spaces. They stimulate our senses via new means and strategies and thus differentiate the product. Differentiation raises the issue of what stimuli are most appropriate for creating sensory appeal.

2. SENSE as Motivator

SENSE campaigns can do more. They can motivate customers to try products and buy them. The key issue is how to stimulate customers without either overloading or understimulating them. With the optimum level of stimulation and activation, SENSE campaigns can be a powerful motivational force.

How is the perfect level of stimulation achieved? This requires an understanding of the "how," the process, of sensory stimulation. As I will discuss shortly, different principles apply at three levels: (1) across modalities; (2) across ExPros; and (3) across space and time.

3. SENSE as Value Provider

SENSE campaigns can also provide unique values to customers. As we will see, this requires an understanding of the type of SENSE that customers desire, i.e., an understanding of the consequences of the sensory appeal.

In sum, there are generally three strategic objectives in SENSE marketing: to differentiate, to motivate, and to provide value to customers by focusing on the senses. These three objectives are not necessarily mutually exclusive: A new product, a communication campaign, a store can at the same be noteworthy through their unusual executions, motivate us to purchase, and can reward us before and after purchase. Indeed, the S-P-C model for achieving sense impact presents a planning tool relevant to all three objectives.

THE S-P-C MODEL FOR ACHIEVING SENSE IMPACT

"S-P-C" stands for the Stimuli, Processes, and Consequences of sensory stimulation. As stated earlier, to differentiate our products through sensory appeal, we need to consider what stimuli are most appropriate for creating it. To motivate customers, we need to identify process principles. Finally, to provide value, we need to understand the consequences of sensory appeal (see Figure 4.3).

Stimuli

As customers, we are bombarded with numerous sensory expressions recorded by our retinas, ears, and nerve cells specialized for tactile and scent information. So which ones do we pay attention to and keep in our minds as permanent experiences?

The decision whether or not to pay attention to and store sensory information is made by the hippocampus, an evolutionarily old, two-winged structure in the center of the brain. The hippocampus is selective in what information it

FIGURE 4.3

The S-P-C Model of SENSE

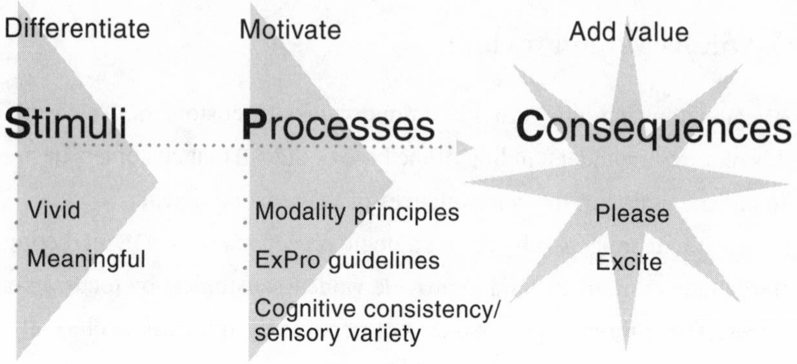

Differentiate	Motivate	Add value
Stimuli	**Processes**	**Consequences**
Vivid	Modality principles	Please
Meaningful	ExPro guidelines	Excite
	Cognitive consistency/ sensory variety	

pays attention to and stores. First, the hippocampus seems to be more interested in the vivid and salient than in the ordinary. Vivid information is inherently attention-getting; more intense sounds, more intense colors, and rough surfaces are more vivid than more subdued tones, pastel colors, and smooth surfaces. Salience refers to information that stands out in contrast to other information. So, sometimes, in loud environments, the understated can be more noticeable.

Second, the hippocampus prefers information relating to what customers already know. In other words, it uses the nets woven by past experience to capture new information. We thus notice things that fit our tastes in primary elements, styles, themes, and overall impressions. And because our backgrounds vary, we pick up slightly different aspects of new sensations.

Process

For process, the "how" of stimulation, different principles apply at three levels: (1) across modalities; (2) across ExPros; and (3) across space and time.

Across Modalities

At the level of the individual ExPro, the key issue is the best use of multimedia—i.e., how best to combine multiple modalities (visual, auditory, olfactory, and tactile) to convey information. Consider a packaging: there is printed text and three-dimensional visual information in the shape of the packaging and the visuals. Or take a web site: there is visual, verbal, and auditory information. In retailing and spatial design, you find visual and auditory information (e.g., background music or background sounds), scents, and tactile information.

Research regarding verbal *vs.* visual information has shown an advantage of pictures over words. "A picture is worth a thousand words," the saying goes, and when it comes to remembering an impression the saying seems to be right. So, whenever you can, try to represent a concept visually. Moreover, meaningful concrete pictures are preferred over abstract ones. Finally, visual and verbal information that is somehow integrated is more memorable than nonintegrated information.[9]

How about written and spoken information? For example, ad campaigns by Delta Airlines and Maybelline use ad claims that alternate between a voice and written display. Is this execution effective?

A former doctoral student of mine, Dr. Nader Tavassoli, who is now a professor at the Massachusetts Institute of Technology, has conducted research on this issue. He finds that compared with a unimodal presentation, in which words are only spoken or only written, verbal information presented in alternating modes is remembered better item by item, but the items are not as well connected. As a result, the overall experience with the brand will not be well integrated. Therefore Dr. Tavassoli warns against the use of the alternating mode in advertising. "Commercials for sport drinks, for example, attempt to maximize the association between 'thirst from being active' with the brand name (e.g., Gatorade) and ad claims such as 'replenishes essential minerals.' The more successful an ad is at integrating those three elements, the more likely consumers will be to think of the advertised brand when they are thirsty after being active." He recommends the alternating mode for online shopping on the Internet because it allows the marketer to convey more information quickly. He concludes, "There may not be one best way to communicate information. Instead the best presentation format depends on the goals of the marketer and the content of the message."[10]

Finally, how about memory for different primary elements? Do customers remember the color of your brand name better, or the color of a brand character? Dr. Tavassoli has also researched this issue. He finds that memory for the color in colored pictures is almost 20 percent higher than memory for color in colored words.

Across ExPros

As part of a research project on sensory impressions in the international hotel industry, sponsored by the Cornell School of Hotel Administration, I collected qualitative and quantitative impressions regarding the degrees of consistency of sensory elements across ExPros. Specifically, for several international hotel chains like the Marriott, the Hyatt, the Four Seasons, the Westin, and others, participants in the studies were shown for the same property (e.g., the Boston Marriott or the Hyatt in Sydney) three parts of the property: the edifice, the lobby, and a typical guest room. The motivational measure concerned their intention to stay in a particular property. The result: consistency in color scheme and overall style was preferred over inconsistency.[11]

Across Space and Time

The hotel project also addressed the issue of the desired execution across space and time by showing participants prototypical slides of the same brand at different locations. The key motivational principle regarding SENSE campaigns across space and time is what I call "cognitive consistency/sensory variety."

"Cognitive consistency" refers to an intellectual understanding of the underlying idea. It refers to the conceptual replication of the styles and themes—i.e., stylistic and thematic repetition. "Sensory variety" refers to the specific executional elements that are used over time (i.e., the colors, slogans, and spokespersons used in an ad; the lighting, structuring, and the service people employed in a particular store; the smell and taste of a particular grocery product; the touch and feel of the 1999 annual report, etc.).

Why is cognitive consistency important? Without cognitive consistency, a SENSE marketing approach ends in clutter. It will not be remembered or understood, and therefore cannot affect behavior. Cognitive consistency provides the structure within which the SENSE approach is presented.

Why is sensory variety essential? Because without it, the campaign will not attract attention in the long term. It will inevitably get boring and be un-motivating.

Unfortunately most companies seem to use only one side of the coin. They either blast their logos, ads, and products in a uniform and ubiquitous fashion, or they switch marketing campaigns too hastily. Companies that successfully use the principle of cognitive consistency/sensory variety such as Absolut vodka or American Express in its "Cardmember" series are still in the minority. Let's examine this issue through a case example that has received a lot of attention, ranging from wild praise to utmost condemnation. The case illustrates how difficult it is to get the idea of "cognitive consistency/sensory variety" right.

British Airways: World Communities

In August 1995, Interbrand Newell & Sorrell was commissioned to translate British Airways' new strategic direction into a forward-looking visual identity and brand image.[12] The main goals were to create a more international and caring image, while maintaining British Airways' strengths as a safe, reliable, high-quality airline.

As part of the campaign, British Airways created a series of "World images." The idea was to commission artworks and to use them as images on the planes' tail fins. These images were made by artists from all over the world and meant to give expression to the moods and heritages of their local communities, thus forming a vast celebration of cultural diversity. The collection of world images was not static but part of an ongoing program of exploration and discovery of the world's cultures. The world images idea has not been without its opponents (some called it "ethnic graffiti"), not least because the artwork replaced the Union Jack on BA planes. In fact, the decision led to a generational split in the United Kingdom: the young loved the new tails; older people tended to dislike them. Former Prime Minister Thatcher was sufficiently offended that she chose to place a handkerchief over the tail fin of a BA scale model.

By May 1998, the British Airways communications director who had been responsible for the campaign championed by CEO Robert Ayling "decided to leave." In July 1998, British Airways dropped the tail-fins design on

British Airways planes at Heathrow airport in 1998

its transatlantic flights, and Mr. Ayling conceded that the majority of business-class travelers were unhappy with the multicultural look.[13]

Consequences

Look at the words customers use to describe their response to sensory input. They either say, "This is so beautiful," "It's so appealing," "How ugly!" Or they say, "This is exciting," "Wild," or "How relaxing." In sum, consequences fall into two categories: pleasing beauty or arousing excitement. As a marketer, you need to decide if you wish to please or to excite.

Brand positioning in terms of consequences offers an "either-or." In fashion Dior, Armani, and Calvin Klein are about beauty (admittedly of different styles). Versace, Gaultier, and Donna Karan are about excitement. In fruit juice Tropicana is beauty; Fruitopia and Mountain Dew are excitement. In cars Jaguar is beauty; Porsche is excitement.

You can have it both ways, however, in spatial facilities. The workout rooms of many fitness clubs in New York are run-of-the-mill air-conditioned boxes with ceiling-mounted TVs and pounding music, but the dressing rooms often offer more sedate environments.

SUMMARY

The objective of SENSE marketing campaigns is to appeal to the five senses and thereby provide aesthetic pleasure or excitement to customers. If managed appropriately, SENSE marketing creates powerful sensory experiences that differentiate companies and products, motivate customers, and convey value to them. To manage SENSE, marketers need to pay attention to primary attributes, styles, and themes in order to create positive customer impressions. I have presented a model that shows how to manage stimuli, the sensory process, and consequences. One of the key principles underlying SENSE (cognitive consistency/sensory variety) presents the organizational challenge of meshing control to ensure consistency with flexibility to ensure variety.

But . . . says LAURA BROWN . . .

Isn't all this SENSE marketing just fluff? Isn't it superficial, and doesn't it distract from the real value of products? Isn't it really meant to fool customers?

5

—

FEEL

FEEL marketing is the strategy and implementation of attaching affect to the company and brand via experience providers. To be successful, FEEL marketing requires a clear understanding of how to create feeling during the consumption experience. Let's look at two examples.

HÄAGEN-DAZS CAFÉS IN ASIA AND EUROPE

A brilliant example of FEEL marketing at the point of consumption comes from Häagen-Dazs in Europe and Asia.[1] Häagen-Dazs cafés are designed as romantic settings where customers can experience the sensual pleasures of premium ice cream and the joys of love. Through skillful FEEL marketing, Häagen-Dazs has linked itself with the idea and pleasures of romantic love.

Product design is a major contributor to the overall FEEL approach. In Asia, Häagen-Dazs offers a line of ice cream cakes with romantic themes, including "Waltzing Romance," "Heart of Hearts," "Truly Deeply Madly," and "Happy Together." Exquisitely crafted and decorated, these cakes are as beautiful as any fine bakery creation. The romantic world of Häagen-Dazs is carried through on membership cards for the Häagen-Dazs cafés, which show a romantic couple embracing and holding an ice cream confection. A brochure for the café pictures a young couple, their mouths wrapped around the same spoon of ice cream. The café's slogan, "Dedicated to pleasure," appears on all printed promotions and reinforces the theme.

The Häagen-Dazs web site offers visitors a whole world of experiences: "Häagen-Dazs is about more than making the world's finest super premium frozen desserts. It is about a commitment to discovering the elements of perfection. It is about distilling the essence of an experience into a flavor. Creating a setting that opens a place for possibility. And defining an inspiration that says satisfaction." The "settings" link takes you along on the romantic adventures of "the Häagen-Dazs world traveler" through journal entries illustrated by photos of Häagen-Dazs cafés worldwide. In Paris, he meets an old love: "April 23. Juliette, looking resplendent in her blue summer dress, caught my eye as I exited the train. In three years she hadn't changed a bit. During the cab ride to her apartment, she asked me a million questions, forcing my tongue to speak the French I thought I'd forgotten." After a blissful visit, it's on to China: "April 27. I had three days in Shanghai but my head was still spinning from the long flight, Paris, and Juliette. I stopped by the prominent Häagen-Dazs Café on Henan and Nanjing East to collect my thoughts over a cup of vanilla ice cream. Gazing out the large window, I watched the countless bicyclists zip past. . . . Leaving the cool and relaxing environment of the café, I ventured out onto the bustling street." If this is November, it must be Manila, and our hero has not forgotten his Juliette: "I wandered down to Makati, the business center of Manila, where I found a Häagen-Dazs café. Realizing I hadn't eaten for quite some time, I stopped in for a little treat. I sipped on a cappuccino as I awaited my feast. Watching the crowds along the promenade, I spotted a woman with long golden hair in a white satin dress. It had to be Juliette. I jumped from my seat and rushed for the door, but the crowds moved too quickly, and the woman was gone. . . ."

A Manila publication hit the nail on the head when it reported on the festivities for the opening of the local Häagen-Dazs café: "The show tied up traffic in the area around the Shangri-La Hotel in Makati City and served strong notice to the young and ice cream fans that Häagen-Dazs has finally moved into the local ice cream market not as a competitor but to add excitement and make people aware of the ice cream market and its possibilities of bringing

Häagen-Dazs café at night in Shanghai (China)

new eating delights to people of all ages."[2] Not as a competitor? Actually, that's right. Häagen-Dazs in Manila, and all over the world, is not so much marketing ice cream as marketing feelings of romance.

CAMPBELL'S SOUP

For decades, the Campbell's soup brand has associated itself with emotional situations. Childhood and family feelings are also the mainstay of Campbell's Soup Company's new FEEL campaign, themed "M'm! M'm! Good for the body, good for the soul." For the campaign's first commercial, BBDO Worldwide created a cloying television spot meant to associate the product with feelings of home and security. A shy foster child is left by a social worker at a new foster home. We then see the frightened little girl, still in her overcoat, sitting curled up alone on her bed, her tiny suitcase unopened. In comes her new foster mother, bearing a steaming bowl of Campbell's soup on a tray. The child's wan face brightens as she says, "My mother used to make me that soup." In a moment of bonding, her new mother replies, "So did mine."

Promotion for Campbell's soup

WHY FEELINGS ARE IMPORTANT

To seek pleasure and to avoid pain—or more generally, to feel good and to avoid feeling bad—is one of the core principles of life. The behaviorist school of psychology (also called "rat psychology") has taught us this lesson over and over. When you hook an electrode into the pleasure center of a rat's brain and link it to a lever that allows the rat to stimulate itself, the rat won't stop pressing the lever—even if it means depriving itself of food and sleep. Deep down inside, organisms are pleasure-seekers.

Feeling good (or avoiding feeling bad) does not have to involve such extreme behavior, although it may in many cases of human behavior as well. Just think about hedonic addictions and obsessions (like smoking, drinking, compulsive gambling, and shopping), behaviors that are often performed at the expense of other valuable activities. Nor is pleasure-seeking the only, or always the primary, motive in human behavior. Many other motives and goals (e.g., seeking variety, status, building satisfactory relationships) that are more cognitive or relational in nature must come into play in explaining customer behavior and developing experiential strategies (see the following chapters). However, all other things being equal, customers opt for feeling good and avoid feeling bad. At various degrees of consciousness, they pose the question "How do I feel about it?" When they feel good, they love the product and the company. When they feel bad, they avoid the product and the company. If a marketing strategy can create consistent good feelings for customers, it can foster strong and lasting brand loyalty.

FEEL marketing appears in advertising, products, and names. FEEL marketing is even used, though less frequently, in building designs. Responding to the Disney CEO's challenge, "What can you do to make people smile?" architects Michael Graves and Robert A. M. Stern created a new Feature Animation Building for Disney's Burbank studio that looks like something straight out of a Disney cartoon.[3]

AFFECTIVE EXPERIENCES

Affective experiences are experiences of degree—that is, feelings vary in intensity, ranging from mildly positive or negative mood states to intense emotions.[4] If we intend to use affective experiences effectively as part of marketing strategy, we need to get a better understanding of these moods and emotions. Figure 5.1 contrasts moods with emotions.

Moods

Moods are unspecific affective states. As psychologist and consumer researcher Alice Isen of Cornell University has shown, finding a nickel in a public telephone can put you in a good mood.[5] This idea has been employed by upscale hair salons, which serve beverages; at airline check-in counters,

FIGURE 5.1

Types of Affect

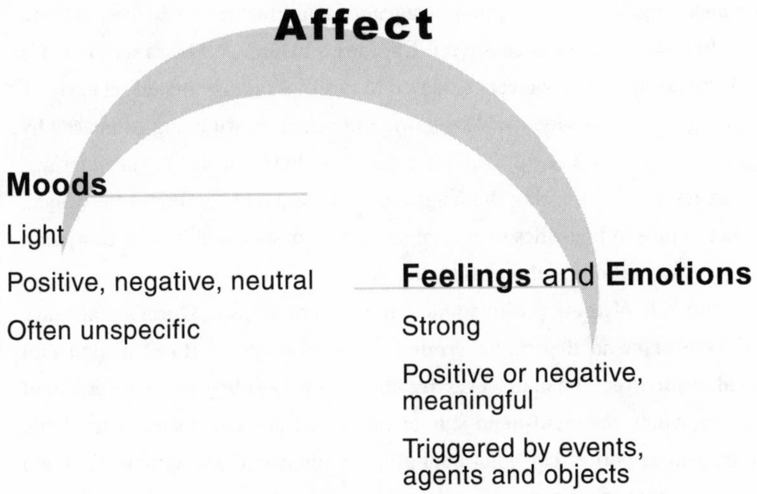

Affect

Moods

Light

Positive, negative, neutral

Often unspecific

Feelings and Emotions

Strong

Positive or negative, meaningful

Triggered by events, agents and objects

where you can get candies; and at restaurants serving an *amuse-gueule*. These techniques work best if they are perceived as unexpected and sincere.

Moods may be elicited by specific stimuli, but customers are often unaware of them. Occasionally, consumers may even misconstrue the source of their affective state. Irritating music in a coffee bar or an inattentive flight attendant may disrupt a conversation with a friend and put you in a bad mood, though you may not be aware that it was the music, or the flight attendant. You just say you don't like the coffee or that you did not enjoy your flight.

Emotions

In contrast to moods, emotions are intense, stimulus-specific affective states. They draw attention onto themselves and disrupt other activities. Just think of anger, envy, jealousy, or even love. These emotions are always caused by something or somebody (people, events, companies, products, or communications). We are always angry about something or at someone, envious about something or jealous of somebody; and we always love somebody or something. For a certain time, these emotions consume all our energy.

EMOTIONAL NAMES FOR FRAGRANCES

The marketing of fragrances and fashion has been traditionally the realm of SENSE marketing. Yet more and more fragrance manufacturers discover the lure of FEEL. In chapter 3, we encountered Clinique's "Happy." Then there is Estée Lauder's "Beautiful" fragrance, presented in ads in a fantasy bridal scenario. A lovely young bride in a wide wedding gown and veil is shown being embraced by an angelic flower girl. The ad draws a connection between the joy of marriage and the experience of wearing the fragrance. The appeal is powerful to women, who either aspire to be brides or warmly recall their special day. The campaign calls up strong emotions and personal dreams.

The flip side of these positive and romantic emotions is Gucci's fragrance "Envy." One print ad depicts an erotic black-and-white photo of a man and woman about to kiss. The man's eyes are glancing very subtly in the direction of the camera. Along the right-hand side of the layout is a color shot of the long, phallic fragrance bottle. The emotional affect is intense, if ambiguous. Wearing the fragrance may inspire envy in others, or the product name may simply invoke a highly sexually charged and passionate world of powerful feelings.

Many emotions are thought of as bipolar. It is difficult, if not impossible, to be depressed and exhilarated at the same time. Even manic-depression comes in periods of mania and depression over time. Moreover, the choice of certain F&B positioning may make it harder to achieve a certain feeling positioning later. For example, Volvo's positioning as "safe" over the years still seems to make it difficult for the car to come across as "emotional" as well.

There are two types of emotions: basic emotions and complex emotions.

Basic Emotions

Psychological research has shown that there are a small number of so-called "basic emotions." Basic emotions constitute the basic components of our affective lives, similar to chemical elements. They include, for example, the positive emotion of joy and the negative emotions of anger, disgust, and sadness. Basic emotions are found all around the globe, and their facial expressions are remarkably similar across cultures. Thus, they are ideal for use in global communications campaigns.

Complex Emotions

Complex emotions are blends and combinations of basic emotions. Most marketing-generated emotions are complex ones.

One example of a complex emotion is nostalgia (a wistful and sentimental yearning for a period gone by). Nostalgia is a powerful feeling that marketers are exploring more and more as the population ages. Yet, as a complex emotion, nostalgia can be invoked only by using the right cultural and generation-specific emotional cues.

Nostalgia can also create intense emotional attachments to logos and other icons, which sometimes presents a dilemma for marketers working to redesign old brands. In fact, nostalgic attachment to an icon has reached massive proportions in the former East Germany, where a familiar street crossing signal is being phased out over howls of disapproval and protest. The figure is the Ampelmannchen, roughly translated as "little traffic light man," a chubby, hat-wearing figure who directs pedestrians to walk or wait. Since Germany's reunification, the Ampelmannchen has been steadily replaced by the west's crossing icon, prompting a nostalgic grassroots movement to save the old vestige of East Germany's communist past. The Ampelmannchen has become a cool icon, the focus of the Committee to Save the Ampelmannchen, displayed on T-shirts, mouse pads, and Internet sites. Marketers have been quick to cash in on this nostalgia-driven craze. One soccer club has adopted the Ampelmannchen as its mascot, and a West German company has begun putting the figure on jars of mustard and gherkins, hoping to boost their sagging sales in the east.

EVENTS, AGENTS, AND OBJECT EMOTIONS

According to an influential psychological model, distinct kinds of emotions (basic or complex) are triggered by three major aspects or changes: events (i.e., things that happen), agents (people, institutions, situations), and objects.

"When one focuses on events, one does so because one is interested in their consequences; when one focuses on agents, one does so because of their actions; and when one focuses on objects, one is interested in certain aspects or imputed properties of them *qua* objects. Central to our position is the notion that emotions are valenced reactions, and that any particular valenced reaction is always a reaction to one of these perspectives of the world."[6]

According to the model, emotional reactions to objects fall into the broad category of "attraction," i.e., like and dislike, or love and hate. Emotional reactions to agents are a bit more differentiated into emotional types of admiration and reproach as well as pride and shame. By far the most differentiated emotional types emerge from reactions to events: joy and distress, happiness and resentment, satisfaction and fear, relief and disappointment.

Let us now consider the types of objects, agents, and events we deal with in marketing. Replace "objects" with "products" or "brands," "agents" with "companies" or "spokespeople," and "events" with "consumption situations," and the model becomes more illuminating. Now it says you can create a general positive or negative feeling, a "like"/"dislike" affect, as long as you think "product" or "brand." Once you add "company" and "spokesperson" (e.g., a testimonial or even a Ronald McDonald–like character in a TV ad), you can get admiration or reproach, and pride or shame. But when you get to the consumption situation, when consumers use your products and experience the brand, when they actually encounter the service and the salesperson, then you can get the most complex emotions: joy and distress, happiness and resentment, satisfaction and fear, relief and disappointment.

AFFECT OCCURS MOSTLY DURING CONSUMPTION

Feelings are most powerful when they occur during consumption. Strong feelings result from contact and interaction, and they develop over time. They are related to personal encounters. Indeed feelings for products arise from contact during consumption over extended periods of time. FEEL during consumption dwarfs FEEL in advertising!

All the goods and services I love—Omaha Steak's filet mignon, the Palm V and VII Organizers, Nokia mobile phones, IWC watches, Häagen-Dazs ice cream (the original, not the low-fat version), the meticulous service on Singapore Airlines, the Jessye Norman recording of Richard Strauss's *Last Four*

THE HEART—A UNIVERSAL SYMBOL

The universal symbol of love, the heart, traces its history to Egyptian art of the fourteenth century B.C. By the sixth century A.D. it had found its way to Europe, where it began to appear on both religious and secular ornamentation. When European settlers came to America in the seventeenth and eighteenth centuries, they brought the heart with them as a symbol of love, friendship, and trust (*Architectural Digest*, June 1998).

The heart has a rich history in American folk art. Pennsylvania German artists adorned baptismal records, babies' cradles, and wooden "sweetheart spoons" with hearts. Sailors fashioned heart-shaped trinkets out of whale bone for their loves on land, including heart-adorned corset stays. By the eighteenth century, the heart was appearing on jewelry boxes, spice boxes, furniture, quilts, earrings, clocks, and dozens of other articles. A carved wooden heart and hand symbolizing friendship and truth was used in nineteenth-century ceremonies of the Independent Order of Odd Fellows. And as a symbol of love, the heart's appeal is still going strong today.

Songs, the raw potency of Bruce Willis action films, and, of course, Yoku Moku cookies and the Amanresorts in Southeast Asia, and now in Jackson Hole, Wyoming (remember my dedication in *Marketing Aesthetics),* as well as skydiving (see the cover of this book)—I have enjoyed many, many times. I may have been impressed with them the first time I encountered them, but my strong emotional devotion to them developed over time and through repeated positive experiences.

Moreover, there are numerous consumption situations that are associated with affect. Having a drink at a bar, going to the mall, going to the movies, seeing a sports performance (or an opera or a theater performance), going to the beach, and driving a car all constitute consumption situations that are often associated with positive affect. Moreover, it is part of the consumption situation of "going to the movies" to consume not only the movie itself but also perhaps a bag of buttered popcorn, a large Diet Coke, a box of Milk Duds, etc. The consumption situation "going to the mall" may include shopping in a variety of clothing outlets, having lunch at McDonald's, and then going to the movies. Think about the opportunity of linking naturally occurring positive emotions to your brand.

Note, however, that not all consumption situations evoke positive feelings. Think about going to the dentist (fear), buying a car (frustration), Christmas shopping on the twenty-fourth of December (anger), trying on a bathing suit after the holidays (self-hatred), and, not so long ago, buying a condom (shame). Buying a car consistently ranks among the most dissatisfying consumption episodes. (Surveys, though, rarely include "going to the dentist," "Christmas shopping on the twenty-fourth of December," and "condom shopping.") Many of these situations are associated with negative feelings because experiential marketing is absent, or poorly done.

Face-to-Face Interactions

In consumption situations, face-to-face interactions are the most important cause of strong feelings. As we discussed earlier, people have strong feelings toward other people. Face-to-face interactions provoke feelings because of the human contact. Services, of course, are a good example. Many services (repair services, consulting and counseling services, services in the travel and hospitality industries) are often delivered face-to-face. Indeed, some of the strongest emotions—good or bad—are experienced in service contexts. Just think about service at the Ritz-Carlton or at your car dealership. Therefore, sales training must include affect management.

High-end fashion designers have long understood the value of the shopping experience and the contribution the sales associate makes to that experience. A long article in *The New Yorker* in 1998 painted a portrait of Victoria Gallegos, then the highest-selling salesperson at Prada's Madison Avenue store in New York and an expert at creating powerful and positive consumption experiences for her clients.[7]

Victoria and her selling approach ("selling approach"—what a trite term—her approach to experiences, to people, to life!) isn't about racking up huge numbers (although she herself sold about $2 million worth of clothing in 1997). It's about personal connections and experiences: "the goal should be to

Ms. Gallegos (and the author) in front of Barney's Christmas window

create great relationships with the clients," she says. The experience starts when the customer walks in the door. Victoria rejects conventional openers like "Can I help you?"—pitches that almost always produce the answer No. Instead, she focuses on the customers themselves, complimenting what they're wearing, making a connection.

When a Brazilian couple in their mid-twenties entered the store one day, Victoria swung into action. The first step was to get a bead on the customers: "What you wear is a little story about your life," she says. She approached João and Maria by complimenting his sweater. He was looking for a jacket, so Victoria steered the couple toward some suits on sale. While João was in the fitting room, Victoria kept chatting with Maria: "You never give less attention to the female than to the man. Just because she's not buying doesn't mean she can't break the sale." João bought the suit. Knowing that South Americans don't mind such questions, she asked João what he did (Europeans, she knew, don't like this sort of question). When he said he was a lawyer, she showed him a briefcase. He bought it. She showed him a matching portfolio. He bought it. The picture of concern, Victoria commented, "You're buying all this stuff—what are you gonna put it in?" She brought out a large black duffel bag with wheels. João and Maria bought that too. By the end of the shopping session, the couple had added a pair of shoes, a belt, and a wallet to their haul—a purchase that totaled over $5,000. While their sale was being rung up, Victoria seated her customers on a sofa and brought them refreshments. After they left, she sent their items on to their hotel with a note reading, "I wish you a magical time in New York City." As *The New Yorker's* Mimi Swartz pointed out, "about an hour and a half had passed since the couple arrived, wanting nothing more than a jacket."

Prada's customers can afford to shop anywhere, and they pay a premium for the clothing they buy. They also pay, although not explicitly, for the personal attention that extends beyond the purchase. Victoria maintains personal relationships with many of her customers, passing on stock tips, recommending interior designers, securing good tables at prestigious restaurants. Victoria is at the center of her own very high class network. She also serves as a kind of friend to some wealthy but isolated customers: when she bought a customer a teddy bear for his birthday, he burst into tears.

It's not just the chic designer shops that recognize the power of emotional experiences for customers. Nordstrom, the Seattle-based department store chain, has built its reputation on its customer service. On a recent visit to Macy's flagship store in New York, it was also clear to me that it wasn't just the selling floors that were being renovated—it was the sales associates' attitudes toward customers as well. Springing back from Chapter 11 status a few years ago, Macy's has installed conspicuous customer service desks on its selling floors and trained its sales associates to give personal attention to customers. Ringing up your sales, associates now take a moment to notice the name on your credit card and to thank you by name for your purchase. "Thank you, Mr. Schmitt" seems like a small thing, but this kind of gesture can turn an impersonal transaction into a memorably pleasant shopping experience.

Unfortunately, face-to-face interactions during service encounters can also be the source of frustration and anger. Just think about your local car dealer (unless you drive a Lexus or Saturn). What can we do about negative experiences? An obvious solution is to take human contact out of the encounter and to replace him or her through automation. It works fine for a routine, low-involvement product, but not for a complex, high-involvement one. The result of this automation of high-involvement products is often sterile goods and services that fail to engage the consumer emotionally. The only adequate approach is to understand the emotions that customers experience.

Which Emotions Are Experienced During Consumption?

Several marketing researchers have developed emotion typologies that are specific to marketing situations. In my view, consumer researcher Marsha Richins has developed the best typology and measurement to date.[8] She covers the emotions that are most commonly experienced in a variety of consumption situations (including anticipatory consumption, purchase, and use of jewelry, clothing, food, cars, and services). The measures are statistically reliable and brief enough to be used by managers as part of survey and field research. Finally, the terms used in the scale are familiar to customers and easily understood.

FIGURE 5.2

Sixteen Types of Consumption Emotions

Anger	**Discontent**	**Worry**	**Sadness**
Frustrated	Unfulfilled	Nervous	Depressed
Angry	Discontented	Worried	Sad
Irritated		Tense	Miserable

Fear	**Shame**	**Envy**	**Loneliness**
Scared	Embarrassed	Envious	Lonely
Afraid	Ashamed	Jealous	Homesick
Panicky	Humiliated		

Romantic	**Love**	**Peacefulness**	**Contentment**
Sexy	Loving	Calm	Contented
Romantic	Sentimental	Peaceful	Fulfilled
Passionate	Warmhearted		

Optimism	**Joy**	**Excitement**	**Other Items**
Optimistic	Happy	Excited	Guilty
Encouraged	Pleased	Thrilled	Proud
Hopeful	Joyful	Enthusiastic	Eager

The sixteen emotions and the respective items to measure them are shown in figure 5.2. As Richins has shown, the sixteen consumption-related emotions may be plotted into a perceptual map of two dimensions. The first dimension is a positivity–negativity dimension. The second dimension is a receptivity (inwardly *vs.* outwardly oriented) dimension.

Figure 5.3 shows exemplary items that fall into each one of the four quadrants formed by the two dimensions. Although not used this way by Richins, this simple model may allow us to predict what happens to an intense emotion when its origin is lost and it becomes transformed into a less intense mood.

Imagine you are on a one-week vacation in a resort and soon after you check into the resort hotel, there is an event that causes one of the four clusters of emotions. For example, you receive an unexpected bottle of champagne after check-in (and a good one, too; say, Dom Perignon, Roederer Crystall, or Krug's Grande Cuvée) and you are in another world: pleased to say the least, more likely exited and enthusiastic. Or you receive a personal,

FIGURE 5.3

Perceptual Map of Consumption Emotions

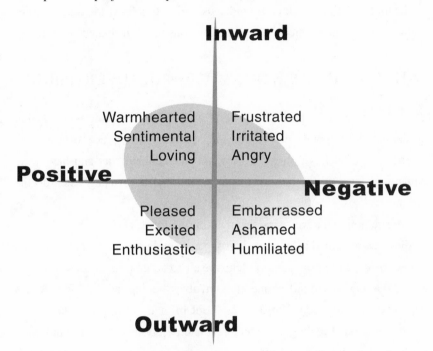

moving welcome card from the guest manager, who remembers you from last year: remembering last year's wonderful stay, you feel warmhearted, sentimental, and loving. Or let's say your shower keeps dripping throughout the night and the resort personnel aren't too responsive: you feel frustrated, irritated, and angry. Or you sleep late the first day and get caught with your pants down by the floor attendant: you feel embarrassed, ashamed, even humiliated.

The labeling of each quadrant of the model nicely helps us to predict what may happen: outward positive emotions are likely to make you walk around and praise, spend money, and recommend the hotel to others; inward negative emotions are likely to turn you into a complainer or, worse, a saboteur who finds fault with everything you encounter from now on. Inward positive emotions make you feel special; you are likely to show understated customer loyalty (but without outward publicity). Outward negative emotions may make you never come back (from fear of being seen by that floor attendant again).

In sum, Richins' research provides us with a typology, measurement instrument, and strategic model for managing consumption-related emotions.

WHAT'S THE ROLE OF EMOTIONAL ADVERTISING?

FEEL marketing works particularly well for complex, involving products that present plenty of opportunities to reinforce feelings during face-to-face interactions. But what if you market a low-involvement product and have little human contact with the customer: can "emotional advertising" then do the job?

Most emotional advertising features smiling faces, crying babies, barking poodles, accompanied by a lot of singsong and jingles. In some rare cases, the product or consumption situation lends itself to an emotional focus. For example, making (personal) phone calls involves feeling, so AT&T's "Reach Out and Touch Someone" made sense. But in many cases, the relation between product and feeling is coincidental and purely driven by a brand manager's or ad executive's decision to jump on the "emotional ad" bandwagon.

These emotional advertising campaigns measure up well in the short run, meaning on some "emotion scale" taken right after the exposure to the ad. But what do these scales really measure? It seems to me most of them measure consumers' memory for certain contents of the ad and how smart the consumer is in guessing what the market researcher has in mind. It is as if the consumer is saying: "All right. You want to know whether after seeing all these happy faces, kids, and dogs, I feel 'warm,' 'full of joy,' and 'glowing with happiness.' Sure. So I'm not a monster after all." In other words, these types of measures have produced massive overstatements regarding the effectiveness of "emotional advertising." Most customers are too smart to be fooled by simple thirty-second commercials (repeated daily). These ads do not possess the power of a three-hour feature like *Titanic* (not to mention the same dramatic qualities), and as a result, they have only a tiny impact. Does this mean that all emotional advertising is wasted? Definitely not. However, if you want your advertising to work, you need to do three things: (1) have patience; (2) hire a good producer; and (3) use ads as an interpretive framework for consumption. All of these techniques require deep pockets. Let me explain.

Have Patience

For emotional advertising to work, you need to transfer the positive affect from an object for which customers already experience strong emotions to a new object (a product or brand) by pairing the two objects. This process is the well-known Pavlovian "classical conditioning."

In a typical classical conditioning consumer experiment, a positive stimulus (e.g., pleasant music) is paired with one product (e.g., a red pen); and a negative stimulus (unpleasant music) is paired with another product (e.g., a blue pen). Using this setting in an experiment, one exposure seems to be enough to get the desired effect: people prefer the red pen over the blue pen. But very likely the finding is what methodologist call a "demand effect": respondents in the experiment guess what the experimenter wants! Using a trickier yet realistic setting, many more trials (up to forty) are needed to get the effect. Therefore, be careful. Do not expect wonders! Classical conditioning requires patience. Only through repetition can you be successful. Repetition breeds familiarity, and familiarity breeds liking. Humans seem to be hardwired through their evolutionary history to respond that way. To like what is familiar and be suspicious of the unfamiliar is adaptive.

Incidentally, in actual retail environments you may do better. Beats per second in music is correlated with walking speed in supermarkets and degree of consumption. This, however, is unspecific choice resulting from a positive mood, not brand choice resulting from strong feelings.

Hire a Good Producer

Do you remember the Taster's Choice ads from a few years ago? Or Grey Poupon? Or the Oreo's cookies campaign with the father teaching the son how to eat an Oreo cookie? And all those Hallmark ads? Coffee, mustard, cookies, and greeting cards are inexpensive, simple products. But nonetheless emotional advertising has worked for them.

Why? My guess is because these ads are produced like movies. They have a narrative; they appear in sequels; they are more like actual program content than disruptive commercials. The Campbell's soup ads described at the beginning of this chapter always use a narrative slice-of-life approach.

If used properly, emotional advertising becomes a powerful, ever-present reminder of the brand's feeling qualities. So, hire a good producer.

Use Ads as Interpretive Frames for Consumption

Emotional advertising can also become a frame, a way of interpreting whatever may happen later during consumption. The feelings then evoked during consumption (but really as a result of the advertising) are the ultimate means of attachment. After seeing a BMW ad, you feel the power of the steering wheel later when you drive the car.

But what if customers have never bought the product? Can we get them to anticipate consumption by designing ads that frame the consumption experience?

Michel Pham, a consumer researcher and colleague of mine at Columbia Business School, believes we can. He argues that customers often picture the consumption situation in their mind and thereby anticipate—and experience—affect.[9] As an F&B marketer, to get somebody to a squash court, you may elaborate on the health benefits of exercise. Dr. Pham, an accomplished squash player, recommends a different track: get people to imagine what it feels like when they are hitting the ball, and create ads that display in striking visual detail the feelings during the play.

Do customers really experience imagined feelings and use them as part of their decision making?

Try for yourself. Imagine you are really late for an international flight. That is, really late: you are leaving your house when you are supposed to have checked in, two hours before takeoff. Under normal circumstances, your ride to the airport takes you about one hour. But it's Friday afternoon, and there is heavy traffic. You sweat through it, barely avoid an accident, just make it to the airport thirty minutes before scheduled departure. The check-in agent refuses to take you; you argue for a while; you speak to the manager. The manager is a nice guy; he rushes you through customs; you make it to the plane, just as they are beginning to pull the jetway away from it. How do you feel now? Do you feel relieved after imagining all this anguish, stress, and fear? Now imagine you had arrived only five minutes later and just missed the plane. Can you now imagine and feel the anger and disappointment? And will you use the affect as part of your future decision making? Will you leave earlier next time to avoid the negative affect?[10] (I certainly hope you will.)

There are numerous consumption situations that trigger consumers' imagery, cause them to experience affect and, as a result, make a decision to take a certain action or not. Imagine how you would feel doing your Christmas shopping on Christmas Day. Are you now willing to shop a bit earlier? Imagine your dentist performing a root canal operation. Are you now willing to brush your teeth regularly and supplement your daily routine with other dental-care measures?

SUMMARY

FEEL experiences can take a variety of forms, ranging from mild moods to strong emotions. The consumption situation is critical for FEEL, although FEEL communications prior to consumption can influence the type of FEEL experienced by providing an interpretive frame for consumption. As an experiential marketer, you need to understand how to induce feelings and how to provide the right level of stimulation for feelings. If you are successful, you have created a strong bond between your brand and the user.

But . . . LAURA BROWN objects:
Isn't FEEL marketing a vicious manipulation of our precious feelings? How dare these marketers treat something so personal and important in such a cynical way?
(By the way, I like Victoria better than Sheila.)

6

THINK

The objective of THINK marketing is to encourage customers to engage in elaborative and creative thinking that may result in a reevaluation of the company and products. THINK marketing has the potential to tap into—and sometimes guide—major "paradigm shifts" in society, as people rethink old assumptions and expectations.

GENESIS ELDERCARE: CHANGING HOW WE THINK ABOUT THE ELDERLY

A marvelous example of THINK marketing comes from Genesis Health Ventures, a company at the forefront of a revolution in caring for older people. Siegel & Gale, a corporate identity firm, has helped Genesis ElderCare develop a THINK campaign for the programs that aim to help older people live full and independent lives.[1] Genesis went to Siegel & Gale with a vision: against the "warehousing" of older people, in favor of independence; against condescension and neglect, in favor of dignity and respect; and against the traditional medical model, in favor of sustaining an independent lifestyle through managing chronic problems and finding their root causes, rather than aggressively treating symptoms.

Ad for Genesis ElderCare

Say for example an older person falls. Standard treatment dictates a quick hip replacement and some rehab, and that's it. There is no systematic or professional understanding of why the fall occurred. Perhaps there was an unfavorable drug interaction? Maybe the person needs new glasses. Maybe the floor was slippery. Another common problem in older people is depression; Genesis wanted to get to the source of it rather than medicating or institution-

alizing the person. Genesis Health Ventures wanted to be a true champion of the elderly, and Siegel & Gale helped them develop a coherent THINK marketing approach for their revolutionary ideas and practices.

Siegel & Gale started with a name, Genesis ElderCare, and a tag line, "ElderCare for a full life." Other language issues were addressed as well, including referring to the elderly as "customers" rather than as "patients." The term "nursing home" was also banished. Staff members were given complete guidelines and training in the use of language to show respect and confer dignity.

Promotional and informational materials for the ElderCare programs depict older people in active settings, enjoying life and enjoying company. The images depict vital people with personalities, values, and relationships. One striking shot shows a confident-looking older woman in the foreground, with her family, slightly out of focus, behind her. Another shot shows an African-American woman in a pew at her church; the copy reads, "Betty still makes hats for some of her lady friends in the choir. They all love her style. And if she keeps working, that's up to her." Yet another shows an older couple getting married, the bride in a white gown and veil, looking at the camera with the headline: "I'm not giving up my independence."

Promotional and informational materials carry a dual focus that represents a perception of aging different from what most of us have been accustomed to. First, the family is highlighted, as is its need for help with caregiving:

"Family caregivers provide the majority of nonclinical care needed by aging adults. Sixty-five percent of caregivers receive no help from anyone or instruction on how to perform the activities they're assisting with."[2] The 1997 annual report from Genesis shows a happy photo of an elderly mother with her daughter, with the copy, "She's getting older. She's changing. And you're not sure what to do or where to turn. First, call us." This emphasis on the family's need for guidance and help answers a crying need for people with aging family members.

The second major focus is on the need—and the right—for older people to keep active if they so choose. One spread shows an elderly man at a filling station in a rural New England setting: "Lester's been pumping gas since it was 10 cents a gallon. He loves being able to still work. If he wants to, he should. At Genesis ElderCare, we assess the individual needs of the elderly and their families and provide health care services through a network of people, places, and programs. That's our vision of eldercare. And why we do all we can to help older people live life to the fullest."

The philosophy of Genesis is carried through in everything they do. Their "brand voice guidebook" offers guidance in the use of corporate communications. Under "How should we use images?" the following advice is offered: "We should use images that are in keeping with our key personality traits— visionary, compassionate, and results-oriented. . . . We believe in using images in our ads and brochures that are credible and that avoid cliches. Images that are engaging—even provocative . . . are a powerful demonstration of how we see the elderly."

Genesis ElderCare is a beautiful example not just of a THINK campaign but also of a THINK service. As society changes its attitudes toward aging and the elderly, Genesis ElderCare provides a model for implementing this new thinking. This is really THINK marketing at its very best.

APPLE COMPUTER'S REVIVAL

In the spring of 1998, Apple's market share was up for the first time in years. After six consecutive quarterly losses, Apple posted quarterly profits, earning over $100 million. And the stock was again a favorite of Wall Street.[3]

Apple was in the process of transforming itself. It decided to get rid of the rainbow colors in its logo because it appeared too reminiscent of the seventies, replacing it with several monocolored logos. It rolled out the iMac (for "internet Mac") in six "flavors" (not colors!), a glitzy new home PC with a blazingly fast processor, and sold 278,000 units in six weeks, making it one of the most successful computer launches ever. *BusinessWeek* voted the iMac one of the best products of 1998 and wrote, "Its translucent teal casing is a bold departure from the acres of putty-colored PCs on desktops everywhere." Steve Jobs, Apple's CEO, said: "Apple is back to its roots, starting to innovate again." And iMac designer Jonathan Ive said, "It's in the genes of this company to be different."

The innovation of the iMac came on the heels of an evocative THINK marketing campaign. Conceived by Lee Clow, an ad executive at TBWA Chiat/Day Inc., who had created the famous "*1984*" spot, the campaign uses the slogan "Think different" over striking black-and-white photographs of "creative geniuses" in various fields—Albert Einstein, Gandhi, Martha Graham, Maria Callas, Amelia Earhart, Rosa Parks, Buzz Aldrin, Muhammed Ali, Richard Branson, and John Lennon and Yoko Ono, among many others. The comprehensive campaign includes television and print advertisements, billboards, wall paintings, bus shelters, and bus wraps. While the campaign urges consumers to think differently about Apple (a linked campaign encourages people to "think different about software on Macintosh"), it also urges them to think differently about themselves and to let their own creative genius shine through by using Apple products. In the words of Steve Jobs, "Think Different celebrates the soul of the Apple brand—that creative people with passion can change the world for the better. Apple is dedicated to making the best tools in the world for creative individuals everywhere."

THE ESSENCE OF THINK CAMPAIGNS

The essence of THINK marketing is to appeal to customers' creative thinking about a company and its brands. THINK marketing is appropriate for a wide variety of products and services. Although Apple Computer and Genesis ElderCare are in radically different businesses, they both appeal to creative thinking. Cutting-edge retailers, termed the "Teach and Sell school of retailing" by the *New York Times,* are also discovering THINK marketing. Examples include the Discovery Channel store in Washington, D.C., which displays a model of a *Tyrannosaurus rex* and an emerald beetle as part of many other interactive educational displays; Mars, a Fort Lauderdale music supply shop where teenagers can take drumming lessons; and Tourneau in New York, where customers learn about the history of watches.[4]

Even the world of fashion and beauty may use THINK campaigns. For example, Eddie Bauer, the women's and men's casual clothing retailer, has used

Apple outdoor billboard

inspirational THINK concepts throughout its stores: "Inspire," "Imagine," "Insight," "Intrigue," "Inhabit (your surroundings)" were terms written all over their retail space, accompanied by sedate pictures of tulips, lakes, and mountains.

It is important, however, to keep in mind who you are communicating with, in what context. Just putting up association-provoking "Think" terms may work for Eddie Bauer but fail in an annual report. As Lucy Kellaway of the *Financial Times* observes: "You might think that the world of annual reports is not particularly fashion sensitive, but you would be wrong. . . . A couple of years ago the trendy thing was to put a picture on the cover showing teamwork. Last year it was back to basics with plain pictures of the products. This year the smart thing is to plaster big words from the mission statement

143

across the cover—making them more prominent than the name of the company itself."[5] She refers to "Future" "Focused." "Value." "Quality." "Growth." "By using one of these lame cliches a company only succeeds in looking just like everyone else."

THINK CONCEPTS: DIVERGENT AND CONVERGENT THINKING

According to psychologist J. P. Guilford, individuals routinely engage in two different types of thinking, which he labeled convergent and divergent thinking.[6] The concepts refer to different modes of operation: narrowing the mental focus until it converges on a solution, or broadening the mental focus in many different directions. Creativity includes both convergent and divergent thinking.

Convergent Thinking

The most specific form of convergent thinking is analytical reasoning or probabilistic thinking involving well-defined rational problems. But any systematic, diligent analysis of a problem may qualify as convergent thinking even if it uses primarily simple heuristics or rules of thumb to arrive at a solution.

For example, evaluating the merits of an argument presented in a communication requires convergent thinking. The evaluation may be done very rigorously and systematically. Are the arguments logical and internally consistent? Is the empirical evidence presented in support of the arguments reliable? Is the evidence valid?

Another way of assessing the merit of an argument in a communication is to use a so-called heuristic. Heuristics are simple rules of thumb that are used to arrive at a judgment. For example, a salesperson gives you several reasons in a row why you should purchase a product; the sheer number of arguments persuades you that you should give it a try. Whether a customer uses rigorous, systematic analysis or heuristics, both represent convergent thinking.

There are sometimes dangers associated with too much convergent thinking. Goethe's Faust, the prototypical frustrated ivory-tower intellectual deprived of real life, yearns for experiences. Convergent, analytical thinking thus can spoil the experience. People who are asked to analyze closely why they like their pizza suddenly tend to like it less.[7]

Another danger is transforming customers from experiencers into greedy penny-pinchers or frequent-miles-program counters. In August 1997, after I had stayed for roughly three months each year in the Shangri-La hotels in China, as well as other Shangri-La hotels in the Asia-Pacific region, Shangri-La Hotels and Resorts made me an "executive member" of their privileged Golden Circle loyalty program. I was thrilled and excited because the glossy brochure promised a number of tangible benefits. Most important, I was promised the even higher—and most exclusive—status of an "Elite" member after twenty-five stays (not room nights) within a year. Interestingly, through this promotion, the hotel chain had inadvertently transformed itself for me from a SENSE and FEEL to a convergent THINK brand, and think and count I did. By January 1998 I had accumulated twenty stays and—just to be sure I was indeed on the right track—I called the Golden Circle Center in Hong Kong. I found out that many of my stays had not been recorded. I was furious! I felt ripped off! The enjoyment of my stays had been obscured by my obsession with collecting bonus points.

Divergent Thinking

In contrast, associative and divergent thinking is more freewheeling, and often more rewarding. It involves what psychologists call perceptual fluency (i.e., the ability to generate many ideas), flexibility (i.e., the ability to switch perspectives easily), and originality (i.e., the ability to create unusual ideas).

Divergent thinking occurs in brainstorming sessions in which participants are instructed to think freely and asked to abstain from any evaluation. Divergent thinking also occurs in dreams, when our analytical self seems dormant.

The Apple Computer campaign described earlier made prominent use of divergent thinking by using striking images of revolutionary personalities to get customers to think about the revolution(s) caused by Apple products.

Like convergent thinking, divergent thinking has its pitfalls if used inappropriately. Divergent thinking does not just happen; it depends on knowledge of a domain. Therefore marketers should not try to be too "multidirectional" (or more precisely, should not target "divergent thinking") unless consumers have a wealth of knowledge about a domain. Moreover, the type of knowledge matters as well. To comprehend the innovation of digital cameras, traditional camera expertise can be a disadvantage, but computer expertise can facilitate the process because it is more useful to think of a digital camera as a scanner than a camera with film. Therefore, it is necessary to appeal to the appropriate thinking frame.

One further caution about divergent thinking: Do not expect your highly original ads, or your sophisticated humor campaigns, to be successful in informational markets. Consumers in other countries often do not share the same product knowledge. Only when they have acquired a lot of product knowledge will they be able to understand appeals to their divergent thinking.

DIRECTIONAL AND ASSOCIATIVE THINK CAMPAIGNS

Marketers need to employ qualitatively different messages to induce convergent or divergent thinking (see Figure 6.1). Moreover, as mentioned earlier, creativity requires both types of thinking. Why? According to psychologists, creativity consists of four phases: (1) an analytical preparation phase, (2) an incubation phase, (3) the illumination phase or "Aha!" experience, and (4) the evaluation phase.[8] Divergent thinking occurs primarily during phases 2 and 3, but the first and the last phases require convergent thinking.

Because convergent thinking requires a specific list of the issues and clear task setting, marketers must be directional in their approach. Directional THINK campaigns spell out precisely what or how customers are supposed to think about the options put in front of them.

Divergent thinking may be targeted through associative THINK campaigns. Associative campaigns make prominent use of more abstract, generic concepts as well as diffused visual imagery.

Moreover, different types of environments are conducive to convergent or divergent thinking. Mihaly Csikszentmihalyi, whom I quoted in chapter 3 and

FIGURE 6.1

THINK Concepts and Campaigns

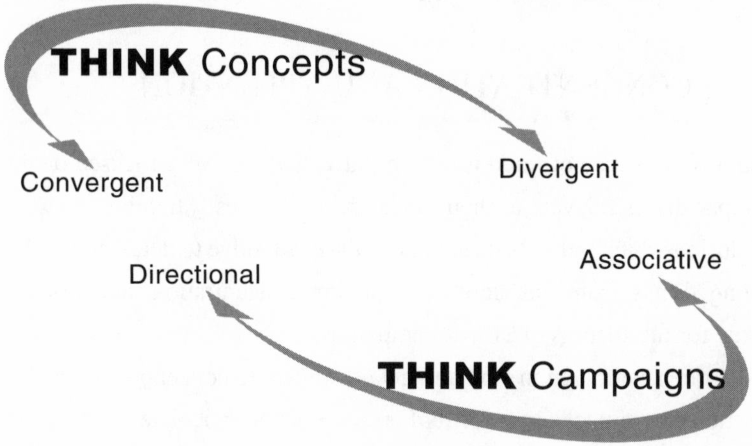

who is author of the best-selling books *Flow* and *Creativity,* stresses the importance of environments for creative thinking. "While novel and beautiful surroundings might catalyze the moment of insight, the other phases of the creative process—such as preparation and evaluation—seem to benefit more from familiar, comfortable settings."[9]

I generally agree with Professor Csikszentmihalyi. However, depending on the type of profession and type of problem, environments do not have to be novel and beautiful to promote divergent thinking. They may in fact have to be exciting, intense, almost overwhelming. That's the charm of many cities.

So, top management, if you want to stimulate your employees' divergent thinking, get them out of the office—up to the mountaintops or into city life. (For everyday convergent thinking, let your employees stay at their desks in the office!) If you cannot afford to send them out of the office, beautify and intensify their office environments.

Corporations are increasingly aware that experiential environments can have a profound impact on creativity at work. Bloomberg in New York has created a high-tech Zen-like atmosphere in its offices. Employees have workstations with radio and television editing equipment right at their desks; at the same time their peace of mind is nurtured by meditative fish aquariums throughout the workspace. Experiential work environments reflect firms' corporate culture and business values: MTV offices, for example, have television screens placed every few feet, showing a variety of dynamic TV offerings.

CONCENTRATION AND ATTENTION

Concentration is a state of mind in which individuals are very focused on detecting input that is relevant to their goals and objectives. Attention is a state of mind during which individuals are particularly attentive to detail and to differentiating things from one another. Inducing concentration, attention, or both is key for the success of THINK campaigns.

Nestlé ran a campaign in China to get customers to concentrate on and to pay attention to the packaging for its Ferrero Rocher chocolate truffles. The company had failed to register its brand on time, and found a Chinese local competitor copying its products right down to the golden wrapping paper that covers each truffle. However, there was one signal to distinguish the copy from the original. Since the Chinese company used lower-quality paper, the gold came off when consumers unwrapped the product, leaving tiny golden flakes on their hands. As a result, Nestlé used this effect to differentiate the product. Ads showed people at a stylish party being offered Ferrero Rochers and commenting to the host that they were original because the wrapper had not flaked off and stuck to their fingers.[10]

THE THINK PRINCIPLE: A SENSE OF SURPRISE, A DOSE OF INTRIGUE, AND A SMACK OF PROVOCATION

So what is the recipe for a successful THINK campaign? What are the ingredients of creative communications, product presence, co-branding campaigns, or any other THINK ExPro? What do THINK ExPros have to achieve?

Here is my recipe (see Figure 6.2). First, create a sense of surprise. Do it either visually, verbally, or conceptually. Then add a dose of intrigue. And finish it all up with a smack of provocation. Let me describe each component in more detail.

FIGURE 6.2

The THINK Principle

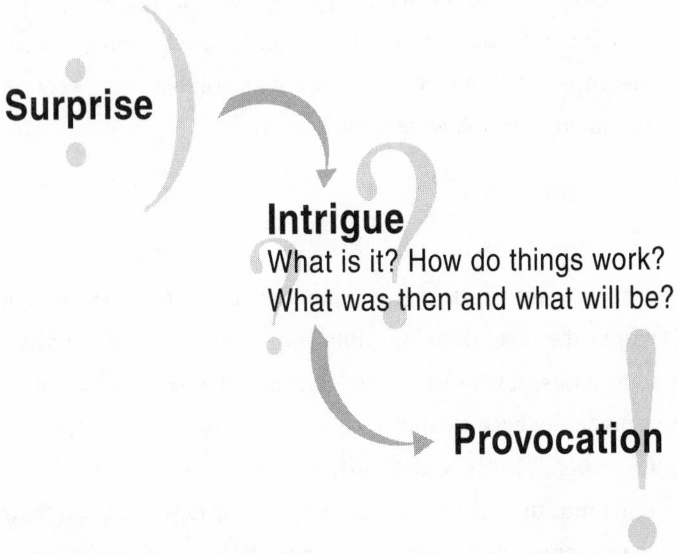

Surprise

Intrigue
What is it? How do things work?
What was then and what will be?

Provocation

Surprise

Why surprise? Surprise is essential for setting up the customer to engage in creative thinking. Surprise results when you depart from a common expectation. The surprise has to be positive. That is, customers get more than they ask for, more pleasant things than they hoped for, or something entirely different from what they expected—and they are delighted.

In its ads for color ink jet printers, Epson shows a striking visual image of a woman in what is ostensibly a bathing suit. The text reads: "At 360 DPI you see a lady in her bathing suit. At 720 DPI you see her bathing suit is wet. At 1440 DPI you see her bathing suit is painted on." (It even works when you just imagine the ad, doesn't it?)

The *Wall Street Journal* uses unexpectedly dynamic fashionlike photographic images to engage potential readers' and advertisers' thinking. The copy of a trade ad makes another surprising point—namely that the "the world's most important publication" is not only informative: "Yes, the *Journal* is essential reading, but it's also great edge of the seat, pass the popcorn entertainment. In fact, if you're after the rapt attention of the most influential audience in the world, it may be the only don't-miss show in town."

Other surprise approaches include the New York Police Department's slogan "CPR," standing for "Courtesy, Professionalism, Respect," and the wonderful Levi's campaign suggesting that major designers got their start wearing 501's ("Calvin wore them," "Ralph wore them," etc.).

Intrigue

Intrigue goes beyond surprise. If surprise is about departure from expectation (i.e., results of "within-the-box" thinking), intrigue reaches "out of the box." Intriguing campaigns arouse customers' curiosity; they puzzle, they fascinate, or challenge one's ingenuity because they challenge deeply held assumptions.

What intrigues people? Intrigue depends, of course, on an individual's reference point. What intrigues some people bores others, depending on their level of knowledge, interest, and prior experience. Broader, generic, more "philosophical" issues have a higher chance of inducing intrigue. Here are three examples.

Ontology: What Is It?

Merrill Lynch is running intriguing ads in which Merrill Lynch managers discuss concepts like wisdom, commitment, and human achievement, and what they mean for Merrill Lynch. Similarly, Harvard Business School Executive Education is pushing beyond the limits of traditional course offerings with a THINK program called "Odyssey." The program is pitched at successful senior-level executives as "a journey of self-exploration and career renewal," an experiential offering designed to respond to executives' needs for personal and professional growth.

Process: How Do Things Work?

The conglomerate Siemens Corporation urges consumers to THINK about the interrelatedness of products, and their own broad expertise, with a simple but compelling print ad. A man is shown in a rowing scull in dark silhouette against a glittering blue river background. Taking a break, he is enjoying a cold drink of bottled water. Superimposed over the scene are the words "Before you drink this, you have to have this [over a small sepia-toned photo of chemical beakers], this [over a shot of Siemens-branded electronic equipment], and this [over a photo of a high-tech assembly plant]." The copy reminds readers that "even the simplest products—a soft drink, a newspaper, a chocolate bar—have a lot of technology behind their manufacture."

Time: What Was and What Will Be?

Microsoft's campaign "Where do you want to go today?" falls into this category. Interestingly enough, the ad slogan is increasingly becoming a tag line as it is used even in Europe with an English slogan.

Digital Corporation ran ads in which it showed its contribution to the success of the movie mega-hit *Titanic*. "For James Cameron's *Titanic*, Digital Alpha Server systems ran nonstop for weeks, rendering the film's complex visual effects beautifully, and blazingly fast. If your business could use that kind of speed, power, and reliability, we're the only way to go." On Digital's web site, we found an even more detailed explanation of the exact process.

Malaysia's campaign "Malaysia. Bullish on bouncing back," designed in

Siemens ad

the middle of the Asian environmental and financial crises in the late nineties, falls into this category as well. The copy describes Malaysia overcoming the "dark clouds" that have been hovering over the country: first the air pollution, which has been remedied; and next the environment of economic uncertainty, which is expected to blow over "soon." This extraordinary THINK pitch for the country as a whole focuses on national perseverance as the path to a bright future.

Provocation

Provocation can stimulate discussion, create controversy—or shock, depending on your intentions and the intended target group. Provocations may appear irreverent and aggressive, and they can be risky if they go overboard, i.e., if they exceed good taste or violate morality.

The classic provocation campaign is the "United Colors of Benetton" ad (e.g., one ad features an African-American girl with her hair styled in horns while a Caucasian child sports little blond ringlets). A 1996 provocative (and some said pornographic) campaign for Calvin Klein jeans featured male teenage models in compromising positions; a 1999 campaign featured children's underwear. Both Calvin Klein and Benetton have attracted not only attention but also scorn. The two Calvin Klein campaigns were discontinued days after their inception; the Benetton ads caused outrage and lawsuits in different countries.

RCN Telecom Services is an East Coast–based company building a broadband fiber-optic network to supply phone service, cable, and Internet access in the Boston-to-Washington corridor. As the first company in America to offer the residential market the choices outlined in the Telecommunications Act of 1996, RCN is playing on its "revolutionary"status to create an integrated THINK marketing campaign. The campaign is organized around political and revolutionary images. RCN's home page on the World Wide Web, for example, shows a header that reads "Welcome to RCN Revolution Headquarters" with a background of clenched fists held aloft. Links on the page are accessed by clicking on what appear to be political lapel buttons with the slogans "Power to the People," "How to Join the Revolution," and "News from the Front." The web site also includes an animated version of an RCN billboard. Over a picture of a Lenin statue with a noose around its neck, the headline flashes, "No Empire Lasts Forever." The next image reads, "Especially one that keeps you waiting five hours for a repairman." The campaign makes consumers THINK about phone and cable service in a new light, and raises the possibility that by choosing RCN they can free themselves from the oppressive bondage of traditional phone and cable companies.

SUMMARY

The objective of THINK is to engage customers' creative thinking. The creative process that customers engage in includes both convergent and divergent thinking. To appeal to creative thinking, managers can use both directional and associative marketing approaches. This requires an understanding of customer knowledge structures and their attentional and concentration resources. The key principle to providing the right motivation to THINK combines surprise with intrigue and (sometimes) a sense of provocation.

But, wait a minute, says LAURA BROWN . . .

Isn't all of this too demanding? Who wants to do all that thinking? It costs enough to buy the products; now these marketers want you to spend your life thinking about them and their companies?

7

ACT

A CT marketing strategies are designed to create customer experiences related to the physical body, longer-term patterns of behavior and lifestyles as well as experiences occurring as a result of interacting with other people. Let's take a look at three recent examples of ACT marketing. The first case, the Gillette Mach3, focuses on a campaign that aims to change men's physical experience of shaving. Case 2, the Milk Mustache campaign, focuses on a specific lifestyle change. Case 3, the Martha Stewart Living brand, illustrates ACT marketing from a broader lifestyle and interaction perspective.

GILLETTE MACH3

Gillette spent six years and more than $750 million in researching and developing its new Mach3, not just a razor but a "shaving system."[1] The company expected the razor to be the most popular razor in America by the year 2000, selling 1.2 billion Mach3 blades each year. Both the name and the sleek design suggest speed, high performance, and aerodynamic flight.

The Mach3 is a high-tech product representing a "quantum leap" in shaving technology, according to Robert G. King, a Gillette executive vice presi-

Gillette Mach3: product and packaging

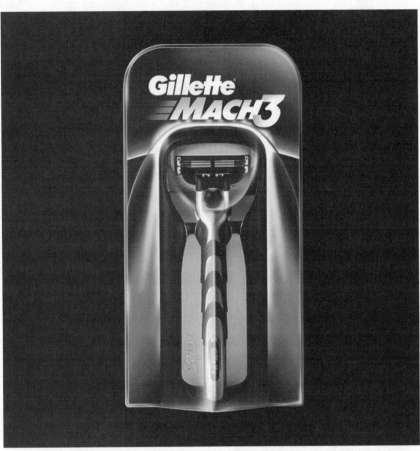

dent. Gillette retooled factories and employed new manufacturing processes for the Mach3, borrowing techniques from aerodynamics and ion-deposition processes used in the making of computer chips. The system carries thirty-six patents and is designed to provide not just a better shave but an entirely new and more satisfying shaving experience. With its innovative three-blade spring-mounted design, the Mach3 is designed to bring sound-barrier-breaking speed to the morning ritual, claiming a closer shave in fewer strokes.

The $300 million global marketing campaign for the Mach3 carries through the experiential appeal of supersonic flight. The brand identity and package design, which reflects speed and technology in its dynamic colors and graphics, was created by Wallace Church Associates. The in-store signage for the Mach3 invites men to try the product with the line, "Test pilots wanted." In one television spot, a fighter jet is shown breaking the sound barrier at Mach 1. As it accelerates to Mach 2, the jet begins to break up. At Mach 3 the pilot is transformed into a man standing in a futuristic bathroom, a sleek razor flying into his hand. The Mach3 media mix includes TV, radio, print, outdoor, and Internet ads, and Gillette has also launched a web site for the Mach3 created by Think New Ideas of New York.

Gillette's introduction of its Sensor razor around the world made marketing history, and Sensor has remained the world's most successful razor. With the Mach3 shaving system, Gillette is betting on an experiential approach in product design and marketing to top the performance of the Sensor.

THE MILK MUSTACHE CAMPAIGN

The "What a surprise!" and "Where's your mustache?" marketing campaigns for milk take a rather unexciting product, whose initial appeal would seem to be in its nutritional benefits, and turn it into an exciting ACT product. Throughout the eighties, milk consumption had fallen out of fashion, and by the nineties the negative consequences of drinking less milk became obvious through increasing incidence of osteoporosis, bone density loss, and fractured hips. To reverse this trend, the milk processors of the United States, the U.S. Congress, and the Secretary of Agriculture decided to launch an educational ACT campaign.[2]

The campaign attempts to correct false beliefs and educate the consumer by providing "surprising new nuggets of information about milk." At the same time, the campaign goes far beyond simply describing milk's benefits; rather it makes a powerful lifestyle statement to promote the beverage. The campaign, created by Bozell Worldwide, an ad agency, and photographed by Annie Leibovitz, the celebrated portrait photographer of American Express's "Membership has its privileges" campaign, uses a wide variety of celebrities—including supermodels like Naomi Campbell, Christy Brinkley, Kate Moss, and Iman; actors and actresses like Matt Fox, Jimmy Smits, Dennis Franz, Jonathan Taylor Thomas, Nastassja Kinski, Lauren Bacall, Isabella Rossellini; athletes like Kristy Yamaguchi, Gabriela Sabatini, Patrick Ewing,

Milk Mustache print ads

Have you seen me sweat? I must lose 10 lbs a game. And from what I hear, it's not just about losing water. It's about nutrients. That's why I drink milk. 2%. It's got nine essential nutrients my body needs, like calcium and potassium. I thought about telling the boys in Chicago, but it's about time they lost something.

MILK

Where's *your* mustache?

and Pete Sampras, as well as many other celebrities like Spike Lee, Ivana Trump, Paul Shaffer, David Copperfield, Larry King, and Martha Stewart—all wearing a "milk mustache." The text for each ad then provides a clever tie-in between the world of the celebrity and the benefits of milk. The Martha Stewart version, for example, is featured in cooking magazines and recommends substituting milk for water in recipes. Jonathan Taylor Thomas, a new teenage heartthrob, targets a teen female market, stating that three glasses of

milk a day help girls grow strong bones. Michael Johnson, Olympic Gold Medalist, wears a mustache on the cover of a recent sports nutrition information pamphlet. Participating celebrities cut across a wide social range, bringing lifestyle appeal and motivation to ACT to many different kinds of consumers. It is a cohesive campaign, easily updated to incorporate the latest "cool" person in any field. The milk web site, carries through the campaign with a page called Famous Faces, a "who's who" of the milk mustaches and why they think milk is cool. Even ads that don't feature mustache-wearing celebrities carry the slogan "Where's your mustache?"

MARTHA STEWART LIVING

She has been called "an icon of American pop culture," a "one-woman marketing concept," and "America's greatest cultural influence since Thomas Jefferson."[3] Martha Stewart is like a literary text that affords multiple interpretations depending on your viewpoint. Some believe she reflects "the American woman's longing for lost domesticity"; they argue that she's fostering a respect for homemaking that American society has lost. Others see Stewart as a retrograde influence, reversing the empowerment of women over recent decades: "American women can't do it all. The last thing we need is something else to feel guilty about." One writer referred to Stewart's magazine, *Martha Stewart Living,* as "pornography for women. We look at all those projects and all that energy and we fantasize, not about sex, but about having that kind of time."

Regardless of your opinion, one thing is sure: in the recent past, there has not been a single better identifier, interpreter, role model, and driver of lifestyles in American culture than Martha Stewart.

She has launched the recent trend of lifestyle books, lifestyle magazines, and lifestyle shows on TV. Her books *Entertaining* and *The Martha Stewart Cookbook* have sold more than 500,000 copies each in hardcover. Her subsequent hardcover titles have covered every imaginable lifestyle topic from gardening and decorating to holidays and weddings. She has built a $200 million empire, wresting control of *Martha Stewart Living* from the powerful Time Warner, and forming her own company, Martha Stewart Living Omnimedia LLC.

A search on Lexus/Nexus revealed more than a thousand hits on "Martha Stewart" and "lifestyles" from January 1998 to January 1999, alone. When the pope arrived in Cuba, Martha was there, sent by CBS to cover Cuban cooking and culture.

But Martha Stewart has also plugged into a trend: According to statistics gathered by Home & Garden Television, a twenty-four-hour cable network, Americans spend $587 annually on building and remodeling, decorating and interiors, gardening and landscaping, crafts and hobbies, as well as home electronics. As Americans' lives speed up and become more technologically centered, Martha Stewart has fashioned herself into an icon of a slow-paced, relaxed, domestic lifestyle.

TRADITIONAL MARKETING AND ACT EXPERIENCES

Traditional marketing has largely ignored the notion of ACT experiences. Even the field of consumer behavior, which is more in tune with perceptions, consumer information processing and behavior, has focused primarily on influencing, categorizing, and predicting behaviors and lifestyles rather than understanding the experiential qualities of ACT as such (see Figure 7.1).

In this chapter, I will first discuss ACT techniques related to the physical body. Then we will focus on broader behavioral patterns and lifestyles. I will conclude with a discussion of techniques for interactions with other people.

FIGURE 7.1

ACT Experiences

Reasoned action

Flesh

Behavioral modification

Motor actions

ACT Experiences

Self-perceptions

Interact

Nonverbal behavior

Lifestyles

PHYSICAL BODY EXPERIENCES

Flesh

The physical body does not only produce sensations and perceptions of the "distant" outside world (e.g., perceptions of products, companies, web sites, etc.). Our body as such—the flesh—is also a rich source of experiences. Just imagine how you feel when you are getting a haircut, a manicure, a shoeshine, or a massage. The proper marketing of these flesh experiences critically depends on creating the right products, stimulation, and atmosphere.

Many products related to body functions and experiences fall into the "taboo" category in many cultures because they are related to personal and private activities (such as washing and cleaning the body, sexuality, disease, substance addiction, etc.). Therefore they require particular attention from marketers due to the sensitive nature of the product categories' applications. Let me give you some examples.

The web site for Victoria's Secret, a division of Intimate Brands, is a great example of tasteful experiential branding for the lingerie category on the Internet. The company is also experimenting with new online ventures to make the purchase easier and more acceptable, especially for men. On February 3, 1999, at 7 P.M. Eastern Standard Time during the Valentine's Day season, Victoria's Secret broadcast its fashion show live over the Internet—direct from Wall Street. Close to 100 million people watched the broadcast. (Unfortunately, I had to attend a tenured faculty meeting at that time, but I was told by a colleague, who was absent during the meeting, that the show was intriguing.) And Intimate Brands' annual report was spiced up with product samples.

Japanese culture has been obsessed with cleanliness and orderliness. They thus make two out of the three characteristics of what Freud called the "anal character complex" (number 3 is stinginess). Not surprisingly, the Japanese home plumbing and toilet market has seen high-tech, high-aesthetics product introductions that avoid any bad associations and enhance the experience. In Japanese households, toilets that allow you to program the temperature and pressure of the wash-water spray (some Japanese avoid toilet paper altogether because they find it too dirty) as well as the temperature of the toilet seat have become standard. The latest model includes a remote control to lift the seat. And this product category is also making inroads into the United States: I recently tested a model at a Sheraton hotel in Los Angeles!

Another Asian product making inroads in the U.S. market is whitening essence. Asians' desire for white skin (tanned skin is considered unattractive) has always been one of the major forces behind cosmetics sales. Now it is reaching the U.S. market as well. Lancôme, Elizabeth Arden, and Clinique all have recently launched scientifically tested skin-whitening products. The Lancôme product with its French brand name, "Blanc Expert," positions itself as an "active whitening spot corrector," "clinically tested on Asian skin." An ad shows the product, accompanied by a white rose. The copy states: "Experience the totally new efficacy of Blanc Expert, the revolutionary whitening spot corrector" and promises customers that they can experience its magic within twelve days.

In his award-winning movie *Saving Private Ryan,* director Steven Spielberg used innovative cinematic techniques in order to create a physical war experience for his audience. The first twenty-eight minutes of the film depict the invasion of Normandy during the Second World War from a close-up, uncompromising point of view. "I'm asking the audience—and it's a lot to ask of an audience—to have a physical experience, so that they can somewhat have the experience of what those guys actually went through," Spielberg said.

Motor Actions

Regarding "motor actions," we can also learn from the Asians. The Chinese theory of Qi Gong holds that certain motor actions produce mental states and experiences. For example, in Taiji, a set of exercises based on Qi Gong, you move your arms describing a semicircle at a certain angle in front of your body—and you'll feel mentally relaxed. But does it really work?

Jens Foerster, a German psychologist, has assumed the role of experimental Qi Gong master by conducting some fascinating research on how people infer their attitudes from their nonverbal behavior.[4] Here is a typical

Foerster experiment: People are asked to move their heads up and down (for some spurious reason) or to move their heads left and right while they watch some stimuli. Later, when they are asked to evaluate the stimuli on an attitude scale, they like the ones for which they used the vertical movement, and they dislike the ones for which they used the horizontal movement. Importantly, they have no conscious awareness that the head nodding or head shaking determined their attitudes. It seems that the sheer body movement has become so automatic that it affects attitudes even once it is stripped of its meaning. (So, now you know why people like TV ads so much. It's because they are performing micro movements of nodding while digesting the potato chips in front of the TV.)

I am convinced that behavioral techniques targeting motor activities work not only when people perform these motor activities themselves but also in social interactions. That is, in sales encounters or on TV commercials, you can include subtle nonverbal cues that, when seen by others, affect their attitudes and behavior without their consciously being aware of it. For example, imagine you are looking for a gift and the salesperson says: "Let me show you a really, really nice gift." Now imagine the salesperson saying this by nodding (while saying "really, really nice")—and I bet you like the gift more. You are subtly influenced by his or her nonverbal behavior, and perhaps, in a ritualistic exchange of signals, have imitated the nodding, thus reproducing in vivo Foerster's experimental Qi Gong.

Body Signals

There are numerous body signals that come into play in social exchanges, which suggest approach and avoidance, preference and disliking, domination and submission; these are parts of our distant evolutionary animal past. We may not be consciously aware of them, but they do not simmer in the Freudian unconscious either. They are signals that we immediately read and understand, and thus they affect our reactions.

Watch animals when they play or fight, and then watch Michael Douglas playing a corporate raider. You will notice—in the body language—numerous similarities between the animal and corporate kingdom, which a superb actor like Michael Douglas knows so well. Then film yourself during a negotiation, and you will see that you are using many of the body signals yourself (like gestures, tone of voice, eye contacts, etc.), and that you subtly affect your opponent. As a marketer, salesperson, and advertiser, you can use the same body signals to affect customer behavior.

Environmental Influences on Physical Desires

As the Bible taught us, and clever marketers have shown us, the "flesh is weak." Therefore, one of the most successful ACT strategies is to locate your marketing close to a place where physical desires are most likely to arise. That way, you not only create an experience but simultaneously reinforce it.

Coca-Cola and other beverage manufacturers place their logos, ads, and vending machines at strategic consumption places in order to activate the consumer's desire to buy a drink. Other brands have used a similar approach. Marlboro displays a huge outdoor ad in Hong Kong's traditional expatriate nightlife area called Lan Kwai Fong, spanning across the street. The location has been chosen in a clever way given that cigarette users are more likely to smoke when going out at night. The ads may thus serve as a retrieval cue and reminder for cigarette smokers to pull out their cigarettes.

Environments also affect brand choice. After a workout during the winter, I avoid the Gatorade Frost or else I'd feel even colder. In a Japanese vending machine, I probably wouldn't even have the choice of the frosty drink. Japanese marketers have figured out in what season at what time of day the customers prefer to drink what. Accordingly, vending machines get restocked several times a day: with preheated coffee in the morning, and a majority of beer brands at night.

LIFESTYLES

"Lifestyles nowadays is about jumping out of the box," states Beth Wareham, director of Simon & Schuster's Lifestyle Publicity Department. "I know a woman who runs a multimillion-dollar corporation, and on weekends perfects the ultimate piecrust with a vengeance. I know a man, a true monument to testosterone, who knits. 'Lifestyle' is everything from hanging out with your dog to re-creating the gardens of Monticello in your backyard."

In the marketing literature, "lifestyle" refers to "the person's pattern of living in the world as expressed in the person's activities, interests and opinions."[5] To express their lifestyles, display it to others—and themselves—consumers need markers and indicators; they need lifestyle brands. As marketers, we therefore need to be sensitive to lifestyle trends—or even better, become drivers of lifestyle trends—and make sure that our brands are associated, in fact, form part of the lifestyle. Only in that manner can we create the most effective lifestyle experience.

One recent lifestyle trend, which originated in California but is now swaying the nation, is the "juice bar." Just as Starbuck's embodies the lifestyles of its customers, so have juice bars been springing up, appealing to a wide spectrum of consumer experiences and values. During a recent visit to California, I discovered Jamba Juice, whose menu guide explains the premise behind the company: "Welcome to Jamba Juice! Month after month, all around the world, fruit growers and farmers carefully tend crops as they ripen to luscious sweetness: mangoes in India, bananas in Costa Rica, red papayas in Brazil. A Jamba Juice buyer visits these crops, talks to their growers, then purchases only the very finest fruits to offer you in your favorite smoothie or juice blend. We first opened as Juice Club in San Luis Obispo, California, in 1990, obsessed with promoting the pleasures and health benefits of fresh juice and fruit smoothies. In 1995 we evolved to an even sweeter state of being by becoming Jamba Juice. Jamba means 'to celebrate,' which is what happens every time we take your order and do that wildly flavorful blender dance that puts liquid delight in your cup. It's our passion for doing this that has made us the leading provider of made-to-order, all natural smoothies and juice blends. But we didn't do it alone. Your comments and your passion for a healthier lifestyle are what brought us here. And it's your continuous comments that fuel our ongoing quest for juice excellence."

The marketing material appeals on a sensory level, with rich descriptions of delicious fruits, and offers a RELATE appeal, not just in terms of the health values of the product, but in terms of its worldwide origins. But the products themselves incorporate many ACT components and suggest an entire lifestyle.

For example, every smoothie contains a "juice boost" of your choice, including an "energy juice boost," an "immunity juice boost," or a "life juice boost." The menu includes wheatgrass juice, with the tag "Ever tasted sunshine?" Customers' special needs are catered to with products like Femme Phenom (offering "superior female nutrition"), nondairy smoothies (for the lactose-intolerant), and even Ghirardelli Chocolossus, for the health-conscious chocoholic! Menus are printed on recycled paper, with bright earthtone colors.

Even Snapple is now jumping on the juice-bar bandwagon. The new Whipper Snapple line is enhanced with ginkgo biloba and packaged in wavy green, yellow, or pink bottles reminiscent of soda shop frappes and soft-serve ice cream. It promises "a unique smoothie blended with juices, purees, and other good stuff!"

How can we induce such lifestyles? There are several techniques.

Induce Acting Without (Much) Thinking

Sometimes pure appeals to action—like "Just do it" in the famous Nike campaign—work. This seems to be the case because customers are often in a fairly mindless state and do not necessarily analyze reasons closely.[6]

Indeed, appeals to the mind can undermine a mindless approach that seems to be working. In 1998, Nike switched from its "Just do it" slogan to "I can" and then "I know I can." But it only ran these ads for a short period of time, perhaps realizing that the simple appeal to action still works the best.

Use Role Models

Another approach to lifestyle experiences includes role models. In contrast to Nike, for years Adidas marketed its products using a features-and-benefits approach. But since the early '90s Adidas, like Nike, has been quietly signing young American athletes as spokespeople. By signing people like Kobe Bryant, the 19-year-old Los Angeles Lakers star, Adidas is hoping to appeal to the 12-to-21-year-old segment now known as "Generation Y." Adidas has also signed Antoine Walker of the Boston Celtics and Jermaine O'Neal of the Portland Trailblazers. Overall, Adidas has kept its celebrity endorsements quieter than Nike's Air Jordan barrage, in keeping with its more conservative European image. Its low-key marketing approach is also reflected in a series of ads created by Leagas Delaney in San Francisco, which follows the exploits of a group of potbellied Yankee fans. The campaign marks "one of the few times you'll even see a fat guy in a sneaker ad," according to Harry Cocciolo, creative director of Leagas Delaney. Finally, Adidas unveiled a series of ads that play on the heritage and history of sports teams (e.g., the Notre Dame football team).[7]

While the Adidas campaign has concentrated on spokespeople in the United States, in Germany the brand has been revived through creative event marketing. Adidas regularly sponsors competitions and street fairs in the old city squares of small German cities.[8]

Appeal to Norms

Finally, some lifestyle changes occur because the new behavior is strongly enforced by social norms (laws, rules and regulations, or implicit group norms or group pressures). We will discuss social influences in more detail in the next chapter. Regarding ACT, it is noteworthy that these initially external norms may over time become internalized norms in the sense of "It's the right thing to do," and thus are no longer felt as norm expectations or pressures.

INTERACT

Aside from physical experiences, and long-term lifestyles, there are experiences related to interactions with others. Interactions do not occur in a social vacuum. Instead, people's behavior depend not only on their own outcome beliefs, attitudes, and intentions but also on the beliefs of reference groups and social norms (see Figure 7.2). We will discuss these issues in more depth in the following chapter on RELATE marketing.

Here I would like to focus on the medium of interaction, because it is

FIGURE 7.2

Theory of Reasoned Action

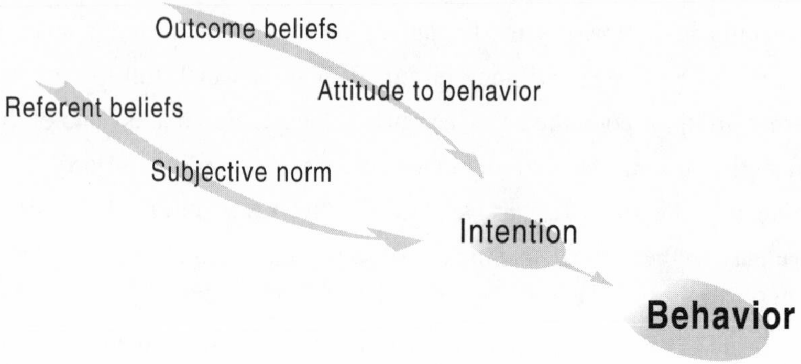

Outcome beliefs

Referent beliefs   Attitude to behavior

Subjective norm

Intention

Behavior

closely related to the physical and social behavior of the interacting parties. The notion of the medium of interaction is highly relevant for the experiences created in learning programs. A former executive MBA student of mine, Kristin Breuss, who manages corporate training for Goldman Sacks, told me that experiences are key for creating the right training atmosphere and image of Goldman Sachs among employees. Therefore the physical environment needs to be structured appropriately to facilitate the right perceptions and interactions. Likewise Jim Tuohy, the food and beverage director at Arden House, a conference facility in upstate New York where I frequently teach as part of Columbia Business School's Executive Programs, makes a concerted effort to enhance interactions among international participants by planning dining events related to various home countries, thus providing an easy conversational opening for participants.

In 1998 I had the opportunity to be, for the first time, the instructor of a long-distance executive program in a course on branding. The three-day program, with three hours of programming every day, was broadcast live out of a TV studio in Dallas and beamed via satellite into subscribing companies as well as some TV studio sites throughout the United States.

Just as on *Larry King Live,* the technology offered two-way audio (i.e., the participating executives could hear me and I could hear them) and one-way video (they could see me but I couldn't see them). This type of program may never entirely replace face-to-face interactions, but it offers an interesting supplement to more traditional forms of executive teaching, with the inclusion of live studio guests or guests brought in via satellite, live phone interviews, high-quality close-up camera shots of products, etc.

It was an interesting interaction experience for me. Rather than having students or participants in front of me, I had to look straight into the camera for several hours and imagine who might be out there. I am sure it was also an interesting interaction experience for the participants, seeing the instructor on a conference screen rather than live in a classroom, using a keypad to get into queue for questions, etc. One becomes aware of the physical constraints—but also freedom from social constraints—that technology creates via distance.

How the medium of interaction can affect experiences is a key issue for any service provider. In chapter 5 we learned that well-trained real-life salespeople are critical for inducing strong positive emotions. The key word is "well trained," or else the opposite occurs: strong negative emotions. Yet, there is the broader issue of what kind of behavior the presence or absence of other people affords. Thus the strategic decision is "Automate or personate?" and the answer depends on the type of service. Ask yourself: for what type of banking transactions (or services in general) do you prefer an automatic teller machine, and for which ones a personal teller? It also depends on the customer. Some customers (older people on a leisure trip) prefer to pick up the key and documents from a car-rental counter (assuming there are no lines); others prefer to go straight to the car and drive off (younger customers on a business trip?). The reasons are not limited to time considerations. The entire experience changes in terms of control, initiative, and feelings of being taken care of.

SUMMARY

ACT experiences move beyond the realm of sensations, affect, and cognition. ACT experiences may sometimes occur privately (especially if they are related to intimate aspects of our bodies); many ACT experiences, however, result from public interactions. As such, they are visible to others and customers may use their actions (e.g., lifestyles) to display their self-conceptions and values.

Lifestyles and interact . . . What? asks LAURA BROWN . . .

Isn't all of this just sweet talk for ostentation? Showing off your new toys on Main Street so that everyone can look at them? Why would anyone want to do this?

8

RELATE

ELATE marketing expands beyond the individual's private sensations, feelings, cognitions, and actions by relating the individual self to the broader social and cultural context reflected in a brand.

Recall the Palm III Organizer, the light handheld computer mentioned in chapters 1 and 2. The Palm III Organizer is not only an exciting lifestyle product but also changes the way we interact with others (e.g., business colleagues). One of the ads for the product focuses on the Palm III Organizer's capabilities to beam one's business card to another user via the infrared port. The ad shows a group of managers exchanging printed business cards and comments on this "passé" ritual. The Palm III Organizer thus changes entirely the experience of interaction and greeting.

RELATE implies a connection with other people, other social groups (occupational, ethnic, or lifestyle, for example) or a broader, more abstract social entity such as a nation, society, or culture. RELATE marketing often results in SENSE, FEEL, THINK, and ACT experiences. However, this outcome is only secondary to the prime objective of building a relationship between the social meaning of the brand and the customer. Using the concept of the sociocultural consumption vector (SCCV) introduced in chapter 1, we can say that our possessions become a summary representation of these more or less abstract so-

Palm III conference ad

cial entities in a variety of consumption contexts. As consumer researcher Russell Belk observed, "we cannot hope to understand consumer behavior without first gaining some understanding of the meanings that consumers attach to possessions. A key to understanding what possessions mean is recognizing that, knowingly or unknowingly, intentionally or unintentionally, we regard our possessions as parts of ourselves."[1]

This is especially true for a brand that is far along the SCCV. As Steve Goldstein, the vice president of consumer research and marketing for Levi's USA put it, "The philosophy and history of Levi's has always been that it's more about the relationship between the brand and the consumer than any product attributes."[2] Unfortunately in the late '90s Levi's had lost touch with customers and culture, and profits shrank.

EXAMPLES OF SUCCESSFUL RELATE CAMPAIGNS: MARTHA, HARLEY, TOMMY, STEVE, AND MAO

RELATE has been used successfully in a variety of recent marketing campaigns. Let's examine some of them.

Let's start with relating to a person. In the last chapter we looked at the ACT appeal of Martha Stewart. Her RELATE appeal is just as powerful and, for some, highly personal. Women who don't admire Martha, as well as those who do, speculate about "being" Martha. One writer describes her tongue-in-cheek foray into the world of domestic perfection: "the idea—regrettably, my own—was to see whether I could be Martha Stewart in time for the holidays."[3] Despite the humor of the topic, many people do relate to Martha as the embodiment of an elegant and relaxed lifestyle.

Reference-group feelings can provide a powerful starting point for a RELATE campaign. Just think about Harley-Davidson, the American icon of free-spiritedness, which draws thousands of motorcycle enthusiasts to weekend rallies staged around the country. Harley-Davidson evokes such strong relations that owners tattoo the logo on their arms or their entire bodies. As Alec Wilkinson wrote in the *New York Times:* "If you ride a Harley, you are a member of a brotherhood, and if you don't, you are not."[4]

On a higher-end scale, we find yet another brotherhood—that of Tommy Hilfiger, the American casual-clothing designer brand. Like Harley-Davidson, Tommy Hilfiger has used RELATE marketing for many years. A recently launched Tommy fragrance uses the tag line "The real American fragrance." Print ads show groups of wholesome-looking young people of different races wearing Tommy fashions and relaxing in casual settings. The atmosphere is one of warmth and easy camaraderie among friends. One setting, on a manicured lawn before a large Cape Cod home, is strongly reminiscent of the Kennedy enclave at Hyannis Port. Tommy's signature colors—red, white, and blue—are carried through in American flags that appear in the background of each shot.

An integrated and successful collection of RELATE products and services is provided by the Franklin-Covey company. Building on the phenomenal success of Steven Covey's best-selling book *The Seven Habits of Highly Effective People,* Franklin-Covey offers a line of Franklin organizers, the Covey Leadership Center, and Covey's books on self-management. They have even opened a line of retail stores, the 7-Habits stores, selling products and services intended to help people get control of their lives.

Finally, RELATE marketing can be serious or playful. A "communist chic" restaurant is all the rage in Singapore. At the House of Mao, waiters wear red stars on their caps and Maoist slogans on their sleeves. A portrait of the late Chinese leader Mao Tse-tung dominates one wall of the restaurant, which is decorated with medals, posters, and copies of Mao's famous Little Red Book. The menu itself mimics the Little Red Book and offers dishes like Long March Chicken and Chairman Mao's Favorite Braised Garlic Pork. This tongue-in-cheek nostalgia is not confined to Asia, either. Shortly after the fall of communism in Europe, a hammer-and-sickle craze swept the region, with pizzerias and cafeterias harking back to the "good" old days in their design and marketing.

RELATE MARKETING AND SOCIAL INFLUENCE

The field of social psychology is concerned with the influence of the actual, imagined, or implicit presence of other people on an individual's thoughts and behavior. "Actual presence" refers to the social influence provided during face-to-face or otherwise personal encounters (e.g., via phone, e-mail etc.). Mutual influence in Harley-Davidson rallies, user groups, and family decision making are good examples. "Imagined presence" and "implicit presence" are more indirect. In "imagined presence" customers believe they can change their identity or their membership in a reference group by purchasing a certain brand. The purchase of a Tommy Hilfiger sweater with "Tommy" printed all over it is an example. In "implicit presence" the customer acts out—often unknowingly—the expected role behavior of a reference group (e.g., by ordering a Bud in the bar after work).

American Girl Place, a retail and entertainment destination site located in Chicago's North Michigan Avenue shopping district, uses imagined and implicit presence as part of its RELATE marketing. Designed exclusively for girls seven and up, it provides a magical experience of the American Girl products, a brand of the Pleasant Company, typically available through the company's catalog. The mission of the American Girl products is "to educate and entertain girls with high-quality products and experiences that reinforce positive social and moral values." To fulfill this goal, American Girl Place features the complete product line, historical exhibits, an elegant café, and a Broadway-caliber musical. The 35,000-square-foot-space, designed by Donovan and Green in close collaboration with Pleasant Company founder, Pleasant T. Rowland, thus raises the level of the experience of the brand to a participatory cultural experience.

Independently of whether others are actually present, merely imagined, or implicitly present, each situation provides a connection between an individual and other individuals via brand purchase and usage. Thus, the essence of RELATE marketing is to get people to relate to other individuals as well as to entire groups and cultures (constituted by these individuals) via brands.

SOCIAL CATEGORIZATION AND IDENTITY

The purpose of relating to others seems to be motivated by a need for categorization and a search for meaning. When we are asked to describe ourselves as individuals, we may describe ourselves in terms of certain individual traits.

FIGURE 8.1

RELATE Experiences

Social Influence

Social roles

Social categorization

RELATE
Experiences

Kin relations

Social Identity

Brand communities

Cultural values

Group membership

But, equally likely, we can use certain social categories to describe ourselves. Or others may describe us in terms of social categories.

Social categories may be characterized by one attribute (e.g., "She's female," "She's from New York," or "She's a lawyer"). Or several attributes may be combined to form a complex category ("a female New York lawyer"). These individual and complex categories are often not merely descriptive but become "prototypical" or "stereotypical" images that are used by showing certain user types in RELATE communications campaigns.

Prototypes serve an important function for individuals: they provide them with a sense of social identity. Social identity is defined as the part of the individual's self-concept, which is affected by the knowledge of membership in a social group.[5]

"Us" *vs.* "Them"

According to Henri Tajfel's social identity theory, the identification involves not only identification but also contrast with another group. Thus, identification is also a need for social distinctiveness. The contrast between "us" and "them" is critical. Indeed, imagined differences may be exaggerated beyond real ones.

The Asian financial crisis has set the stage for a RELATE-based "buy Korean" campaign. The country's foreign-exchange crisis and IMF bailout have raised concerns about buying imported goods and further draining the country's reserves. Advertisers for products from sneakers to leather goods have jumped on the patriotic bandwagon; one ad for Pro-Specs sneakers pictures a foot wrapped in dollar bills with the headline "Are You Wearing Dollars?" The government is ambivalent about these campaigns, concerned that they may alienate foreign investors. But the RELATE message seems to be getting across: one college student was quoted in the *Asian Wall Street Journal* as saying, "Buying [Korean products] is really all I can do to help our country."[6]

"Us *vs.* them" does not always carry a belligerent undertone. In 1994, Nickelodeon, the cable channel for kids with its flexible approach to logos (see chapter 3), made the decision to transform itself from a channel simply running children's shows into a creative organization by, for, and about kids. To do this, they hit on the notion of "us *vs.* them." Everything was reevaluated in light of this "Big Idea": "'Us vs. Them' became, and remains today, the Nickelodeon battle cry. We stand up for kids, expose their injustices and celebrate their triumphs. 'Us vs. Them' is the 'big idea,' the informing principle behind everything we do at Nick. It's the flame that burns in our hearts and the standard by which we measure everything from new shows and marketing plans, to the people we employ. And most importantly, 'Us vs. Them' is an idea that really means something to kids. It doesn't mean that Nickelodeon is anti-parent or anti-adult, it just lets kids know that Nickelodeon understands what it's like to be a kid and that Nick will always be there for them."[7] This "Big Idea"—RELATE to kids on all levels—is carried through in everything that Nick does, from programming to copywriting to graphics to products. Nick provides an unusually organic, and very successful, example of identity RELATE marketing.

Kin Relations

Preferential feelings and preferential treatment of the ingroup *vs.* the outgroup seems to be a generalization from a fundamental biological mechanism: the love of one's own kin. Steven Pinker of MIT explains this phenomenon from an evolutionary point of view: "The love of kin comes naturally; the love of non-kin does not. That is the fundamental fact of the social world, steering everything from how we grow up to the rise and fall of empires and religions. The explanation is straightforward. Relatives share genes to a greater extent than nonrelatives do, so if a gene makes an organism benefit a relative (say, by feeding or protecting it), it has a good chance of benefiting a copy of itself. With that advantage, genes for helping relatives will increase in a population over the generations."[8]

Thus, once we know we are related, the social psychology of kinship kicks in. "We feel a measure of solidarity, sympathy, tolerance, and trust toward our relatives, added on to whatever other feelings we may have for them. . . . The added goodwill one feels toward kin is doled out according to a feeling that reflects the probability that the kind act will help a relative propagate copies of one's genes. That in turn depends on the nearness of the relative to oneself in the family tree, the confidence one has in that nearness, and the impact of the kindness on the relative's prospect of reproducing (which depends on age and need). So parents love their children above all others, cousins love each other but not as much as siblings do, and so on."[9]

RELATE advertising and other RELATE campaigns (e.g., transfer of frequent flyer miles) reflect this law of nature. I have not counted the number of RELATE ads reflecting parent-child relationships, sibling relations, and relations between cousins. My hunch is that their frequency of occurrence is correlated with relationship strength as indicated by biological relations.

Social Roles

Besides kinship, relationships may also be formed with other individuals in a more generalized/abstract fashion via social roles. For example, a female consumer may feel an affinity with other female consumers—not necessarily her female friends but women in general. As a result, she may be particularly attuned to RELATE campaigns that feature the social role of women in society and their relations with men and women.

Wonderbra, the push-up bra that has been a huge success, launched an unusual RELATE campaign in 1998.[10] Print ads and posters show an underwear-clad model in an action pose, airborne, hair flying. The text proclaims defiant independence. One reads, "First date. Disagree on foreign policy. Last date." Another shows a model nearly in flight, with the text announcing her freedom from a bad relationship, "Later, Mr. Wrong, it's not me, it's you." The campaign is counterintuitive and powerful—an item that makes a woman's breasts appear larger becomes an agent for her empowerment, the nearly nude model a strong modern image for her to RELATE to. The 1999 campaign ("Let 'em think it was luck") has similar appeal.

Interestingly, the advertising campaign for Wonderbra (managed in Europe by Playtex) takes, in France, a diametrically opposite approach. A series of print ads depict a woman whose clothes have been suddenly torn away, revealing her bra. In one, a sweater is being unraveled by a dog, in another a jacket is being caught and pulled off by a construction crane. In both cases, the distressed woman is being observed by male bystanders. According to Nick Houghton, Wonderbra's marketing director, the campaign was well researched among French women and had been very well received. And Mercedes Erra, of the Parisian advertising agency BETC, characterized the campaign as a paradoxically liberating RELATE strategy: "We wanted to get away from the image of the woman who is in control of everything." However, the campaign met with strong opposition in the United Kingdom, where Dr. Rosalind Gill of the London School of Economics commented, "I think [the ads] are horrendous, borrowing heavily from pornography." The campaign did not make the channel crossing. RELATE marketing involving social roles is particularly dependent on cultural values, and to be successful, international campaigns must take into account the local cultural norms.

CROSS-CULTURAL VALUES

Values may be viewed as general beliefs that transcend specific situations. They pertain to desirable end states and people often rank them implicitly in a hierarchy of priorities.

Shalom Schwartz, an Israeli psychologist and the leading theorist on values, has distinguished ten value types, which he claims are universal. To date, these values have been verified in over 200 samples of respondents in over sixty countries involving a total of 100,000 respondents. Strangely enough, the model has received little attention in marketing.[11]

Professor Schwartz often represents the ten values in a circular structure, indicating that the pursuit of a value may be in conflict or compatible with another value depending on their proximity to one another. The Schwartz model can be used universally to make sure that in RELATE campaigns compatible values rather than incompatible ones are targeted.

One concept that has frequently been used to describe cross-cultural differences is individualism/collectivism. As a result of religious, philosophical, and historical developments (e.g., Christianity *vs.* Buddhism; enlightened rationalism *vs.* Confucianism, etc.), members of individualist societies like the U.S.A. are characterized by self-reliance, individual achievement, and an emphasis on personal goals. In contrast, members of collectivist societies (e.g., many Asians) describe themselves as part of groups, subordinate personal goals to group goals, and derive strong attachments from belonging to a group.

Individualism/collectivism has consequences for the view of the self (independent *vs.* interdependent self), goals (a preference for personal *vs.* communal goals), cognitions (an emphasis on needs and rights *vs.* obligations and duties), and evaluations (a focus on a rational analysis of relations *vs.* a focus on developing and keeping relations).

Appeals to self-reliance and assertiveness work better for individualists than collectivists. But RELATE marketing that appeals to reference-group norms works better for collectivists than individualists. Moreover, individualists want to differentiate themselves from others; they want to be unique. Collectivists want to assimilate themselves with the reference group. For them, to stand out—even in a positive way—is not really desirable. Thus an understanding of reference-group norms is a prerequisite for designing a successful RELATE campaign.

Specific Values and Attitudes

RELATE marketing may also focus on specific values—values of a lower order than Schwartz's general values—or on specific attitudes. If values can be specific to a particular culture, RELATE marketers must be sensitive to these cultural differences and design their marketing campaigns accordingly. Here is an example of certain qualities that some claim are specific to Chinese culture.[12]

- Abasement
- Modesty and self-effacement
- Pragmatism and compromise
- Respect for authority
- Relationships
- Reciprocity of actions
- Face saving

These Chinese cultural values have important implications for structuring service encounters (e.g., in a hotel for Chinese guests) in terms of actual face-to-face treatment, general ambience, marketing communications before and after the service encounter, etc. Moreover, behavioral exchanges and mannerisms during service encounters or business meetings can also make or break a transaction. For example, whereas Americans tend to be casual and friendly at first sight, such behavior may be interpreted as lack of proper respect among Chinese, especially toward an elder.

Reaching Asian Consumers in the United States

AT&T is one of the pioneers of multicultural marketing. Recognizing the size, growth, and bottom-line business impact of the Asian consumer population in the United States, AT&T took upon itself to address various Asian consumer segments in the United States. In the spring of 1997, it asked its Asian-American advertising agency, Kang & Lee Advertising in New York, to create a brand campaign. The campaign used the overall brand positioning of "It's all within your reach," with targeted executions for Chinese, Japanese, Korean, and Vietnamese consumers to create the right cultural experience for them.

For example, to target the Japanese market, Kang & Lee focused on businessmen who come to the United States for only a brief period of time, and hence are not highly nostalgic about Japan. Instead, they choose to live an

"American lifestyle" for this short period. Taking this into consideration, Kang & Lee created an ad revolving around a Japanese expatriate family: a Japanese businessman takes the day off work, choosing instead to "telecommunicate" from home, because his wife is ill, and he wishes to take care of her.

For the Chinese market, the advertisement had a very different focus. It depicted a Chinese student in the United States calling his girlfriend, who is in Asia, and telling her the moon outside is beautiful. When she says she cannot see it, as it is daytime in Asia when it is nighttime in the United States, the man says he will send her the moon (and uses AT&T's Worldnet Service to do so). This execution was chosen because many Chinese in the United States are foreign students who experience prolonged separations from family and friends in Asia.

The Image in the World Community

In global campaigns, marketers may choose entire cultures to provide attractive RELATE campaigns. This requires that the culture as a whole has positive associations and is valued in such a way around the world. The United States has been very successful in defining attractive cultural values. As a result, U.S. cultural images are dominating global ad campaigns. American movies and American novels are displacing homegrown competitors. Disney theme parks are a big success wherever they open (even in France, after an initial glitch). Restaurants based on U.S. cultural themes, like Planet Hollywood, are popping up around the globe.

THE NEED FOR CONFIRMATION

Because others play a critical role in the formation of the self, people systematically seek out information that verifies their self-concept.[13] We surround ourselves with people who flatter us, admire us, and share our opinions. We dump those who threaten our self-concept.

Moreover, we display relevant identity cues to lay claim to a certain self-concept. Suppose an individual is committed to a self-definition of "consultant," then she lays claim to this definition through the clothing and briefcase she chooses, the language and jargon (lots of use of "planning," "strategic," "value," "bottom-line," etc.), and the car she drives (a BMW, perhaps).

THE CASE OF MICHAEL JORDAN FRAGRANCE

How can marketers establish a RELATE association for their brands? Endorsers are a frequently used means to relate a brand to a specific reference group or to induce an identification of the brand with a celebrity. Celebrities have always attracted consumers to products through endorsements of everything from cars to laundry detergents to snack crackers.

The naming of products for celebrities, as well as the attaching of celebrity images to them, presents another great opportunity for powerful RELATE marketing. An especially strong example is Michael Jordan men's fragrance, the first fragrance developed—not just endorsed—by a major male athlete. The campaign is a highly integrated one that has lifestyle appeal on its own. The fragrance was developed in conjunction with the designer Bijan, Jordan himself collaborating on all aspects of the product from scent to packaging. To coordinate with the launch of the fragrance, Bijan designed an entire wardrobe for Jordan, a wardrobe that would cost $2.5 million at Bijan's retail price. The line was not designed for retail but presages the team's planned entry into casual sportswear.

The packaging of the Michael Jordan fragrance capitalizes on the star's identity: each product is merchandised in a matte black carton with a velvet-texture finish.[14] Openings in the front and back panels of the carton reveal a basketball etched on the glass bottle inside. The base and cap of the bottle are made of black rubber, the base resembling the tread on a sneaker and the cap bearing Jordan's signature. The $20 million advertising campaign, jointly developed by Jordan, Bijan, and Ground Zero Agency, includes television, radio, and print campaigns.

The campaigns all focus on the tremendous appeal of Jordan himself. Early television spots featured the sound of a pounding heart as Jordan's "chrome-dome" head slowly took shape as a black silhouette. The silhouette image was followed through much of the product promotion. Jordan used his celebrity status to promote the fragrance on television, on *The Tonight Show* with Jay Leno and *Larry King Live,* for example. Jordan explained how the components of the fragrance represent aspects of himself. According to Jordan, the product contains five different fragrance essences. The first is Rare Air, "Air" being a famous nickname of his, and is composed of cedarleaf and grapefruit. The second is called Cool, which is made up of cognac, geranium, and cypress. The third, Home Run, representing Jordan's love of baseball, contains green tea and clove leaf. The fourth is a golf association, Pebble Beach, which contains clary sage, lavender, and fir. The fifth is called Sexy Sensual, containing sandalwood, patchouli, and musk.

This RELATE product bears the identity and image of the man himself—Olympic Gold Medalist, Chicago Bulls superstar, most valuable player, All-Star, charismatic class act. It aims to capture the essence of Michael Jordan, on and off the court.

BEYOND CATEGORIZATION AND IDENTIFICATION

Thus far, we have focused on social categorization and group or personal identification (real, imagined, or implicit) and the role that brands may play in this process. As part of this process, marketers need to accomplish four tasks: (1) they need to create or allude to a certain social category X; (2) they need to get customers to apply the label "I am X"; (3) they need to persuade them that labeling themselves as "part of X" provides a positive experience; and (4) they need to show them that they can create this positive experience by consuming a certain brand.

Once these four goals have been accomplished, customers will feel good about themselves because group membership (real, imagined, or implicit) makes us feel good about ourselves. Robert Cialdini, a prominent social psychologist, and his associates have called this tendency BIRG (pronounced "burge") or "basking in the reflected glory."[15] Moreover, consumers may, in a way, take true possession of a brand by establishing "brand relations" similar to human intimate relationships and/or by forming "brand communities."

Basking in the Reflected Glory of the Brand

How does BIRG manifest itself? At several universities Mr. Cialdini found that students wore more school sweatshirts, baseball caps, scarves, and pins after the football team won than after it lost. Even a rather arbitrary incident can change the RELATE experience. People who find out they share a birthdate with a "bad guy" feel worse; those who share it with a "good guy" experience BIRG.

There are, however, limits to BIRG. Let's say you want to win the Boston Marathon. And let's further assume that another person who is very close to you won it two years ago. Will you BIRG because he won? It depends on two things. First, how close you are to the other person (was he your brother or your neighbor?) and how important winning the marathon is to you. If winning is a goal but not exactly the goal of your life, then you may BIRG in your brother's success. If winning is really important, you may be disappointed and engage in sibling rivalry. Sometimes we love to bask in the glory of loved ones; other times their success is painful for us. Furthermore, we are not always free to choose our comparisons. Sometimes we have to make a presentation after the best presenter in the company, and may feel envious and resentful.[16]

Establishing Brand Relations

Susan Fournier, a consumer researcher at Harvard Business School, has used an anthropological model to understand the personal relations that consumers form with their brands.[17] Conducting in-depth interviews with consumers, she finds that consumers use descriptions of their relations to brands that are strikingly similar to descriptions of their relations with people. Brands thus acquire animistic qualities, which include:

- Brands seem to be possessed by the spirit of the past. Thus, a brand of air freshener that Mother used or a floor cleaner that the ex-husband used can become so associated with the past-other that the person's spirit is evoked in each brand usage.

- Brands become anthropomorphized, i.e., they assume human qualities of emotionality, volition, and thought. Fournier cites Charlie the Tuna and the Pillsbury Doughboy as examples.

- Brands become close relationship partners that consumers long for, admire, or love. One of the interviewees stated: "Well, when Mary Kay changed that lipstick color on me, well, I near died. I just never thought they would do that to me."

Brand Communities

Albert Muniz and Thomas O'Guinn, respectively of the Walter Haas School of Business at the University of California at Berkeley and the University of Illinois at Urbana-Champaign, describe brand communities as "a structured set of social relationships among brand users."[18]

Brand communities are widespread. You can find them in Macintosh user groups, Harley-Davidson outings, "teenage idol" web sites on the Internet, and Saturn user groups.

You find these brand communities not only in real groups. For example, I experience an instant bonding with a stranger who wears my brand of watch, carries my brand of briefcase, or uses my brand of laptop. We usually hit it off immediately and start talking about our great watches, briefcases, and laptops for quite a while.

Muniz and O'Quinn identified four key characteristics of brand communities. Let me illustrate each characteristic with a quote that they provided from a Saab or Bronco user.

First, there is a consciousness of kin among users:

"When I see another Saab, and I think about it for a second, I not only have a feeling for the Saab, but I kind of know what that guy is like . . . he's kind of like me . . . or she's kind of like me."

"Who else drives Broncos? Guys like myself and guys who like engines. And preppy guys who drive them because they are 'in' right now. My Bronco won't be popular with them (because it's not new), but I don't care."

Second, users feel a sense of moral responsibility toward community members:

"On the way home from work . . . last week I get off the interstate and I see this car sitting there. . . . I drove him into the gas station and had club cards with me and said, 'Here, you want one of them?'"

"Yeah, we see another Saab on the side of the road, we pull over to help, no matter what it is."

Third, users share rituals, symbols, and traditions:

"If you drove a Saab, whenever you passed someone else driving a Saab on the road, you beeped or flashed your lights.

"Or you'd wave at each other. I did it today, I was driving around downtown Kenosha, and it was a four-door, nothing special, but that's OK, 'Hey, how you doing?' You were part of a select and crazy group. Yeah, I still flash my headlights at people."

Finally, users share personal experiences with the brand over and over again:

"A good friend of mine ran from the cops once in my car with new Michelins on it. I had just put the Michelins on a few days before. John had been racing another car when the cops started chasing both cars. The other car pulled over, John kept going. He lost the cops by turning off his lights and driving through a park and dodging trees."

The notion of brand communities is an important one. Think The Grateful Dead, Saturn, Versace, Hermès ties, Brooks Brothers shirts. Or think baseball fans, football fans, and soccer fans. Or specific baseball teams, football teams, and national soccer teams. Through brands we relate to one another and create barriers to others. As long as brand communities are alive, we are far away from creating a world community.

The concept of brand communities requires a revision of traditional communication models. Classic mass media communication models assume that the company communicates directly to the end consumer or to the decision maker in an industrial selling situation. The company offers products (designed without customer input), selects the distribution channel, and bombards customers with mass-media messages. In contrast, a market-driven relationship marketing model considers this process to be, in part, a two-way street. The brand community model adds to this by adding links between customers: they communicate with one another. Moreover, since it is a social system, there may be social roles such as opinion leaders in the community that set up web sites, user groups, and brand events. Customers create shared brand experiences, which may take the brand into a direction that management may not want to go.

So, to what degree does management have control over brand communities? Should management encourage or discourage brand communities, and how should it do so? Figure 8.2 shows some of the advantages and disadvantages of brand communities.

SUMMARY

RELATE experiences range from relatively straightforward reference-group identification, in which consumers feel connections with other users, to the highly complex formation of brand communities, in which consumers actually view a brand as the center of social organization and take on a marketing role themselves. RELATE marketing thus provides powerful experiences that result from the interplay of the sociocultural meaning and the customers' need for a social identity. The key challenge of RELATE is the selection of the right

FIGURE 8.2

Advantages and Disadvantages of Brand Communities

Brand Communities

Advantages

Strong bond to brand

Enriches the brand through communications

User groups attract attention and promote themselves

Disadvantages

Can turn into negative influencers

Can become clannish and unnecessarily adversarial toward other groups

Distort the brand

reference group and reference appeal that creates a differentiating social identity for customers by celebrating the group or culture that customers want to
be part of.

But . . . wonders LAURA BROWN . . .

*Who wants to relate to a thing like a brand? Or to another person via a
brand? What kind of communities are these "brand communities"? What
about communities of real people?*

PART THREE

STRUCTURAL, STRATEGIC, AND ORGANIZATIONAL ISSUES

9

EXPERIENTIAL HYBRIDS AND
HOLISTIC EXPERIENCES

In chapters 4 through 8, I discussed the five strategic experiential modules (SEMs) of SENSE, FEEL, THINK, ACT, and RELATE that form the basis of experiential marketing. As we saw, when using a particular SEM, managers need to give careful consideration to its objectives and principles. For each SEM, I have provided a set of tools, concepts, and techniques that managers can use once they have decided to use a certain SEM.

SEMs may be viewed as the fundamental building blocks upon which the edifice of experiential marketing rests. As such, they are the starting point—not the end goal—of experiential marketing. The ultimate goal of experiential marketing is to create what I call "holistic experiences." In the middle ground on the way to the holistic experiences, we find experiential hybrids (see Figure 9.1). In this chapter, I discuss the structural issues of building hybrids and holistic experiences. Moreover, I will introduce the "Experiential Wheel" as a tool for building hybrids and holistic experiences. Let's first look at some examples.

FIGURE 9.1

The Experiential Hierarchy

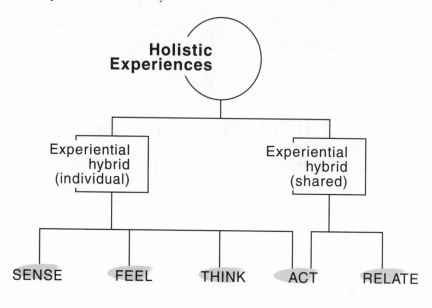

THE NEW BEETLE

Volkswagen's much-heralded return of the Beetle is steeped in experience.[1] Clearly America has an emotional bond with the Beetle that is very unusual for a car. More than that. The Beetle is a truly holistic experience.

The decision to relaunch the Beetle goes back to an idea that Volkswagen Chairman Ferdinand Piëch had in 1993. When I served on Volkswagen's Council of Consumer Affairs, I had the pleasure of meeting Mr. Piëch several times; he is passionate about cars and has cunning instincts for new business opportunities. At the time, Volkswagen lost $1.1 billion worldwide and had a U.S. market share of less than 1 percent but—against all odds—Mr. Piëch ordered up a new Beetle prototype in a bid to recapture Volkswagen's former glory. By 1994 a prototype, known as Concept One, was ready and presented at the Detroit auto show. Concept One was greeted with enthusiasm. One New Hampshire woman sent in a $500 check as a down payment—quite unusual for a car that was not in production! What to do next was straightforward. Says Piëch: "To say the least, we were overwhelmed. From the very first moment, it

Old campaign for the Beetle

seemed that we were almost forced by the customer's voice to make a 'real car' out of Concept One."

Volkswagen aimed for more than a straight nostalgic throwback to the model that was discontinued in 1979, however. Sure, the quirky round shape that invites a smile is still there. But the New Beetle is also a thoroughly modern car that offers everything the modern driver has become used to, such as

New campaign for the New Beetle

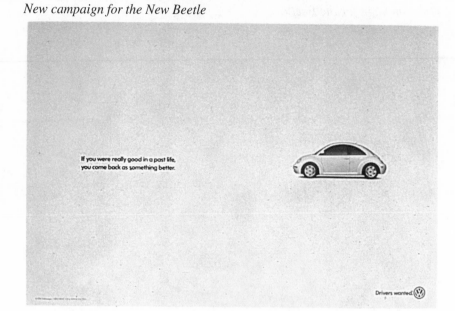

four air bags, power outlets for cell phones, an adjustable steering wheel, a premium sound system, and a central locking system with remote control. The New Beetle is also slightly bigger on the outside and markedly roomier inside. The price reflects the fact that the Beetle has grown up, as have its most likely customers: while in today's dollars you could have bought an old Beetle for $8,300, a typically equipped new one will run about twice that. So while this car clearly acknowledges its roots and taps into the emotional context and value system surrounding the old model, it is also very clearly a car of the late '90s. (Although the sticker price of $15,200+ probably renders it out of reach of your average just-out-of-college GenXer, for them there's a whole assortment of Beetle accessories, ranging from watches and key chains to jackets and T-shirts.) Just as the old Beetle came to represent the '60s, the new one fits perfectly with these pragmatic times in which corporations are headed by former "flower children" and college students take out their nose rings before presenting themselves on Wall Street. The payoff for Volkswagen: sales at an eighteen-year high!

Targeting for this car is deliberately very broad. Says board member Jens Neumann: "You might wonder how we plan to market this car to such a broad audience. Let me share with you some of our observations in our pre-marketing studies: Whenever and wherever we showed the New Beetle design concepts, we noticed an amazing reaction. People of all nationalities, all ages, divergent life experiences, different incomes, different religions—all behaved the same way when they first saw the car. They smiled." He continues: "These pre-marketing observations gave us insight into how we should bring this car to the attention of the American people: Simply show the car, show its shape, don't try to describe it, don't explain its features, don't spoil individual dreams and memories by talking hardware. Get out of the way and let people define this car in quite personal terms, let them establish their own personal relationship, and let them want to drive the car." This strategy of "show them the car and get out of the way" makes a lot of sense in this case, and is definitely refreshing as far as car marketing goes.

The advertising campaign—estimated at about $35 million a year—stays true to the above principle to stay out of the way and leave the car's wonderful shape to do the talking. The only copy is tongue-in-cheek tag lines such as: "If you sold your soul in the eighties, here is your chance to buy it back," "A car like this comes around only twice in a lifetime," and "Less flower. More power." In self-deprecating reference to the old Beetle, one ad asks: "0–60?" then replies, "Yes."

Promotional tie-ins are chosen to reinforce the Beetle's hippie past. For instance, Volkswagen sponsored the 1998 edition of Lilith Fair, the funky touring showcase of female songwriters.

Piece by piece, the Beetle is a marvelous example of a holistic campaign, that is, a campaign that unites all five SEMs in an integrated experiential appeal:

SENSE. In a car market where at a distance of a hundred yards automotive executives would be hard put to tell their own models apart from their competitors', the beautiful, circular shapes of the Beetle make it visually as distinctive as a car can ever hope to be.

FEEL. The emotional appeal of this car is just as distinctive as its design. Said an advertising executive involved in the taping of the pre-launch commercials: "When I parked one in front of a restaurant, it drew crowds. It was like being a rock star. But when I went inside, people were still looking at the car and not at me." On first sight, this car elicits feelings of warmth, affection, and nostalgia. One ad asks simply, "Hug it? Drive it? Hug it? Drive it?"

THINK. In its past incarnation, in an era of cars the size of small ships, the Beetle, with its legendary "Think small" campaign, singlehandedly changed the way an entire generation thought about its transportation needs. Today's car has lost nothing of that aura. The Beetle is retro and futuristic at the same time; as the ad puts it, "Twice in a lifetime."

ACT. This is definitely a car that makes a bold statement and encourages you to be an individualist. Many people are buying it as a fun lifestyle car that lets them change their behavior.

RELATE. This car is today as much as ever an icon of the flower power era. Ex-hippies can relive their youth, and GenXers, who have adopted '60's chic as cool, can relate too.

SHISEIDO'S 5S STORES

Now let's look at holistic experiences in a very different setting. In the heart of New York's trendy, artistic Soho district, Shiseido is redefining the art of marketing cosmetics.[2] From the outside, the 5S store looks more like an art gallery than a retail store—high ceilings, large windows letting in natural light, pale wood floors, and plenty of open space. Entering the store, you find yourself embraced by a world much like a contemporary museum. Just inside the front door is a panel that announces the holistic philosophy behind the store: "A woman's beauty is a function of the way she thinks, the way she lives, and the way she feels at any given moment. Each woman's beauty is ethereal, changing every moment. Beauty is deeper than age, nationality, and status. Every woman has her own beauty and it is this beauty that 5S was designed to enhance. 5S is skincare and makeup for the whole woman—mind and body. We use aromas, colors, plants, and natural extracts that amplify each woman's unique beauty by enhancing her mind and her body."

Moving around the spacious room, one sees products displayed almost as though they were art objects. A collection of bottles on a tabletop is accompanied by a lighted panel that describes the virtues of the natural herbal ingredi-

5S Store

ents of the product. Displayed on the walls behind these tables are beautiful photos of women of different ethnicities in natural settings. Videos on the same motifs are playing on monitors, accompanied by ambient music.

The environment is comfortable and accommodating. Information is abundant but unobtrusive; stand-alone touch-screen computer stations answer questions about skin care; brochures are free for the taking. A wooden rack displays the latest beauty and fashion magazines, as well as a reference collection of books about natural foods and herbal teas. A *Soho Guide* is displayed for sale next to a computer screen showing information about the local area. A thermos of herbal tea is available for sampling by customers. Salespeople quietly make their presence felt without jumping all over customers— it is possible to walk the full circuit of the store without ever being accosted, and yet not feel ignored.

5S is tuned in to ecological concerns. A brochure, printed on recycled paper, explains, "When we gave birth to 5S, we wanted an eco-conscious policy that was environmentally sound and cared about our global community." Packaging is minimal and recycled whenever possible. Recycled materials were even used in the architecture and design of the store itself. Whenever possible, products are made with natural ingredients and herbally based.

That music you hear? It's 5S music. "It evokes the world. It reflects women. It invokes the five senses. It's challenging, but it's beautiful. It's water, wind, birds, the sea, flutes, guitars, women singing, speaking, whispering, reading poetry in ten languages. . . . It's totally new and it's impossible for me to describe," says Mark Badger, one of the composers. The brochure goes on: "And then there's the way you listen to it, on DVD, in SurroundSound, enveloped in the scent and space of the 5S store, accompanied by the saturated colors and images of the ambient video. . . . The 5S music experience is a complete sensory event, designed to sweep your mind and body away on a trip as breathtaking and unique as the products."

It's hard to imagine anything more different from the typical cosmetics counter at a department store! The 5S store has created a holistic approach to cosmetics and fragrances that encompasses product design and display, and links ideology with the values and lifestyles of contemporary women.

HYBRIDS AND HOLISTIC EXPERIENCES IN THE SUPERMARKET

Let's now leave the rarefied environment of 5S and turn to a much more mundane setting—the supermarket. Follow me as I push my cart around, and look at what's happening, especially with newer brands. We'll find the shelves full of experiential hybrids and holistic experiences.

Let's start with the beverage aisle. Sometimes it's hard to tell what's what by looking casually at the array of bottles. Various beverage lines compete not just within product categories but across them—iced teas competing with fruit drinks competing with spring waters—and they are all using experiential marketing. (As I am writing this, I am nipping on a New Age soda called "Tribal Tonics." Its motto is: "Tribalize & Revitalize," and on the bottle they define the word "tonic" for me: "stimulating mental, physical, or emotional vigor, increasing strength and tone.")

Among the most creative are the Arizona Iced Teas, which have several lines of products with distinctive packagings. Their Green Tea drink, for example, has a celadon green bottle painted in a Japanese motif with pink cherry blossoms and Asian characters—it looks more like a work of art than a drink. Their ginseng extract is painted with Southwest Indian symbols, including a buffalo, lightning bolts, and a masked warrior figure. Arizona's line of diet teas are in bottles painted like old-fashioned fruit packing labels, with rich, sumptuous colors and idealized fruits. Their Honey Lemon flavor actually reprints old lemon packing labels on a burlap background. Their "Lite" line includes a chocolate fudge drink adorned with a nineteenth-century image of a lovely, rosy-cheeked woman draped with the American flag. Beside her is an idyllic early pioneer scene. This retro look is carried through into their line of Cowboy Cocktails, including the Colada Cocktail displaying a cowboy riding a bucking horse.

Fruit drinks by SoBe (for "South Beach") rival Arizona in their evocative power, if not in their spectacular packaging. Printed on the bottle of their Power Line drink, in lettering reminiscent of Celtic manuscripts, is the following text: "Naturally healthy orange and mango juices enhanced with herbs whose properties promote calm and focused thought, ginkgo to sharpen the mind, St John's wort to help impart a feeling of well being, and gotu kola to help rejuvenate the brain. Power * Wisdom * Energy." The brand's logo, a lizard, is molded into the glass bottle. Other SoBe drinks include: "Wisdom" and "Eros." The company sold $67 million in 1998 alone.

An early pioneer of experiential marketing, and one that is still going strong, is Celestial Seasonings teas. Each of their various products is marketed in a holistic way, with ideas carried through from names to package artwork to poetry quoted on the back of the box. Mint Magic, for example, is packaged in a blue box with white stars, showing a painting of a wizard summoning a gold, jewel-encrusted grail from a thicket of mint leaves. By his side is a charming unicorn wearing a wreath made from the same leaves. On the back of the package, next to a painting of the same golden teacup, is printed the poem "New Friends and Old Friends" by Joseph Parry: "Make new

Arizona: Nine bottles and stationery

1212 SYCAMORE STREET, CINCINNATI, OH 45210 - TEL. 513 784 9898 - FAX 513 357 4754

friends, but keep the old/Those are silver, these are gold. . . ." Sleepytime tea, one of their most popular lines, shows a cozy scene of a bear wearing a night-cap and nightshirt, a cat curled up in his lap, sitting before a comforting fire. The back of the package quotes "Learning to Pause" from the best-selling author Sarah Ban Breathnach's book *Simple Abundance: A Daybook of Comfort and Joy.* Chamomile tea is packaged with a sunny painting of a woman—with

SoBe Wisdom bottle

long blonde hair and a romantic pink dress—swinging in a flowering tree before a thatched-roof cottage. The text on the back is from Dr. Stanley Frager's phenomenally popular *Chicken Soup for the Soul* series: "A lesson in heart is my ten-year-old daughter Sarah, who was born with a muscle missing in her foot and wears a brace all the time. . . . " The experiential appeal is very strong for the busy women who make up Celestial Seasonings' primary consumers.

Spring waters, whose popularity soared along with our interest in health and fitness, rely almost exclusively on experiential marketing to appeal to consumers. Many water brands use names that suggest unpolluted natural settings, such as Spa, Appalachian, and Crystal Geyser. And to suggest purity, snow-capped mountains appear on the packaging of almost all the major brands: Poland Spring, Evian, Volvic, and Crystal Geyser. Spa's packaging shows lush green fields.

Celestial Seasonings herb teas

Even Perrier, the traditional French brand that led the charge of mineral waters into the U.S. market in the 1970s, has turned in the direction of experiential marketing in a limited edition of its holiday bottles. Perrier has retained its basic label design but updated it with SENSE and FEEL appeal. The new labels are colorful: bright green with stars, swirls, and "floating" Perrier bottles that mimic the sparkle of the water. Perrier's flavored waters are adorned with labels showing juicy lemons and limes, and their lemon label has been printed in bright yellow.

A particularly interesting experiential water is Fiji natural artesian water, drawn from a spring on the Fiji Islands. Fiji is packaged in a distinctive square

Perrier 1998 holiday bottle

pale blue bottle, reminiscent of Bombay Sapphire gin. The label design suggests an island paradise. On the front of the bottle, under the gold-outlined word "FIJI," is a bunch of tropical flowers. Seen through the bottle, on the inside of the back label, is an Edenic South Pacific scene, with a white waterfall and lush vegetation. Viewing this scene through the bottle gives the sensation that we are underwater, and suggests that we are drinking this very waterfall. On the back of the bottle is a map of the Fiji Islands. This multivalenced packaging suggests a myriad of sensory, affective and lifestyle associations—from fine liquor to tropical paradise to exotic travel.

Hey, I didn't think they could sell liquor in a supermarket! Oh, it's not liquor—it's water: Crown Natural Spring Water from Australia. Its plastic packaging is molded in a honeycomb pattern, its dark blue label printed in elegant silver type, and it's topped with a coordinating blue cap. Casually glancing at the market shelf, I took it for a bottle of vodka!

A new entrant in the water market is Wazu, a Canadian spring water that self-consciously positions itself against the paradisiacal visions of its competitors. (Yes, you guessed right! By now, I have emptied my "Totem and Taboo" tonic and am literally nipping on the oh-so-Freudian-designed nipple of "the TRUE WAZU," which encourages me: "wet yourself.")

Wazu's packaging has a strong experiential appeal for the twenty-something consumer (or the twenty-something-something consumer like myself). It carries a dark label with misaligned typewritten characters in multiple bright colors. Comments scattered on the label are in sync with the irreverent and cynical flavor of the packaging: "If the rules don't work . . . change the rules." "WARNING: Open your mouth before pouring!" "So here's the deal. WAZU is new. What we want to do is provide great products without the annoying attitude. So we won't proclaim utopia!" Of course, the product has an attitude of its own: "WHAT? There's no MOUNTAIN on this label? Listen, if this really WHACKS YOU OUT, drop us a line on the INTERNET and we'll see what we can do." Even the name of the company suggests the antithesis of pure mountain springs and ethereal experiences: "All trademarks and copyright are the property of Urban Juice & Soda Company, Ltd. (Our lawyer told us to say that.)"

Experiential marketing of water is all the rage not only in the United States but in other markets as well. From Canada comes "Aquator," a glacial water. In the United Kingdom, the London design firm Coley Porter Bell has created an experiential water for its client Eden Valley Mineral Water. Their product, Ten Degrees sparkling water, is so named because it flows from its source at 10 degrees centigrade. The package design carries through this sense of cool purity: the glass bottle is tinted blue, the printing a sophisticated navy blue. The bottle shape is based on that of a claret bottle, its neck elongated to give it elegance. A black foil seal tops off the product, making it a suitable table companion for a bottle of fine wine.

The experiential imagery of water has even been extended to the wildly successful Brita water filtration pitcher. A print ad shows a deep blue stream flanked with delicate banks of melting snow. Lines of text, arranged as if they were cascading down the stream, read, "There was a time/When it was perfect. Clean. Untouched. You can have this taste." The product itself appears in only a small photo at the lower right-hand corner of the spread—what's important is its experiential setting.

Now it's on to the checkout line, where the usual array of candy bars is beginning to look very different. Candy bars are not just candy bars anymore. Dotted among the older brands are the new "experience bars."

For the exercise-conscious are the "Balance" and "Think" bars. "Think" pitches itself as good brainfood, hardly a new idea, but its packaging breaks new ground in linking with the experiences of consumers. The wrapper is designed as a computer screen, the word "Think" appearing as a file name under a tool bar. The Balance bar is another experiential nutritional product with a strong lifestyle appeal. Packaging bills the bar as "the complete nutritional food bar," and advertising links nutritional needs to busy lifestyles at work and at play. The Balance bar is promoted as intelligent nutrition for active people, with the slogan "You can do anything on it."

Another entrant is the Clif bar, a product of Clif Bar Inc. of Berkeley, California, with sales more than $22 million in 1997. The Clif bar is a pretty ordinary energy bar, full of rolled oats, brown rice syrup, rice flour, oat bran, cornmeal, dried fruit, the works. However, it has only 2 grams of fat and no cholesterol, which qualifies it as a "natural energy bar." The packaging has holistic appeal. On the front, there is a cartoonlike picture of a mountain climber on a cliff, with red mountains glowing in the sunset. On the back, we read a statement by "Gary of Clif Bar Inc.": "Clif Bar is named after my father, Clifford, who was my childhood hero and companion through the Sierra Nevada mountain range. Maybe you'll spend an afternoon on the bike or a few days climbing a granite wall. Or it might be a 14-hour work day. Under these conditions, your mind as well as your body require extra carbohydrates to sustain a peak level of performance." Sounds like Outward Bound in a snack.

Clearly, just like Internet stocks, not all these products will be successful in the long run. But the sheer pervasiveness of experiential hybrids and holistic appeals in today's supermarkets is undeniable. And another word of caution. No amount of experiential marketing can rescue a bad product.

Clif bars

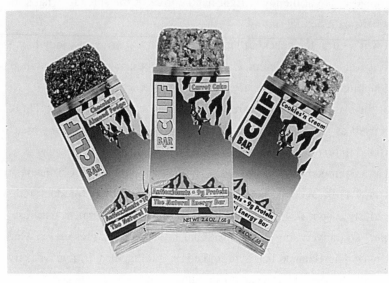

According to *BusinessWeek,*[3] the candymaker Mars is withdrawing its trendy new energy bar VO2 Max. The problem? Its taste. Loaded with proteins and carbos, the VO2 Max was found to be deficient in flavor.

Isn't it fun to be in a supermarket at the turn of the century?

EXPERIENTIAL HYBRIDS

Experiential hybrids combine two or more SEMs. With experiential hybrids, we move from mono-experiential brands and marketing campaigns to multi-experiential—though not yet holistic—brands and marketing campaigns.

Roughly, SEMs fall into two categories: "individual" and "shared" (i.e., sociocultural) experiences. SENSE, FEEL, and THINK are individual experiences. That is, the marketing strategies designed to induce these experiences target the perceptions, feelings, and creative thinking of individual customers. In contrast, ACT and RELATE are "shared": RELATE experiences typically occur with respect to reference groups (real or imagined), and ACT experiences generally happen in the presence of others, although certain body experiences and behaviors may be considered purely individual (see Figure 9.2).

FIGURE 9.2

Types of Experiential Hybrids

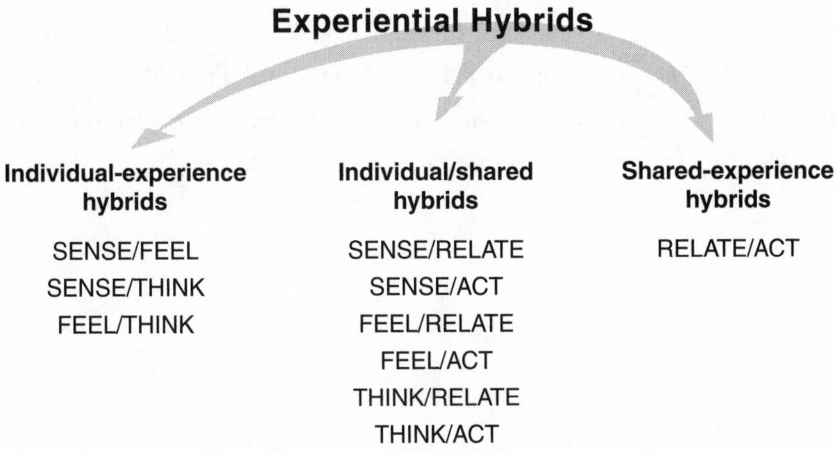

Experiential Hybrids

Individual-experience hybrids	Individual/shared hybrids	Shared-experience hybrids
SENSE/FEEL	SENSE/RELATE	RELATE/ACT
SENSE/THINK	SENSE/ACT	
FEEL/THINK	FEEL/RELATE	
	FEEL/ACT	
	THINK/RELATE	
	THINK/ACT	

Individual-experience hybrids come in the form of SENSE/FEEL, SENSE/THINK, and FEEL/THINK. Individual/shared hybrids combine individual appeals to sensation, feelings, and thinking with shared actions and broader social/cultural appeals. The shared-experience hybrid combines a relational appeal with an opportunity for individual action.

More Than the Sum of the Parts

Hybrids typically add something beyond the sum of the two (or more) SEMs—namely, a new experiential appeal resulting from their interaction.

Finlandia vodka has launched a tongue-in-cheek hybrid campaign that plays on popular interest in spiritualism and reincarnation. One print ad shows a woman in a white bathing suit, floating in a cool blue pool of lily-pads. The handwritten text reads, "In a past life I was a mermaid who fell in love with an ancient mariner. I pulled him into the sea to be my husband. I didn't know he couldn't breathe underwater." At the bottom of the page appears a bottle of Finlandia vodka, with the text "In a past life I was pure, glacial spring water." Past lives—and reincarnations—have captured people's imaginations, and marketers are playing with these ideas. (In its creative campaign for the New Beetle, for instance, Volkswagen runs a print ad showing a simple shot of the car, with the tag line "If you were really good in a past life, you come back as something better.") The Finlandia campaign nicely illustrates the interaction of hybrids—the more than the sum of the parts—that I mentioned earlier. It is not just FEEL + THINK but FEEL AND THINK AND FEEL AND . . . A note of caution, though—Finlandia's campaign, for all its wit, may be a bit too esoteric to appeal to a wide audience.

Finlandia ad

In a past life I was a mermaid who fell in love with an ancient mariner. I pulled him into the sea to be my husband. I didn't know he couldn't breathe underwater.

In a past life I was pure, glacial spring water

A TOOL FOR BUILDING HYBRIDS: THE EXPERIENTIAL WHEEL

The question remains, when—and how—do you create them? Very often, experiential hybrids are not built from scratch. They arise when a company feels that its current corporate identity, product presence, or communications are no longer appropriate for its customers, lack competitive advantage, or are too simplistic. As a consequence, the company decides to extend its experiential approach beyond the realm of a single SEM.

A planning tool for building hybrids, which I have employed in my consulting with clients, is the "Experiential Wheel." The Experiential Wheel may be compared with advertising's hierarchy-of-effects models used in traditional F&B marketing (see Figure 9.3).

The hierarchy-of-effects models in advertising are guided by the notion that it is necessary to achieve several sequential communication objectives before an ad campaign impacts sales. Figure 9.3 shows the learning hierarchy, which starts with awareness, followed by comprehension, attitude formation, and purchase. In other words, an ad campaign must first draw attention to the

FIGURE 9.3

A Hierarchy-of-Effects Model

Awareness

Comprehension

Attitude

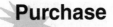
Purchase

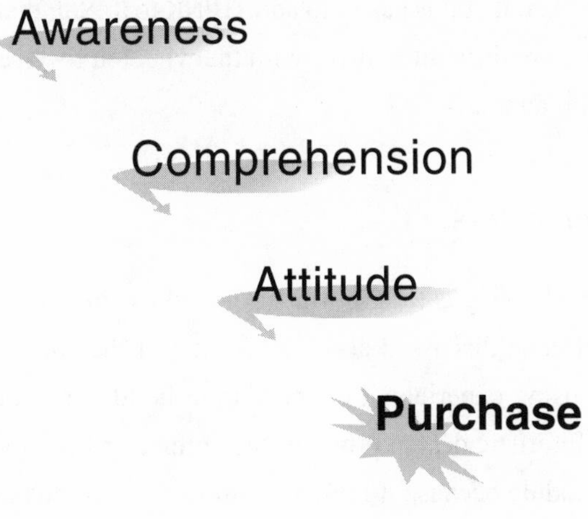

ad or the brand, then get consumers to comprehend the features and benefits of the brand, then get them to form a positive attitude; all these steps will result in a purchase intention and ultimately in purchase.

The Experiential Wheel works in much the same way, to a certain degree. As in hierarchy-of-effects models, there is a certain natural sequence and priority of objectives for building hybrids. If you start from scratch, the recommended sequence is the order in which I discussed the SEMs in this book: SENSE - FEEL - THINK - ACT - RELATE. SENSE attracts attention and motivates. FEEL creates an affective bond and thus makes the experience personally relevant and rewarding. THINK adds a permanent cognitive interest to the experience. ACT induces a behavioral commitment, loyalty, and a view to the future. RELATE goes beyond the individual experience and makes it meaningful in a broader social context.

At the same time, it is useful to think of the SEMs not as self-contained, insular modules like the communication objectives of hierarchy-of-effects models but as structures that are interconnected (as shown in Figure 9.4). The Experiential Wheel thus becomes a strategic tool for building hybrids by adding more and more connectors, thus increasing the overall gestalt far beyond the sum of the parts.

These connectors mean that it is possible to reverse the direction of the wheel if necessary. If you are starting with a pure THINK or ACT brand, for example, you can "go back" and add SENSE and FEEL to your experiential mix. The model does suggest, however, that it is easier to add THINK to SENSE than to add SENSE to THINK. It is more difficult to drive with the wheel in reverse, and doing so requires careful planning.

Using Experiential Connectors

The key issue in experiential wheeling is the identification and use of experiential connectors. The New Beetle discussed at the beginning of the chapter provides a good example of using experiential connectors to build a holistic experience. The funky retro-futuristic design provides the connector from the SENSE module to the FEEL module because it makes us smile and reminds us

FIGURE 9.4

Experiential Wheel

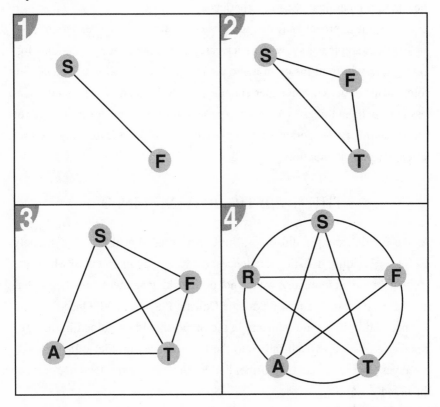

of the car's earlier models in the '50s and '60s. This memory can be further intensified and enriched through communications, web sites, and sponsorships, for example, thus developing an all-out FEEL module. Parts of this FEEL module (such as the unusual hype, excitement, and nostalgic feelings) may then be used to connect the FEEL module to the THINK module: what type of car is this that everyone loves and feels so sentimental about? The THINK module may be further built by allusions to the '60s advertising campaign and the quirky features of the earlier cars and their drivers. Through the uniqueness and individualism of the cars, we provide a connector to ACT, especially for those drivers who wish to add a little spice to their lifestyles (e.g., corporate executives who drive a Lexus or BMW during the week but want to lead an entirely different lifestyle on the weekend). As in the '60s, this counterculture attitude may become the connector to the sociocultural aspects of the car, thus creating a RELATE experience.

The same approach may be used for adding any other new experience. As the Beetle example has shown, in each case, management needs to ask the following question in terms of strategic planning: How can we leverage certain components of our current experiential approach for the new experience? Unless management thinks in terms of experiential connectors, it runs the risk of simply putting two experiences next to each other without leveraging their interrelations and interactions.

THE HOLISTIC PLAYING FIELD

As the Beetle example illustrates, the Experiential Wheel is also extremely useful for building holistic experiences. As we are adding new SEMs to the product, brand, or company, we are not only making an incremental contribution but also creating a new field—the Holistic Playing Field. Once this field has been built, future investments in the brand should be guided in terms of whether a given approach falls into the Holistic Playing Field. If it does, it leverages joint resources and further builds the holistic experiential aspects of the brand.

Holistic experiences may be created gradually over time, using the Experiential Wheel as a step-by-step planning tool for yearly communication, sales, or web site campaigns. Alternatively, holistic experiences may be built from scratch, using the Experiential Wheel as a planning tool for new product development and for launching the new product. Indeed, although we just analyzed the New Beetle experiences step-by-step, the holistic experiential qualities of the New Beetle were not added gradually; this car was launched as a holistic brand from the start.

Holistic experiences often result from intensifying, broadening, enriching, and interconnecting experiences (see chapter 10). Holistic experiences may also be created, however, for one given ExPro—in product design, retail design, or in an advertising campaign. Let us take a look at a product-design example.

Pottery Barn's Beach Boy Transistor Radio: A Holistic Experience in a Box

An offering from Pottery Barn for the summer of 1998 was the holistic "Beach Boy Transistor Radio." The bright packaging with intense colors and sunburst images has a strong SENSE appeal, and pictures of a '60s couple frolicking at the beach create a charming FEEL of nostalgia. In fact, the box itself proclaims "Summer Nostalgia from the Sixties." Upon closer inspection, the back of the box looks like the back of an old record album (THINK), with descriptions of the radio in several languages appearing in the place of song titles, and the "Beach Boy" reference uses the ageless pop group to help consumers RELATE to the sixties. The radio itself echoes 1960's product design, resembling at once a radio, an old electric shaver, and a pack of Lucky Strikes. Another component of the product is ACT—this is a product pitched for summer fun—take it to the beach!

SUMMARY

The New Beetle, Shiseido's 5S stores, and several manufacturers of consumer packaged goods found in the supermarket offer hybrids and holistic experiences that serve as best-practice examples for their industries. Hybrids and holistic experiences occur not only at the "macro" level of the firm but also at the "micro" level of each ExPro. Hybrids and holistic experiences are built via a process and methodology called the Experiential Wheel. If this process is used successfully, connections are built that result in the whole being far more than the sum of the parts: we are creating the Holistic Playing Field.

Isn't this getting really perverted now? wonders LAURA BROWN. Weren't these "modules" enough, and now we've got them adding up to "hybrids" and "holistic experiences"?

10

STRATEGIC ISSUES OF EXPERIENTIAL MARKETING

S trategic issues are issues of choice. They are governed by certain determined objectives. Strategic decisions in marketing are not made in iso-
lation; they are made after a careful consideration of customer and
competitive issues. In this chapter, I discuss strategic issues of experiential
marketing regarding the choice of SEMs and the use of the Experiential Grid,
introduced in chapter 3, as well as broader issues of brand architecture (corporate branding *vs.* sub-branding), new products, brand extensions, partnership strategies, and global experiences (see Figure 10.1).

ISSUE 1: WHICH SEM?

Why should you select a SENSE marketing approach rather than FEEL, THINK,
ACT, or RELATE? Or why THINK over FEEL, or RELATE over SENSE? In other
words, why should you run a certain type of experiential marketing campaign? How do you make this decision? Moreover, once you have decided on
the type of SEM, how exactly should you execute it in images and messages?
The choice of the type of experiential marketing approach is driven by customer, competitor, and trend analyses. Key questions in these analyses include:

FIGURE 10.1

A List of Strategic Issues

Strategic Issues

Which SEM?

Strategic issues related to the experiential grid

Corporate branding and sub-branding

New products, brand extensions, and partnership strategies

Global experiential branding

- Who are your customers?
- What do they appreciate most about your products: a SENSE, FEEL, THINK, ACT or RELATE appeal?
- What approach have your competitors used? Have they been successful?
- In which direction is the industry going? Has there been a small competitor who has been very successful with a unique approach?

Once you have focused on the appropriate SEMs to use, decisions about the precise execution of strategy need to be explored in a similar manner. These decisions can be made by examining relevant concepts discussed in chapters 4 through 8 and asking pertinent questions, such as:

- For SENSE: Should we pursue an aesthetic approach or an entertainment/excitement approach? Which senses should we appeal to? Do we have the resources and creative potential to use a consistently executed approach that also provides sensory variety over time?

- For FEEL: What is the goal of the FEEL approach—to induce a mood or a specific emotion? Which emotion? How can we emotionalize the entire consumption experience?

- For THINK: How can we stimulate creative thinking? Should we focus primarily on convergent or divergent thinking? Can we create surprise, intrigue, and perhaps provocation?

- For ACT: Should we target bodily experiences, lifestyles, or interactions with our brand? What approach should we use to induce lifestyle changes?

- For RELATE: What are the relevant reference people, groups, or cultures for our target customers? How can we get customers to identify with these groups? Should we promote brand communities?

ISSUE 2: STRATEGIC ISSUES RELATED TO THE EXPERIENTIAL GRID

Figure 10.2 shows the Experiential Grid. The SEMs are listed as rows and the ExPros are shown in the columns.

Expanding the Basic Grid

The Experiential Grid is extremely useful for experiential marketing planning. In fact, depending on the planning needs of the organization, it can be expanded into three dimensions to develop further strategic insights. For example, suppose you run a service business (like AT&T or United Airlines) and you are interested in analyzing and planning SEMs and ExPros at every point of customer contact (e.g., before purchase, during purchase, during first contact, during repeated consumption, etc.). In that case, a useful third dimension may be the progression of the service (represented as steps or blueprints of the service encounters over time). Or imagine you want to take your experiential marketing approach global; then the third dimension might represent different countries with different cultural values. In this case, you will complete a three-dimensional experiential grid by filling in SEMs and ExPros on a country-by-country basis. The grid is adaptable in numerous directions, depending on your company's needs and objectives.

FIGURE 10.2

Strategic Issues of the Experiential Grid

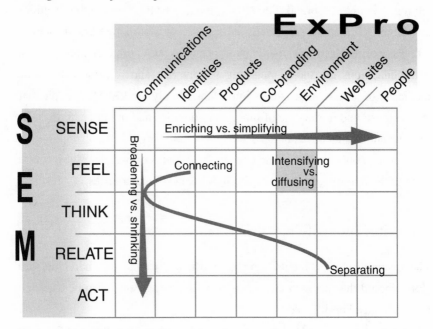

The Relation Between SEMs and ExPros

Before we proceed with strategic issues, using the two-dimensional grid for sake of simplicity, it is important to note that although any SEM may be instantiated via any ExPro, certain ExPros fit certain SEMs better than others. For example, for sensory experience, the starting points are often identity and signage, and product presence. To be sure, after the sensory experience has been established, it can and should be enriched by other ExPros such as communications, spatial environments, electronic media, and to a degree by co-branding and people. However, identity and signage and product presence are the places to start, and unless you manage them well, a SENSE campaign may start off on the wrong foot.

As was discussed in chapter 5, people and communications are key for affective experiences: people to deliver feelings at the point of consumption (e.g., of the service), and communications to "frame" the consumption experience. Again, other ExPros may enrich the experience, but without the appropriate people, management, and communications it is difficult to create a satisfying overall FEEL brand. For THINK, the key ExPros are communications, co-branding initiatives (especially in the case of a corporate brand), and, in today's world, electronic media. For personal ACT, product presence and communications are most important; for interact and lifestyles, electronic media are becoming increasingly important. Finally, for RELATE, people matter the most, and in the case of brand communities and brand gatherings, the Internet and spatial environments can be pivotal.

Let me now move on to the key strategic issues of the grid. These are related to the intensity, breadth, depth, and linkage of experiences.

Intensity: Intensifying *vs.* Diffusing

The intensity issue ("Intensifying *vs.* Diffusing") concerns individual grid cells. Should the specific experience provided in a given ExPro be experientially enhanced or diffused?

Let's say you are Hallmark Cards, and you are creating a FEEL experience during the *Hallmark Hall of Fame* by showing a FEEL commercial. (You know, those "slice-of-apple-pie" two-minute commercials showing the brother coming home [almost] late for Christmas dinner, just in time to sing a Christmas carol with his younger brother.) The question is: What is exactly the right level of intensity to get viewers to dab their eyes and feel good about Hallmark, without overdoing it and coming across as tacky? This is not an easy balance to strike. According to Brad Van Auken, Hallmark's director of brand management and marketing, it requires careful copy testing to get it just right.[1] Without this kind of testing, you can overshoot your mark or fall far short.

Breadth: Enriching *vs.* Simplifying

The breadth issue ("Enriching *vs.* Simplifying") concerns the management across ExPros. Should the organization enrich a given experience by adding

Hallmark Christmas commercial: older and younger brother

additional ExPros that provide the same experience, or simplify the experience by concentrating it into certain ExPros?

Again, you are Hallmark. Should your retail stores be experiential FEEL environments in order to enrich the experience, or should they be more functional selling spaces? Or conversely, should you even drop the FEEL advertising described earlier and use a more simplified approach by relying solely on the messages and imagery of the cards themselves?

Hallmark's choice has been to enrich the experience, creating new Hallmark Creations shops in collaboration with the retail specialists at the design firm Donovan and Green.[2] In late 1998, Hallmark had over eighty Creations stores with plans to open about another fifty in the following year. Sales surpassed Hallmark expectations. The stores enhance the brand's FEEL appeal by providing a warm and welcoming atmosphere. According to Donovan and Green, "The emotional content of the product drove the new store." There are quiet spaces for selecting cards (rather than rows and rows of card displays), comfortable writing surfaces with child-sized tables and chairs and boxes of crayons available, and themed displays ("Kids' Party," for example, or "Adult Birthday"). Shoppers are welcome to sit down and have a cup of coffee while they plan a party or select a Mother's Day gift. Using retail space to enrich the Hallmark experience has meant a dramatic increase in the volume of sales as well as amazing results in customer perception of the brand.

Depth: Broadening *vs.* Shrinking

The depth issue ("Broadening *vs.* Shrinking") concerns the management across SEMs: Should the organization broaden its experiential appeal from individual experiences to experiential hybrids and holistic experiences, or should it stick—or shrink—to one single experience?

For example, as part of its strategic planning, Hallmark may ask, "How can we keep our leadership and relevance in the electronic age? What is the function and meaning of greeting cards in the electronic age? Does it still make sense to send greetings via mail? And what if greeting cards are sent by e-mail, or personally created and stored on web sites?" As these questions illustrate, in the electronic age, Hallmark has the chance to broaden its experiential approach from FEEL to THINK and perhaps even explore RELATE and ACT. In fact, the company has capitalized on these opportunities by inaugurating one of the most interesting and thought-provoking sites on the World Wide Web.

Linkage: Connecting *vs.* Separating

Finally, the linkage issue ("Connecting *vs.* Separating") concerns the interrelations among SEMs as well as ExPros. It is often not enough merely to add SEMs. SEMs need to be connected with one another. Yet, in some cases it may be beneficial to separate experiences that have become too broad and thus run the risk of being meaningless.

Should Hallmark create linkages and connections between its traditional FEEL approach and its new THINK approach by, for example, adding multimedia to its physical greeting cards? Or should electronic greeting cards and printed ones be run as separate businesses with separate customer targets?

Hallmark Creations store

Successfully managing these strategic issues requires making a commitment to an experiential approach to marketing. Most companies, having practiced features-and-benefits marketing for many years, initially generate impoverished experiential marketing strategies: they use an approach that is too diffused and simplified, focusing on one type of experience only or using multiple, yet unconnected, experiences. For them, the strategic task clearly requires intensifying and enriching current experiences, adding new types of experiences, and interconnecting them with one another gradually. As a result, major investments in experiential marketing are needed because the strategy approach often calls for a stepwise review and revision of all ExPros and the addition of experiential elements into communication hitherto used for features-and-benefits marketing.

ISSUE 3: CORPORATE BRANDING AND SUB-BRANDING

This issue concerns corporate/brand architecture as it is projected to customers (suppliers, business customers, or end consumers). Typically, a company that has very high corporate visibility (e.g., Ford or Nestlé) must create an experiential identity for itself. But it must also create experiential identities for its brands and products, and these should not clash with the corporate identity. A corporation that has created strong stand-alone brand identities (such as General Motors and Procter & Gamble) may forgo experiential branding because it has less visibility as a corporation. But it still needs to manage the experiential identities of its products and brands very closely.

Swatch, the Swiss manufacturer of casual watches, tends to build its brand architecture experientially. Swatch has created specific experiential identities for many of its products. But Swatch has also organized them along experiential types (e.g., watches that appeal to SENSE; FEEL watches with romantic symbols like red hearts or pictures from Hollywood movies; conceptual THINK watches; exercise ACT watches; and RELATE watches for cultural events). Swatch has thus created a holistic identity for Swatch as a company, which gets reinforced in its corporate advertising (e.g., a commercial asking "What is time?" and showing sensory, affective, cognitive, behavioral, and re-

EXPERIENTIAL MARKETING AT SONY

In 1998, Sony dedicated an entire issue of its internal newsletter, *Branding Matters*, to the experiential marketing framework presented in this book and featured me in an interview. To prepare for this conversation, I brought myself up to date on Sony's market presence by visiting Sony Style and retail outlets in the United States and Japan, examining Sony products, logging on to the Sony web sites, and scanning through recent advertising.

In the past, Sony has focused on traditional marketing and branding, and as such used quality and innovations, primarily the Sony name and the Sony logo. Over the years, however, Sony has introduced experiential approaches into its marketing strategy.

The Freq: one of Sony's new walkmans

A prime example of SENSE marketing is the superslim Sony VIAO laptop computer. It has been heralded as the first ultrathin, stylish new laptop launch in the computer industry. Another example is the "Freq," an exciting Walkman for the tough street life (complete with "bumper guard").

Then there is THINK. In particular the new "What's Next" campaign—e.g., the ad with the boy in the lake. A television advertisement, in monochromatic colors, depicts a young, fair-haired boy wading through the waist-high water of a lake. Light music accompanies the soft narrative voice-over: "He doesn't know what a phonograph is. He's never heard of eight-track. The only time he saw an LP was in his grandparents' attic. CDs and diskettes are his parents' toys. What will his be?" Subsequently the screen shows the words: "Walkman. Discman. CD. Minidisc. What's next?" And then the Sony logo appears. This is very much a THINK ad, because it gets you to reflect on the future of technology: "What is Sony Electronics going to do with the next generation?"

Sony also uses ACT. The best example is the Walkman, an ACT example because of lifestyle. It defines the fast-paced movements of our time, the need for relaxation and distraction. It is the ideal manner in which to unwind on the way to work, or the perfect accompaniment to a "power walk."

The RELATE approach appears in several marketing campaigns, for example in the *Playstation Underground* CD magazine, which relates the product to its customers in an innovative way.

The only experiential component that has been somewhat neglected by Sony is FEEL. Also, as soon as Sony manages to integrate different types of experiences, it will be on the way toward a holistic corporate brand.

lational images). The company stands for excellent experiential marketing at the corporate level, and it segments the market at the brand and product level by experiential appeals.

ISSUE 4: NEW PRODUCTS, BRAND EXTENSIONS, AND PARTNERSHIP STRATEGIES

Using the traditional F&B approach, the goal of new product development is often seen as adding new features and benefits, "improving" old products or old technologies. Traditional marketing models view brand extensions in terms of the fit between product categories and the transfer of positive equity from the current brand to the extension product.

In contrast, new product and brand extension decisions using an experiential marketing approach are driven by three factors: (1) the degree to which the new product and extension category enhances the experiential image of the company or brand; (2) the degree to which new products and brand extensions add new experiences that can be leveraged in additional new products and further brand extensions; and (3) the degree to which they help in the creation of holistic experiences. In other words, when Lipton considers extending into teahouses or Johnny Walker into apparel (as both brands have done recently—Lipton with a Starbucks-style teahouse in Pasadena and Johnny Walker with a boutique in Bloomingdale's), the key issue is whether the overall experience will be right.

Similar considerations will also drive the selection of other companies for strategic partnerships. Such experiential considerations may have been behind the mid-'90s decision of Swatch and Daimler Benz to form a joint venture to manufacture a new car—a decision that puzzled many industry experts. The resulting product—the Smart car—is a new automotive offering that is experiential from beginning to end. The Smart (at this point available only in Europe) reflects the best of both of its parents' worlds. Its appeal derives from its design, which couples attention to safety with a customizable fashion look. The Smart car is a mini, designed to fit in any parking space in any crowded city in the world; its thought-provoking slogan is "reduce to the max." The Smart is conceived as a completely new product—an innovative solution to the problems of city driving. And small is big again—not only in city cars in Europe but also in Asia. Despite its size, the Smart is passing rigorous safety tests, and safety is a central design concern. The Smart is also fun. Its distinctive look—tiny, somewhat triangular, and modern—sets it apart from all others; this car looks like nothing so much as a sneaker! Its distinctive two-tone color scheme is customizable to consumer specifications, and its interior design employs modular parts, making it possible to stylize the car quickly and cheaply. In fact, the Smart represents the realization of a car as a safe and well-designed fashion accessory. What else would you expect when Daimler Benz and Swatch team up?

GENERATIONAL EFFECTS

Peter Levine of DGA Consulting has done extensive research on three different generations and how they respond to different types of communications.[3] Levine focused on the Baby Boomer generation (ages 34–52, or what he calls the "Us" generation), the GenX generation (ages 24–33, the "I" generation), and the GenY (ages 22 and younger, the "All" generation). Because these generations differ in their prior life histories, it is necessary to take a person's age and experiences into account in order to determine appropriate marketing strategies. For instance, having experienced the Vietnam War and protests, the Baby Boomers respond well to quality and comfort. Additionally, since they were strongly influenced by television and rock 'n' roll, they admire icons and authority and have a preference for escape and fantasy. GenXers are known to be more pessimistic and realistic; they respond to independence and are less influenced by marketing or television programming, as many are children of divorce and have grown up in an era of AIDS, gangs, and violence. Finally, the GenYers are more optimistic, brought up in an era of psychology, and in an era of the "future." Thus they respond to new ideas, prefer companies with a philosophy, and have a sense of community. Mr. Levine's research suggests that different generations may prefer different SEMs. He also believes that GenXers and GenYers are more prone to respond to experiential marketing than the Baby Boomers, who primarily want features and benefits and quality.

ISSUE 5: GLOBAL EXPERIENTIAL BRANDING

Experiential branding extended into the global arena raises a range of complex issues, including the following:

- Do customers in different countries expect and appreciate the same type of experience?
- Are there cultural differences in preferences for types of SEMs? For example, do customers in one nation prefer FEEL, in a second nation THINK, and in a third RELATE?
- How about specific experiences? For example, are certain nations more

attuned to aesthetics in SENSE, while others love excitement? Or do some like nationalistic RELATE appeals but others global RELATE appeals?
• Do different ExPro executions appeal to customers in different countries?

As we saw in chapter 8, nations differ in terms of cultural values. In addition, cross-cultural research in image management, advertising, and consumer behavior has provided positive answers to all of the above questions.

The next question to ask is how strong these differences are. If they are overwhelming, then a localized strategy is the best course.

Experiencing impressive growth in revenues in the nineties, Ohio-based Service Corporation International (SCI) strives to deliver the best service and business practice as the world's largest death care provider. Providing its burying and cremation services with accompanying ceremonies to families of numerous cultures, languages, nationalities, religions, and tribal affiliations, SCI must localize the experiential aspects of its services.[4]

On the other hand, if there is some flexibility and openness to learning, or if the experience is less value laden, then a standardized strategy is worth trying. Bear in mind, though, that adaptation takes time, and a standardized approach may require patience in some countries.

Consider another, more mundane example: Oreo cookies, launched in 1912, has been one of the most successful product introductions ever, commanding over 10 percent market share in the cookie category in the United States and still growing substantially in sales. Kinship bonding across generations has been the major theme of the advertising for Nabisco's Oreos. In the emotional RELATE campaign, "How to eat an Oreo cookie," a grandfather teaches his grandchild the art of eating an Oreo cookie with milk. The campaign has been adopted in foreign markets as well, although in a slightly modified form (e.g., in Argentina a father teaches his son).

Interestingly enough, in China—one of the most family oriented countries in the world—the campaign has not been used yet. The reason is that ad executives think it is too early. Although Oreo has gained awareness very quickly in China and reached trial rates of 75 percent following a massive introductory advertising and sampling campaign in 1996, repeat purchase intention in 1998 was 32 percent and declining. According to Frank Wong, managing director of Nabisco China, the sensory experience of Oreos may not be quite right for the Chinese. Chinese customers are not used to eating a (slightly) bitter chocolate in what, for them, is an unappealing dark color. Until they acquire this taste, a FEEL/RELATE marketing may not be possible in China. Judging from the experience of Japanese consumers, though, there is hope: A bitter chocolate pretzel stick called Pocky, made by Osaka-based Ezaki Glico, is all the rage in Japan and has even recently branched out into the milk chocolate category with its "Royal Milk Pocky" (what an experiential name!). If the Chinese can adapt to the unusual experience of Oreos, experiential marketing won't be far behind: according to Wong, "Around the world, Oreos has moved way beyond product attributes. Oreos is about connecting."

Having the patience to shape experiences over time in a cross-cultural setting can provide us with a unique opportunity. Using the Experiential Wheel introduced in chapter 9, we can begin to create holistic experiences for global customers over time, in the process creating a truly global holistic brand.

SUMMARY

The strategic issues of experiential marketing include the selection of appropriate SEMs, and the relationship between these SEMs and the ExPros, including questions of intensity, breadth, depth, and linkage. But there are also broader strategic issues beyond the Experiential Grid of SEMs and ExPros. Experiential branding involves creating identities for product lines and for entire corporations and managing new product introductions. Global experiential marketing raises important standardization/localization issues in terms of creating a global or local experience.

NO, NO, NO . . . screams LAURA BROWN . . .

Experiences for everything and everybody. Experiences for the World. For Planet Earth. And all managed and strategically planned. A smiling Big Brother? Is the world going nuts?

ASSESSMENT TOOLS FOR EXPERIENTIAL MARKETING

Over the years I have developed easy-to-administer assessment tools to measure the concepts provided in this book. The tools consist of specific instruments for measuring SENSE, FEEL, THINK, ACT, and RELATE. They have been used in consulting projects to

- Audit a company's experiential marketing approach in its entirety
- Assess the experiential aspects of various ExPros
- Plan ExPros and SEMs for company brands
- Make strategic and implementation recommendations

In conjunction with Josco Brakus, a doctoral student at Columbia Business School, I have also created a short and straightforward scale to find out whether a specific ExPro (a logo, an ad, an interior space, a web site) appeals to a specific SEM. The scale consists of several items per ExPro, accompanied by seven-point ratings scales ranging from "not at all" to "very much." Following common measurement practice, the scale has been tested for reliability and validity. Please note that some of the scales are negatively worded and need to be coded reversely. Below, these items are indicated by a minus sign; the positively worded items are indicated by a plus sign.

Here are some sample items.

SENSE:

- The (ExPro) tries to engage my senses.(+)
- The (ExPro) is perceptually interesting.(+)
- The (ExPro) lacks sensory appeal for me.(–)

FEEL:

- The (ExPro) tries to put me in a certain mood.(+)
- The (ExPro) makes me respond in an emotional manner.(+)
- The (ExPro) does not try to appeal to feelings.(–)

THINK:

- The (ExPro) tries to intrigue me.(+)
- The (ExPro) stimulates my curiosity.(+)
- The (ExPro) does not try to appeal to my creative thinking.(–)

ACT:

- The (ExPro) tries to make me think about my lifestyle.(+)
- The (ExPro) reminds me of activities I can do.(+)
- The (ExPro) does not try to make me think about actions and behaviors.(–)

RELATE:

- The (ExPro) tries to get me to think about relationships.(+)
- I can relate to other people through this (ExPro).(+)
- The (ExPro) does not try to remind me of social rules and arrangements.(–)

This scale may be used in combination with other measures for

- Strategic experiential modeling
- Experiential perceptual maps
- Experiential profiling of various brands

Finally, these experiential marketing methodologies may be related to broader brand equity measures (such as brand awareness, brand associations, brand esteem, and brand-customer relations) as well as financial brand valuation measures.

11

BUILDING THE EXPERIENCE-
ORIENTED ORGANIZATION

I n chapters 9 and 10, we discussed hybrids, holistic experiences as well as marketing and business strategies of experiential marketing. These issues can be addressed, resolved, and planned best if the organization is oriented toward experiential marketing. In the final chapter, I address the challenge of building an experience-oriented organization, which requires rethinking the role of marketing and business in general.

This chapter will sketch the outlines of the ideal type of organization for dealing with experiences (see Figure 11.1). As we will see, what is needed is not really a new organizational chart but rather a new spirit that pervades the entire organizational culture. I call such a culture, described more fully below, the "Dionysian Organization." Moreover, an organization that is serious about experiential marketing places an emphasis on creativity and innovation and, following along the sociocultural consumption vector (SCCV) discussed in chapter 1, looks for broad, long-term trends in the environment ("taking the helicopter view"). Moreover, the experience-oriented organization treats the creativity and innovativeness displayed by its employees as its most critical intellectual capital. As a result, hiring, training, and experiential growth—as well as attention to the physical environment—become key human resource

FIGURE 11.1

Characteristics of the Experience-Oriented Organization

The
Dionysian culture

Creativity
and **innovation**

Taking the
helicopter view

Attractive
physical environment

Experience-Oriented Organization

Experiential growth
for **employees**

Integration in
working with **agencies**

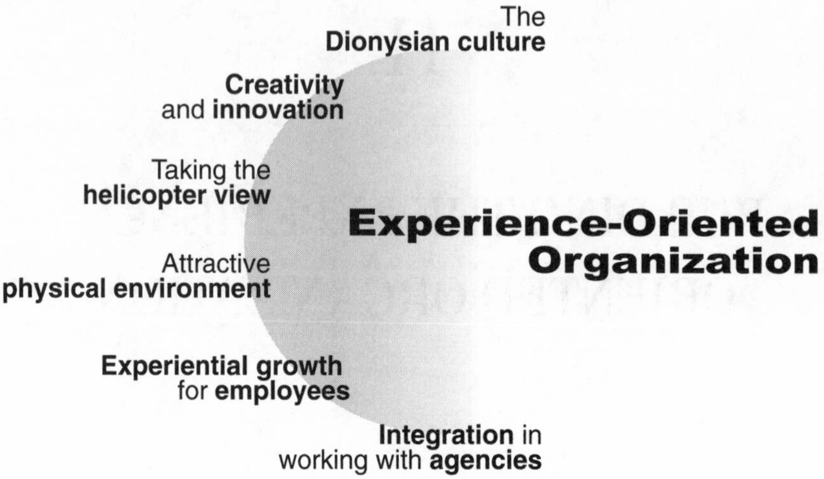

and "internal marketing" requirements. Finally, in the process of strategizing and developing experiential programs, the organization will rely on the expertise of outside constituents. In this regard, I will discuss integration in working with creative agencies.

Before we start, here are a few points to keep in mind as you read through the chapter.

First, the type of organizational culture and outside agencies that I will discuss hardly exist in today's business environment. Even if your organization is market-oriented (i.e., it pays attention to customer needs and competition, works cross-functionally, collects market information, disseminates the information, and acts on it), it does not mean that your market-oriented organization is experience-oriented.[1] Many market-oriented organizations are very functionally oriented and focused on strategic planning, and lack the culture to promote creativity and innovation within the organization. As a result, they are unable to launch breakthrough products and innovative campaigns.

Second, the creation of an experience-oriented organization requires the involvement of top management. So those of you who are CEOs, owners of small or large organizations, department heads or task leaders will find it useful to see the outlines of such an organization and some guidance on how to create one. But this does not mean that the chapter is irrelevant for those of you who are not (yet) holding such a position. Many of the ideas presented can be used as part of your everyday work as a brand manager, product manager, sales manager, advertising manager, product designer, etc. And even if you are not in the functional marketing area, you will benefit from learning more about the organizational issues of experiential marketing.

Finally, the underlying assumption of this chapter is that it is easier as a company employee to create exciting experiences for your customers if you are attuned to experiences in your life (work and private). Although this chapter focuses on experiences from an organizational viewpoint, I will also share some insights with you that may improve your own "experiential lifestyle." Don't worry—I am not going to ask you to light candles, turn on New Age music, and soak yourself in a bubble bath. But I will point out a few less intimate experience-enhancing personal strategies that will sharpen your skills as an experiential marketer.

THE DIONYSIAN CULTURE

The terms "Apollonian" and "Dionysian," both drawn from Greek mythology, have been used to describe diametrically opposed ways of thinking and views of the world. "Apollonian," derived from the Greek god Apollo, refers to the structured, the balanced, the reflective. The term "Dionysian" is connected with the cult, myths, and festivals held for the Greek god Dionysos, from which the Greek drama is supposed to have originated. Dionysian festivals were traditionally revels where celebrants experienced inspiration bordering on madness. "Dionysian" is thus associated with the ecstatic, the passionate, the unbounded.

Applying the terms to present-day organizations, we can contrast as ideal types the Apollonian and the Dionysian organizations. The Apollonian organization is of a rational nature: harmonious, ordered, and planned. It is, ultimately, the result of the spirit of enlightenment. The Dionysian organization is born out of a different understanding of reality. The Dionysian organization is of a passionate-creative nature; it thrives on chaos.[2]

Both the Apollonian and the Dionysian organization have their drawbacks: too Apollonian and the organization stagnates; too Dionysian and the organization may disintegrate. Clearly, an experience-oriented organization needs both elements: the planners who plan and manage and measure, as well as the creatives—internal and external—who communicate the message to key customer targets.

But, all else being equal, it is the Dionysian organization that provides the best environment for experiential marketing. Most organizations are too timid, too slow, too bureaucratic in their decision making. I would rather have people around me buzzing with new ideas than arthritic, command-executing automata. I would rather receive too many e-mails with ideas than too few. In the transition phase from F&B marketing to experiential marketing, in particular, Dionysian processes and initiatives are clearly preferable. What you may lose in predictability you more than make up for in creativity and vision.

However, it is key to make communications as transparent as possible in a transition from F&B to experiential marketing, and to gain strong support for the approach within the organization. Remember the British Airways' "World Communities" campaign in chapter 4? Reactions to the tail-fins campaign were hostile at practically all levels, from flight attendants to shareholders. Cabin crew as well as shareholders were offended when they were asked to give up "Britishness." It is difficult to secure support externally when you do not have it internally.[3]

What are some of the specific characteristics of the Dionysian organization, and how do we create one?

Objective: To Dream

Forget "strategy," "planning," "the bottom line," and "research" for a moment. Instead, start dreaming. Ask yourself: What experience do we want to create in the long term for our customers, and how can we get it done in an unusual, interesting, eye-catching way? Make a list, in a group or as an individual. Discount the common solutions. Go for the wild ones! Encourage your people to be passionate and enthusiastic. Encourage them to dream.

Send in the Iconoclasts

Bring in people who question or challenge established beliefs, structures, customs, and ways of thinking. Bring them in as consultants, through agencies, even as your CEO. A stiff organization may benefit from a "Ben & Jerry" type of casualness, while a granola culture (like Ben & Jerry's) can benefit from a more analytical CEO. Both types are iconoclastic compared with the dominant culture. Hire people who will shake things up.

Numerous organizations have benefited from this approach: IBM by hiring Gerstner, the Guggenheim Museum by hiring an ex-ad executive, Hermès (the traditional French leather goods manufacturer) by hiring Martin Margiela as its designer. The latter example shows that even in the fashion business, an iconoclast may be necessary. Here's another example. Bernard Arnault, chairman of LVMH Moët Hennessy Louis Vuitton, has hired John Galliano, the flamboyant English designer, to head the house of Dior, and Alexander McQueen, another young Brit, to head Givenchy. Of course, as an aggressive, business-minded wheeler and dealer who shook up and transformed the French luxury industry, Mr. Arnault may be viewed as an iconoclast himself.[4]

Quit the Bull

In chapter 1, I discussed what I considered to be the "good, the bad, and the ugly" of traditional marketing. Now it's time to act on this understanding. Get rid of meaningless terms, strategy gibberish, management pretense. Get employees to express themselves more honestly, directly, and creatively. Encourage them to explore new methodologies. Think of new ways to generate ideas, new ways to communicate, and new ways to present information in meetings. Go so far as to establish new rules for meetings and presentations, e.g., "anyone who uses bullet points gets shot!"

Infiltrate the Organization

What do you do if you truly believe in the value of experiential marketing but are not in a decision-making position and face opposition to your ideas?

Don't despair. Start with guerrilla strategies. Live by example, and infiltrate the organization bottom-up with your ideas. Start with small projects that get the attention of top management. Find people with similar minds who share your vision. Bring in people (e.g., consultants, speakers, advisors) to whom top management is more receptive because they are deemed more objective. Identify case examples and best practices from other industries. Become an experiential "crew-sader" (see www.exmarketing.com).

Does it all sound a bit wild, a bit unfamiliar? Good! It should. The spirit of Dionysos is the spirit of ecstasy, creativity, inspiration. Let a bit of this spirit breathe in an organization, and watch how things change.

CREATIVITY AND INNOVATION

In the spring of 1998, as part of a speaking engagement at the annual conference of the Corporate Design Foundation, I met Gerald Hirshberg, the fascinating founder and president of Nissan Design International. Hirshberg is a firm believer in the key role of creativity within an organization. "Making room within an organization for creativity is one thing. Designing an organization around creativity itself is quite another. This is not simply to advocate an increase of the role of creativity *in* business. It is to advocate creativity as the principal role *of* business."

In the sixties and seventies, Hirshberg headed design for Pontiac and Buick. In his book *The Creative Priority: Driving Innovative Business in the Real World,*[5] he describes General Motors at the time when the company designed such extraordinary vehicles as the Chevy Corvair, the Buick Riviera, the Pontiac Firebird, and the early Corvettes:

"When I first arrived, GM was the supreme icon of power and success for America. And it was the pinnacle for anyone wanting to design cars in this country. There was a spectacular array of talent under the fiery leadership of

William Mitchell, the VP of styling, upon my arrival. Passionate about cars, motorcycles, and racing, his veins were saturated with gasoline. . . . I moved into management fairly quickly and had considerable opportunity to experiment with leading the creative process. . . . Mitchell's ability to mobilize an entire department (and most of the corporation) around his cause left a deep impression on me."

Do you recognize this type of company? Do you currently work for such a company? Can you imagine the excitement that such a culture invokes?

At the same time, Hirshberg noted a certain myopia in Mitchell's and GM's attitude—an attitude that can also be found among some of the creative, passionate cultures of today. This attitude ultimately dethroned GM. Today the company has about half the market share it enjoyed during the fifties, when it was close to 50 percent.

"Mitchell had no patience . . . for listening to a designer (or anyone else) explain the theory behind a design, describe its intended customers, or talk about the world in which it would exist." And it was this attitude that ultimately brought GM down: "The emergence of Ralph Nader, consumerism, safety, environmental concerns, and imports all made the sixties and seventies a time of growing turbulence for the automobile industry. But GM continued to display a dangerous reluctance to seriously engage its creative energies and resources in response to these issues. They were seen as obstacles, not as fresh opportunities for new thinking. . . . GM's resistance to outside change was mirrored by an increasingly stifling corporate culture within, the walls thickening between the departments, each becoming a bastion of protection for well-worn procedures and assumptions buttressed by past successes."

In 1980, Hirshberg left GM for Nissan. There he headed up a new autonomous facility called Nissan Design International (NDI), dedicated to bridging the gap between American design excellence and Japanese technological sophistication. Like GM in earlier decades, this unique corporate hybrid became a hotbed of automotive innovation, producing such cutting-edge designs as the first Nissan Pathfinder, Altima, Maxima, Pulsar NX, and Quest minivan, the Infiniti J30, and the Mercury Villager for Ford. "NDI began life as a cauldron of boiling and colliding cultures abrading against one another's workstyles, rhythms, and priorities. . . . Everything was discussed by everyone, and the atmosphere was noisy, intense, irreverent, and by turns joyous and abrasive."

We have discussed creativity from an individual's point of view in chapter 6. But what principles, structures, processes and decisions are required to make creativity the principal driver of business?

Hirshberg, the Dionysian, is a firm believer in the creative energy generated by opposites—a process that he calls "polarity." Polarity manifests itself in retaining, as a division or organization, conflicting viewpoints without discarding either one, in hiring divergent pairs of employees, and in encouraging employees to adopt an alien, even threatening viewpoint to get a new perspective on an entrenched position. Hirshberg quotes the physicist Neils Bohr, who said, "The opposite of a correct statement is a false statement. But the opposite of a profound truth may well be another profound truth."

Although I have become familiar with Mr. Hirshberg's ideas only very recently, I remember this principle very well from a class on creativity that I took as a student with Professor Norbert Groeben at the University of Heidelberg many years ago. Like Hirshberg, Groeben, a psychologist, characterized the essence of the creative process paradoxically as "bipolar integration." To this, he added another important notion: the idea of oscillating between polar extremes over time in order to create a higher-order synthesis. The term "synthesis" originated in the philosopher Hegel's theory of dialectics ("Thesis—Antithesis—Synthesis") and represents a qualitatively higher stage of truth.

I have applied the dialectic process of oscillation between extremes in my own work with high-performance executive teams. This is how it works in a nutshell.

- *Step 1: Thesis.* You ask a group for their true opinions on an issue.
- *Step 2: The formulation of two antitheses.* You divide and physically separate the group and ask each half to push their current view into a more extreme position, yet in different directions.
- *Step 3: Synthesis.* You then bring the groups together to share their new positions and force them to arrive at a new solution.

- *Step 4: Iteration of steps 1–3.* You reiterate the process, starting again with step 1, followed by step 2, followed by step 3 and another solution. If possible, you perform another iteration.

The final result represents a creatively enriched solution that is far superior to any elaboration, clarification, or brainstorming procedure performed on the original position. Although I described the concept as a group exercise, a creative individual can also perform it alone when seeking a solution to a problem. Moreover, the entire process may also be played out visually—e.g., by identifying visuals that represent customer experiences or instantiations in ExPros, for example. Finally, the dialectical process of oscillation between extremes may be thought of as an organizational model as well; in this sense, the entire organization produces constant higher-level renewal by deliberately experimenting with extreme ends of a spectrum, which ultimately results in higher-order syntheses.

TAKING THE HELICOPTER VIEW

Recently I received an invitation from Nick Shore and his team at nickand-paul, the brand agency, for a "SuperGroup" discussion on long-term trends in technology, entertainment, the body, and home/lifestyles. The invitation said: "A firestart before you come—we are taking the helicopter view of four big societal movements—so before you come, think a little about one of the four and bring along an article or something you find interesting for a cultural 'show and tell.'" The idea for this think-tank discussion about trends at the turn of the millennium was born of internal branding discussions at nickand-paul, and sessions were being held in the United Kingdom, Japan, and rural America. The group of participants was intentionally eclectic: an architect, a cultural anthropologist, a brand manager, a publicist, a research principal, a founder of a high-tech Internet firm, etc.—and myself.

The discussion was exhilarating, full of "out of the box" thinking, bringing diverse perspectives to each problem. I can highly recommend this kind of process to any company. At least once a month, set aside time for a two-to-three-hour "helicopter perspective discussion," or make sure that your employees attend one at another firm or public gathering.

Another good technique is to get as close to your customers' world as possible, and then take the helicopter view with them. I am sure you are all aware that teens are very market-savvy: you cannot easily fool them. Teens want authentic products; they know what's real and what's not. But teens are also an excellent source for trend research. For example, finding out that teens use the Internet for anything from shopping to chatting with friends helps you with future projections of this medium in terms of its SENSE, FEEL, THINK, ACT, and RELATE impact. Attending teen panels (real or virtual) also gives you information about their lifestyles and desired relations.[6]

In Japan, high school girls are considered an invaluable source for new trends and experiential product suggestions. As the *Wall Street Journal* observes: "As Japanese companies have long known, the nation's high school girls have an uncanny ability to predict which products will be hits with consumers of all age groups. What's more, a select pool of these teens can create a buzz that turns a new product into a nationwide smash."[7] Some examples of schoolgirl suggestions that turned into cash:

- For a fermented milk drink by Coca-Cola Japan: "Use a short, stubby bottle with a pink label instead of the tall, skinny blue-labeled bottle"
- For a breath-cleansing drink by Meiji Milk Products: "Blend the cleansing substance with oolong tea instead of fruit juice"
- For a low-priced Shiseido cosmetic product: "Drop the name 'Chopi' and change the container's color from black, white, or silver to beige."

Another useful technique is long-term scenario planning. Shell is a company that exceeds in long-term scenario planning to deal with turbulence and change in their environment. The objective of the scenario building is to identify trends before they are discussed in *The Economist.* Every three years Shell builds entirely new scenarios, including new people in the scenario team. Every second three years they bring in a new (iconoclast) scenario builder.[8]

PROMOTING EMPLOYEE AND GROUP CREATIVITY

What proven techniques exist to promote the creativity of the individual employees as well as groups in the organization?[9]

Brainstorming comes to mind first. Unfortunately, it does not seem to work. In a brainstorming session, an instructor asks a group of managers (e.g., product, brand, or communications managers, or mixed teams) to generate as many ideas as possible about a domain. The instructor gives the explicit instruction that participants should not edit their ideas: any idea is acceptable and participants should use one another's ideas as a spinoff point. After this divergent-thinking phase, the group evaluates the generated ideas.

There are several problems with this procedure. The first is group dynamics. Some individuals who may not necessarily generate the best divergent ideas may assume the role of group leaders and monopolize the discussion, thus quashing the creativity of other participants. Second, individuals not only get stimulated by others' ideas, they also get distracted; just when you're getting started with a new idea, someone else may jump into the discussion and, without fully understanding your idea, take it in the "wrong" direction. Third, because the same individuals evaluate the ideas that they generated, they do not edit them sufficiently. They overestimate the creativity of the ideas because they have—so to speak—personal investments in them.

As a result, brainstorming, though enormously popular (and sometimes fun), is rarely the most effective procedure for generating creative ideas. Brainstormers go for quantity, not quality: they produce lots of ideas but not necessarily good ones. Indeed, asking the same individuals to sit down in a quiet room on their own and to generate unusual ideas often produces better results.

What's the alternative? To avoid the problems of brainstorming discussed above, it is necessary to avoid the leadership phenomenon, avoid distractions, and separate "idea generators" from "idea evaluators." Rather than creating a storm of ideas, it is necessary to get individuals to engage in "brain focusing."

Electronic brain-focusing sessions are typically conducted over an intranet within the company, or through some other electronic medium. Unilever has used the procedure with as many as three hundred managers and consultants in a global session. Electronic brain focusing shares many features with brainstorming. But it also has important differences that get around the problems mentioned earlier.

> Each person sees each other person's idea on a screen. The idea-generating person, however, remains anonymous. Each person can use the screen input to generate his or her own ideas, or may look away from the screen to collect thoughts or develop an idea. Once the ideas are generated, they are typically passed on to a second group for evaluation (e.g., to individuals higher in the organization). The second group may choose certain concepts and give them back to the "idea generator" group for further elaboration. In fact, the evaluators may also participate in the discussion at any time, providing direction or asking for evaluation, impressions, or further associations. The latter approach is a modification of Edvard DeBono's "Six thinking hats" approach.

THE PHYSICAL ENVIRONMENT

Appropriate types of stimulation are key for creativity and innovation and for creating attractive experiences for customers. As a result, organizations need to pay more attention to the physical surroundings at work. This may include the architecture and design of the building and office, as well as unusual work or meeting spaces. For example, Lucent Technologies has created an internal creative center called "Idea Verse," with music, books, videos, and toys in the room, where employees can work and meet. Clif Bar Inc. (featured in chapter 9) has two climbing walls, provides lengthy breaks for aerobic exercise, and pays for spa, ski, and camping weekends for its sixty-five employees.[10]

Prince Street Technologies, a custom carpet mill located in Cartersville, Georgia, has devoted tremendous care to designing its workspaces to promote employee morale and involvement. Having built a reputation in cutting-edge craftsmanship in the 1980s, Prince Street nevertheless found itself in financial trouble by the mid-'90s. In 1994, Prince Street was acquired by Interface, Inc., moved to its new location in Cartersville, and began a transformation that led to a growth in annual sales of $55 million over the past two years.

At the center of this transformation is the plant itself. A space that combines manufacturing, corporate, and showroom areas, the facility is designed to maximize employees' contact with nature. The architectural firm of Thompson, Ventulett, Stainback & Associates of Atlanta designed a glass-and-brick structure landscaped with wildflowers that do not require watering or fertilizing. The focal point of the building is a large glass spire, designed to capture light and direct it into the design studio and showrooms. The building is rich in skylights and large windows: "Nobody has natural light like this," according to Joyce LaValle, Prince Street's former president and CEO. "Most manufacturing is done in the dark. All beauty comes from nature and everybody has the right to see it."[11] Other earth-friendly features of the facility include rooftop air-conditioning units that use non-ozone-depleting refrigerants and modular workstations made of recycled materials.

Prince Street's green mind-set is more than just political correctness: it reflects an entire company culture that makes good business sense. The abundant natural light in the building is credited with fewer employee mistakes, and the cleaner, safer plant resulted in a year with no lost-time accidents in 1997, versus twenty-six such accidents in 1995. The plant is tobacco-free, and the company has worked actively on the issue with its labor force, 75 percent of whom were smokers at the onset of the policy. Recycling and reducing waste are seen as a responsibility of the entire Prince Street "family": "waste" refers not just to materials but to wasted time, and employees are actively engaged in streamlining operations at all levels. Prince Street's company philosophy is manifested physically in its workspaces, and employees have eagerly embraced the teamwork and sense of community the plant embodies.

So what if your office looks like the pits? Do something about it! You may not be able to get the entire office redesigned, but you can improve on it here and there. Change the lighting, move your desk, bring in some props. If you are a true believer in experiential marketing, you know that your environment will affect you. So do not let the environment drag down your senses, feelings, creative thinking, actions and relations.

HIRING, TRAINING, AND PERSONAL EXPERIENTIAL GROWTH

In the brain-powered economy of the information age, most of a firm's capital is inside employees' heads. Robert Kelley, who teaches at Carnegie Mellon's business school, asks us to imagine that spaceships hovered above Microsoft's headquarters and fired rays that pickled the brains of Microsoft's brain-powered workers. "Sales would dry up almost immediately, since customers would know that current products could not receive technical support and that no new product would be forthcoming. Microsoft could not recover, even with massive hiring, since new employees couldn't rise to the expert levels of the competition quickly enough to keep pace."[12]

Employees thus represent intellectual capital that can be bought and that must be invested in. With respect to experiential marketing, this capital consists of acquired knowledge and expertise as well as the creativity and innovation for generating experiential strategies and implementations. Consequently, companies must hire employees who are knowledgeable and experienced about this new form of marketing as well as creative and innovative. Ideally, these individuals should have received prior training or taken courses in the concepts, principles, and methods of experiential marketing.

Unfortunately, these types of courses are difficult to find, especially at business schools. Marketing departments in business schools typically train rational decision makers and view experiences as "superficial," "vague," and largely irrelevant (see chapter 2). They rarely offer interdisciplinary courses that bring together business students with students in the so-called "creative fields" (such as design, architecture, or advertising). Finally, while courses on team building and interpersonal skills have entered the curriculum, training in creativity and innovation is largely unheard of.

The situation among academic marketing researchers is not much better. Most academic journals value methodologically sophisticated modeling applications of the F&B type or highly specific dissections of consumer information processing. The only marketing journal that has even slightly opened up to experiential concepts and relevant methodologies has been the *Journal of Consumer Research*. Yet most of the articles in this journal have a clear anthropological slant and are thus much more narrowly conceived than the perspective advocated in this book.

I, therefore, suggest that you broaden your search. Go to design schools, architecture schools, anthropology departments, even journalism schools to get your new marketing staff. Among business school MBAs, look out for the ones with joint degrees or those that have taken nontraditional courses.

Closely inspect the courses that applicants have taken, and take their hobbies and interests seriously. Most important, look for passion, fire, and creativity during the interview.

Regarding training, the situation is similar. If you want to get away from F&B, stay away from your traditional group of consultants. Go for iconoclasts (see above). But do not fall for graying ponytails with Carlos Castaneda stories. Experiential marketing is a topic too serious to be taken lightly. Also, since experiential marketing is a new approach to management, as a PR manager you should make sure that the training is attended by a diverse group of employees and cross-functional teams—not just the marketing department. Send your staff to conferences and meetings at the fringes of their business. Get them to read fringe magazines, especially "on line."

Finally, you and your company need to promote personal experiential growth. Make sure you use your free time and vacations not only to relax or to overcome your burnout. Go to new travel destinations. Pick up new hobbies. Challenge yourself to experience unusual places, people, situations. Get out of the comfort zone.

And make sure your work is challenging and that your colleagues feel the same way. Nokia Mobile Phones (featured in chapter 4) has created a culture that buzzes with creativity and fun. Let me quote Mr. Nuovo, the VP of design, one more time:

"I could liken it [the process] to improvisation in a jazz quartet, where good ideas come from everywhere and they gel and become a whole. Soloists do well, they are interesting and they make tremendous contributions. But there's nothing like a quartet, nothing like a sextet or octet. And when you get into a big band, you have to have more order. There are still contributions but they are more orchestrated, because there are so many people involved. A lot of the spirit in Nokia is this jazz quartet, this improvisation, this feel and this working with each other and making good music. That comes from not just talking about it but living it."[13]

Similarly, Richard Branson, founder of the Virgin brand, wrote: "Fun is at the core of how I like to do business and it has informed everything I've done from the outset. I am aware that the idea of business being fun and creative goes against the grain of convention, and it's certainly not how they teach it at some of those business schools where business means hard grind and lots of discounted cash flows and net present values."[14]

WORKING WITH THE RIGHT EXTERNALS

As we saw in chapter 10, several key strategic processes of experiential marketing require the integration of ExPros. For this integration, collaboration among areas of expertise is required, not only internally but, in most cases, also externally. There are firms that do not outsource their advertising, design, packaging, or web sites for that reason; some of them, like Calvin Klein, have been successful with this approach. However, most firms, especially larger ones, do use outsourcing for creative issues.

So what are the options?

One option is to deal with advertising and marketing conglomerates that offer services across all ExPros. Consider, for example, WPP, the largest advertising and marketing services company in the world. In 1997, the WPP Group had more than 20,000 employees in 40+ companies in over 750 offices in 83 countries. WPP's service sectors included media advertising (e.g., J. Walter Thompson Company, Ogilvy & Mather Worldwide, and Cole & Weber), market research (e.g., Millward Brown International, Research International, and Simmons), public relations (e.g., Hill and Knowlton, Carl Byoir & Associates, and Ogilvy & Mather Public Relations), and what they call "specialist communications" such as direct marketing, sales promotions, and identity and design (such as Anspach Grossman Enterprise and Sampson Tyrrell).[15]

The stated goals of WPP are to be the preferred provider of multinational services and to provide clients with a comprehensive and, if appropriate, integrated range of marketing services, both strategically and tactically. One of the key issues in accomplishing these goals is the cooperation and coordination among the disparate parts of WPP. As Martin Sorrell, CEO of WPP, put it, "Given the wealth of talent that we have—there is no competitor like us—can you harness those resources given the tribes that you've got into a coherent form? Can the fact that you have J. Walter Thompson, Ogilvy & Mather, Hill

& Knowlton, a Research International, and an Anspach, Grossman & Portugal add value to clients' businesses and to people's careers?"

The integrated agency is a viable idea for experiential marketing. Besides WPP marketing conglomerates (like Y & R) are experimenting with integration. Thus far, it has had only limited success. "Certain agencies paid lip service to integration just because they thought it was what the clients wanted," says Robert Gray, managing director of Mercier Gray.[16]

In order for integration to work, the following structures and processes must be in place:

- The one-stop shop must be integrated from an accounting and organizational point of view. If the ad agency views a web-site design firm that is part of the same group as a competitor because the ad people believe they could do the job of the designers, then integration will not work.
- The creatives must have diverse but high-quality skills. They must know how to put together diverse forms of communications (e.g., print and TV ad copy, promotion packs and annual reports, as well as web sites).
- The one-stop shops needs a framework similar to the one presented in this book, which allows the firm to assist their clients in the planning of a holistic experience, thus demonstrating the value to the client.

The alternative to the one-stop shop of the integrated agency is specialized agencies combined with integration within the firm. That is, a team within the client firm takes on the bulk of experiential planning and works in conjunction with different agencies that are specialized in individual ExPros. In other words, as long as the end solution is integrated, specialists may work together just as well as members of one agency. This approach, however, requires a high area of expertise within the client firm.

Currently, an attractive third alternative seems to be the developing hybrid between the one-stop shop and the implementation specialists: the so-called brand agency. Brand agencies take on the strategic planning for the client and coordinate the experiential marketing efforts. Like a general contractor, brand agencies provide integration and planning across other outside consultants.

SUMMARY

The experience-oriented organization has neither a particular organizational structure nor special processes. It is unique in other ways. First, it is a Dionysian organization and focuses on creativity and innovation. Second, it takes a broad, helicopter view focusing on long-term trends, pays attention to its physical environment, and views employees as human capital. Indeed, the experience-oriented organization is keenly interested in promoting its employees' experiential growth. Finally, the collaboration with external agencies focuses on guaranteeing integration across experience providers. In sum, it is quite different from the typical organization oriented toward order, structure, analysis, and short term.

Hm . . . I might consider . . . says LAURA BROWN . . . in a daydream but can any human or any group of humans really reach this Dionysian paradise?

EPILOGUE

"I raised to my lips a spoonful of the cake . . . a shudder ran through my whole body and I stopped, intent upon the extraordinary changes that were taking place."

Marcel Proust, *Remembrance of Things Past*

This book has been about customer experiences provided by SENSE, FEEL, THINK, ACT, and RELATE marketing campaigns and their integration in holistic marketing practices.

There are, however, entirely different types of experiences—experiences that are somewhat "deeper," "more substantial," and "more involving." They are more dazzling to the senses, more touching to the heart, more involving intellectually than any of the marketing campaigns described in this book. These types of experiences can utterly change our worldview, our priorities, and the way we live our lives. They relate us to a new dimension and a new world. Some of us refer to them as deeply personal or interpersonal experiences. Others call them religious or spiritual. I prefer to call these types of experiences existential or "Proustian."[1]

Most brands and marketing campaigns, most of the time, are unable to provide these types of experiences—even temporarily. As a result, we may be inclined to conclude that experiences created by marketing campaigns are, in a way, inferior to "true" experiences—deceptive and, ultimately, fake. We may become cynical and conclude that experiential marketing should not be trusted because it is superficial, manipulative, abusive, and destructive to the individual and society because of its fake, commercial character. Perhaps this is the gist of many of LAURA BROWN's comments at the ends of the preceding chapters.

While I am sympathetic to the view that the experiences created by marketers are mostly not existential experiences, I find this broad critique of experiential marketing, quite frankly, too grand, undifferentiated, and pretentious. Our organisms have not been built to undergo intense, personality-shaking experiences all the time. Religious, spiritual, and existential experiences often result in dogmatism, obsession, and serious delusions of reality. Somewhat mundane experiences of medium intensity—and even fake experiences—may in fact be the precondition for happiness. As such, they have an important role to play in enriching our ordinary, daily lives.

Indeed, many people enjoy stylizing and accessorizing their lives. They like to be the key players in their own personal movies. If experiential marketing may not have to play a role in the truly special aspects of life, it certainly does in the *ach so menschlichen,* the "oh-so-human" world.

We have now reached the end of our path. Well, almost. I still owe you an answer to the question I raised in the Preface: Who is LAURA BROWN?

After reading this book, I am sure you realize this answer can't be an easy one. Is LAURA BROWN a transcendental figure? Is she just a product of our imagination? Is she a virtual figure like Kyoko Date in chapter 1? Here is the honest answer:

LAURA BROWN is a writing consultant in New York, a Columbia University Ph.D. with a flair for words and ideas. She has been working with me on this book for many months. She has researched and written cases for the book and has been a critic, an editor, and a sounding board throughout the process. Her contributions have exceeded those of an ordinary consultant to such a degree that I had only one choice: to put her name into each chapter in addition to her voice.

I am sure that you are not fully satisfied with this answer. I do not know how you were imagining LAURA BROWN's identity—but I am sure you did. Perhaps you were even a bit disappointed to learn the truth. But it is the beauty of the name "Laura Brown" that it lends itself to all types of identities and experiences. So, even though I have revealed her identity now, it is up to your imagination to re-create her each time you pick up this book. More important, each time you think about your customers, you should also think about her, because her questions will be their questions.

You see, this is the true power of experiential marketing: *Even if LAURA BROWN did not exist, a clever marketer surely would have invented her.*

Author in his Zen Master outfit underneath the eyes of Laura Brown.

NOTES

Preface

1. The term "experiential marketing" has been used in a variety of contexts including event marketing, sponsorships, shopping mall design, online marketing and different forms of communications. For example, McCann-Erickson World-Group has established "Momentum Experiential Marketing Group" as a separate entity to provide services related to sponsorships and event marketing. MasterCard, Gillette, and the Coca-Cola Company have used the term in a similar way. Bruce Kelley of National Mall Network has used the term to refer to shopping mall environments. Intuitive Communications, based in San Diego, uses "experiential marketing" to target the "inner experience" through communications. Jim Nail of Forrester Research speaks of "experiential marketing" in the context of interactive Internet services. Jack Morton provides "experiential communications." Finally, the academic research tradition regarding the "experiential aspects of consumption" was established more than twenty-five years ago by my Columbia Business School colleague Morris Holbrook and co-author Elizabeth Hirschman. (Sources: "Branding on the Net," *Business Week,* November 9, 1998; Rana Dogar with Timm Gossing, "Too Much Is About Right," *Newsweek,* June 15, 1998, p. 35; Antoinette Coulton, "With Sports Alliances, Cards Make Big Play for Fans," *American Banker,* October 2, 1997, p. 1; Morris Holbrook and Elizabeth Hirschman, "The Experiential Aspects of Consumption: Consumer Fantasies, Feelings, and Fun," *Journal of Consumer Research,* September 1982, vol. 9, pp. 132–40; as well as brochures and web sites of the respective companies.)

1. From Features and Benefits to Customer Experiences

1. Mike Mills, "Satellite 'Constellation' Wires the Earth," *International Herald Tribune,* May 19, 1998.
2. John Markoff, "Taking a Step Toward Converting the Home into a Supercomputer," *New York Times,* July 15, 1998, p. 1.
3. Nicholas Negroponte, *Being Digital* (New York: Vintage Books, 1996).
4. Michael Dertouzos, *What Will Be: How the New World of Information Will Change Our Lives* (San Francisco: Harper, 1997).

5. "Japan's Latest Gizmo: A Theater on Your Face." Article posted on CNN's interactive web site www.cnn.com, July 5, 1998, 3:54 P.M. EDT.

6. Based on an "interview" with "Ms. Date" posted on www.dhw.co,www.tv3000.nl, and www.geocities.com.

7. Tom Peters, *The Cycle of Innovation: You Can't Shrink Your Way to Greatness* (New York: Knopf, 1997).

8. "Brand Builders Perceive Pattern," *Financial Times,* June 23, 1997.

9. Richard Branson, *Losing My Virginity: How I've Survived, Had Fun, and Made a Fortune Doing Business My Way* (New York: Times Business, division of Random House, 1998).

10. Regis McKenna, *Real Time: Preparing for the Age of the Never Satisfied Customer* (Boston: Harvard Business Press, 1997).

11. "Here Is the News," *The Economist* (U.S. ed.), July 4, 1998, p. 13.

12. Michael Hammer, *Beyond Reengineering: How the Process-Centered Organization Is Changing Our Work and Our Lives* (New York: HarperCollins, 1997). Gary Hamel and C. K. Prahalad, *Competing for the Future* (Boston: Harvard Business School Press, 1994).

13. B. Joseph Pine II and James H. Gilmore, "Welcome to the Experience Economy," *Harvard Business Review* (July/August 1998), pp. 97–105. See also Pine II and Gilmore, "The Experience Economy" (Boston: Harvard Business School Press, 1999).

14. Philip Kotler, *Marketing Management,* 8th ed. (Englewood Cliffs, N.J.: Prentice-Hall, 1994), p. 295.

15. Michael Porter, *Competitive Strategy: Techniques for Analyzing Industries and Competitors* (New York: The Free Press, 1985), p. 14.

16. John R. Hauser and Don Clausing, "The House of Quality," *Harvard Business Review* 66, no. 3 (1988), pp. 63–73.

17. Kotler, *Marketing Management,* p. 261.

18. James Engel, Roger D. Blackwell, and Paul W. Miniard, *Consumer Behavior* (Hinsdale, IL.: Dryden Press, 1994). See also John Howard, *The Theory of Buyer Behavior* (New York: John Wiley, 1969).

19. Nick Shore, "Dateline London: Cultural Shifts," *Brandweek,* January 5, 1998, p. 14.

20. Actually, some researchers do view brands as a bundle of functional attributes. For example, C. Whan Park, Sung Youl Jun, and Allan D. Shocker ("Composite Branding Alliances: An Investigation of Extension and Feedback Effects," *Journal of Marketing Research* 33 [November 1996], pp. 453–66) write: "A brand can be understood in terms of a set of attributes, each at a particular performance level." (p. 454).

21. David Aaker, *Managing Brand Equity: Capitalizing on the Value of a Brand Name* (New York: The Free Press, 1991), p. 15.

22. James Watson, *Golden Arches East: McDonald's in East Asia* (Stanford, Calif.: Stanford University Press, 1997).

23. Figures presented at *The Economist* meeting on Branding in Beijing, China, June 18, 1998.

24. Gerald Zaltman, "Rethinking Market Research: Putting the People Back In," *Journal of Marketing Research* 34 (November 1997), pp. 424–37.
25. Richard Branson, *Losing My Virginity: How I've Survived, Had Fun, and Made a Fortune Doing Business My Way* (New York: Times Business, division of Random House, 1998).
26. Russell W. Belk, Melanie Wallendorf, and John F. Sherry, "The Sacred and the Profane in Consumer Behavior: Theodicy on the Odyssey," *Journal of Consumer Research* 16, no. 1 (June 1989), pp. 1–38.
27. Based on materials provided by the company.
28. Morris Holbrook and Elizabeth C. Hirschman, "The Experiential Aspects of Consumption: Consumer Fantasies, Feelings, and Fun," *Journal of Consumer Research* 9 (September 1982), p. 132.
29. Gerald Zaltman, "Rethinking Market Research: Putting the People Back In," *Journal of Marketing Research* 34 (November 1997), pp. 424–37.

2. The Breadth and Scope of Experiential Marketing

1. Rana Gogar with Timm Gossing, "Too Much Is About Right," *Newsweek* (Atlantic ed.), June 15, 1998, p. 35.
2. I thank Ogilvy & Mather for providing the Jaguar videos.
3. I thank Ms. Richardson for discussing the Amtrak project with me and providing useful materials.
4. Based on: Jane Levere, "Singapore Airlines and Delta Take Different Approaches to Premium Service for Passengers," *New York Times,* September 16, 1998, sec. C, p. 6; Singapore Airlines web site; conversations with Singapore Airlines management; and Sandra Vandermerwe and Christopher Lovelock, "Singapore Airlines: Using Technology for Service Excellence" (case study, International Institute for Management Development, Lausanne, Switzerland, 1991), Case #M408.
5. The Auntie Anne's Soft Pretzels story is based on material provided by the company and the following articles: "East Coast Treat Finds a Home in South Valley," *The Fresno Bee* (Valley ed.), February 20, 1998; "Auntie Anne Ties Snack Business in Knots," *The Stuarts News,* May 8, 1997.
6. Rana Gogar with Shehnaz Suterwalla, Judith Warner, Stefan Thell, Hideko Takayama, and Barbie Nadeau, "It's a Woman's World," *Newsweek,* May 18, 1998, p. 13. Nina Munk and Suzanne Oliver, "Woman of the Valley," *Forbes* magazine, December 30, 1996, p. 102.
7. I thank Mr. Tony Spaeth, an identity consultant, who has worked on Polartec, for providing me with materials.
8. "Revolution in the Air," *The Economist,* March 22, 1997, p. 16.
9. "Art as a Product, Love the Brand; Get the Picture," *The Economist,* May 23, 1998, p. 79.
10. Roy S. Johnson, "The Jordan Effect: The World's Greatest Basketball Player Is Also One of Its Greatest Brands. What Is His Impact on the Economy?" *Fortune,* June 22, 1998, p. 138.

11. Gregory Carpenter, Rashi Glazer, and Kent Nakamoto, "Meaningful Brands from Meaningless Differentiation: The Dependence on Irrelevant Attributes," *Journal of Marketing Research* 31 (August 1994), pp. 339–50.

3. A Framework for Managing Customer Experiences

1. Mihaly Csikszentmihalyi, *Flow* (New York: HarperCollins, 1991).
2. Peter Drucker, *The Practice of Management* (New York: Harper and Row, 1954), p. 37.
3. Earlier versions of the framework have been presented in the following articles of mine: "Superficial Out of Profundity: The Branding of Customer Experiences," *The Journal of Brand Management,* 5, 1997, 92–98; "Experiential Marketing: A New Framework for Design and Communications," *Design Management Journal,* Winter 1999; "Experiential Marketing," *Journal of Marketing Management.* Vol. 15. 1999.
4. Maurice Merleau-Ponty, *Phenomenology of Perception* (London: Routledge and Kegan Paul, 1962).
5. Edmund Husserl, *Ideas: General Introduction to a Pure Phenomenology* (London: Allen and Unwin, 1931). Franz Brentano, *Psychology from an Empirical Standpoint* (London: Routledge and Kegan Paul, 1973).
6. Roger Brown and Deborah Fish, "The Psychological Causality Implicit in Language," *Cognition* 14, no. 3 (1983), pp. 237–73.
7. John Holland, *Emergence: From Chaos to Order* (Reading, Mass. Addison-Wesley, 1998); Murray Gell-Mann, *The Quark and the Jaguar: Adventures in the Simple and the Complex* (New York: Freeman, 1994).
8. Steven Pinker, *How the Mind Works* (New York: Norton, 1997).
9. One of the clearest expositions has been presented by Steve Pinker, a professor of psychology and director of the Center for Cognitive Neuroscience at MIT. In *How the Mind Works* Pinker dedicates one chapter each to the "organs" or "modules" of the mind: sensory perception ("The Mind's Eye"), feelings and emotions ("Hotheads"), creativity and reasoning ("Good Ideas"), and social relations ("Family Values"). (Unlike other psychologists, Pinker leaves out a motivational or action component, because he is interested primarily in mental computation rather than behavioral action.) Describing the specific structures of each module, Pinker subscribes to a computational theory of the mind, which is controversial. In contrast to Pinker's view, the alternative "embodied cognition" view emphasizes the role of the body in mental structures and claims that the mind is a *perceptual* symbol system rather than a *computational* one (see George Lakoff and Mark Johnson, *Philosophy in the Flesh: The Embodied Mind and the Challenge to Western Thought* [New York: Basic Books, 1999]; Lawrence Barsalou, "Perceptual Symbol Systems," *Behavioral and Brain Sciences,* in press). However, the embodied cognition view does not necessarily call into question the notion that the mind is organized in a modular fashion. That is, the debate regarding computation *vs.* perceptual symbols is a psychology debate which, unlike the "modularity" view, is largely irrelevant to the objectives of this book. Moreover, Laurette Dube and Jordan L. Le Bel of McGill University ("Are all pleasures the same? An empirical test of unitary and differentiated views of pleasure,"

Working Paper, McGill University, 1999) have empirically distinguished four experience prototypes, which they labeled "sensorial/physical," "emotional," "intellectual/spiritual," and "social." (Note these authors combine the SENSE and ACT experiences into one category.) To summarize, researchers in a variety of disciplines are increasingly giving up a unitary, one-dimensional view of experiences in favor of a modular view.

10. Daniel Goleman, *Emotional Intelligence* (New York: Bantam, 1995). Joseph LeDoux, "Emotional Memory Systems in the Brain," *Behavioral and Brain Sciences* 58 (1993). Antonio Damasio, *Descartes' Error: Emotion, Reason, and the Human Brain* (New York: Grosset/Putnam, 1994).

11. "Counter Culture," *South China Morning Post,* November 16, 1997, p. 18; Florence Fabricant, "Food Stuff," *New York Times,* October 15, 1997, sec. F, p. 2.

12. Bernd H. Schmitt and Alex Simonson, *Marketing Aesthetics: The Strategic Management of Brands, Identity, and Image* (New York: Free Press, 1997).

13. *Ibid.,* p. 18.

14. Stuart Elliott, "Clinique Is Introducing Scent in Bid for Share of Premium Market," *New York Times,* September 30, 1997, sec. D, p. 6.

15. Anna Marie Cox, "Microsoft Is Trying to Make You Forget About Its Nerdy CEO Through a Multimillion-dollar Sleight of Hand," *Mother Jones* 23, no. 1 (January 1998), p. 42.

16. Timothy Egan, "The Swoon of the Swoosh," *New York Times,* September 13, 1998, p. 66.

17. "New Brands/Brand Extensions," *Brand Strategy,* May 23, 1997, pp. 18–27.

18. Dana Canedy, "The Media Business: Advertising," *New York Times,* July 2, 1998, sec. D, p. 6.

19. Materials were collected from the Newspaper Association of America web site at www.naa.org and an article in *PR Newswire,* January 15, 1998.

20. Materials provided by the company.

21. Melanie Warner, "Cool companies 1998," *Fortune,* July 6, 1998, pp. 69–80.

22. The materials were gratefully provided by Mr. Hellmut Lischer of Ciba Chemicals.

23. Herbert Muschamp, "Blueprint: The Shock of the Familiar," *New York Times Magazine,* December 13, 1998, sec. 6, pp. 61–66; Rem Koolhaas, Interview in *Kunstforum International,* June 1997.

24. Based on a report on CNN's *Business Unusual* (with Lou Dobbs), Saturday, January 30, 1999.

25. Paul Lukas, "New Headline, Same Great Column," *Fortune* magazine, February 16, 1998, p. 42.

26. Ken Miller, "What's Next in Beverage Packaging?" *Brand Packaging,* October/November 1988, pp. 12–14.

27. Based on materials provided by Wallace Church.

28. *Ibid.*

29. Antoinette Coulton, "With Sports Alliances, Cards Make Big Play for Fans," *American Banker,* October 2, 1997, p. 1.

30. I thank Mr. Dowley, who spoke in my Corporate Identity class at Columbia Business School in the spring of 1998 and provided useful materials on event marketing.

31. Kate Fitzgerald, "Sampling & Singing," *Advertising Age* 69 (June 8, 1998), p. 32.

32. Wayne Friedman, "Promo Power Fueling H'wood," *The Hollywood Reporter,* January 19, 1998.

33. John Bowen, "Brand Culture: Going Beyond Brand Positioning to Enhance Consumer Loyalty and Trust" (speech at "Branded Environments," conference organized by The Strategic Research Institute, Orlando, Florida, December 3–4, 1998).

34. "Blue Is the Color," *The Economist,* June 6, 1998, p. 65.

35. "Oil Companies Must Look Beyond Own Industry to Stand in Increasingly Crowded C-Store Field," *PR Newswire,* July 14, 1997.

36. From a chapter entitled "Reinventing the Coffee Experience," in Howard Schultz and Dori Jones, *Pour Your Heart into It: How Starbucks Built a Company One Cup at a Time* (New York: Hyperion, 1997).

37. James Kaplan, "Designer by Design," *New York Magazine,* July 20, 1998, pp. 34–40.

38. See www.clubmed.com.

39. William Gates, *Business @ the Speed of Thought* (New York: Warner Books, 1999).

4. SENSE

1. Bernd H. Schmitt and Alex Simonson, *Marketing Aesthetics: The Strategic Management of Brands, Identity, and Image* (New York: Free Press, 1997).

2. Kevin Waters, "Dual and Extension Branding: Using Research to Guide Design Decisions and Branding Strategy," *Design Management Journal* 8, no. 1 (Winter 1997), pp. 25–33.

3. The ITT Industries case is based on materials provided by Landor Associates. For a more general discussion of the issues, see Bernd H. Schmitt, and Alex Simonson, "Coupling brand and organizational identities through partnering," *Design Management Journal,* 9, 1998, 9–14.

4. This research was conducted by Eric Johnson and his colleagues at the Wharton School of the University of Pennsylvania.

5. "Hold the Phone! Nokia Takes No. 1 Spot in Cellulars," *International Herald Tribune,* October 24–25, 1998, Business/Finance, p. 1.

6. "Spirit of Nokia's Human Technology," *Business Times Singapore,* November 24, 1997, pp. 8–9.

7. Vanessa L. Facenda, "A Different Side of Sears," *Discount Merchandiser,* April 1998, pp. 14–16.

8. Schmitt and Simonson, *Marketing Aesthetics.*

9. John Anderson, *Cognitive Psychology and Its Implications,* 4th ed. (New York: W. H. Freeman, 1995). Susan T. Fiske and Shelley E. Taylor, Social Cognition, 2d ed. (New York: McGraw Hill, 1991).

10. Nader Tavassoli, "Language in Multimedia: Interaction of Spoken and Written Information," *Journal of Consumer Research* (June 1998), 25, no. 1, pp. 35–36.

11. Bernd Schmitt, "Visual Corporate Identity in the Luxury Hotel Industry" (report submitted to the Center for Hospitality Research, Cornell School of Hotel Administration, Cornell University, 1997).

12. Simon Jones, "British Airways for the New Millennium," *Design Management Journal* 9, no. 1 (Winter 1998), pp. 47–52.

13. Nigel F. Piercy, *Tales from the Marketplace: Stories of Revolution, Reinvention, and Renewal* (Oxford: Butterworth-Heinemann, 1998).

5. FEEL

1. Jojo T. Nones, "Ice Cream Privileges," *Business Daily,* March 3, 1998. "Häagen-Dazs Dream Site," *Advertising Age,* May 12, 1997, p. 62; Häagen-Dazs web site: www.haagen-dazs.com.

2. *Businessworld* [Manila], May 21, 1997.

3. Frank Rose, "The Dream Factories Reborn," *Fortune* magazine, February 16, 1998, p. 106.

4. Important review literature on affect includes: Andrew Ortony, Gerald L. Clore, and Allan Collins, *The Cognitive Structure of Emotions* (Cambridge: Cambridge University Press, 1988); Joel Cohen and Charles S. Areni, "Affect and Consumer Behavior," in Thomas Robertson and Harold Kassarjian, eds., *Handbook of Consumer Behavior* (Englewood-Cliffs, N.J.: Prentice-Hall, 1990).

5. Ms. Isen has published numerous studies on this phenomenon. For example, see Alice M. Isen and Stanley F. Simmonds, "The Effect of Feeling Good on a Helping Task That Is Incompatible with Good Mood," *Social Psychology* 41, no. 4 (1978), pp. 346–49.

6. Ortony, Clore, and Collins, *Cognitive Structure of Emotions.*

7. Mimi Swartz, "Victoria's Secret," *The New Yorker,* March 30, 1998, pp. 94–101.

8. Marsha L. Richins, "Measuring Emotions in the Consumption Experience," *Journal of Consumer Research* 24 (September 1997).

9. Michel Tuan Pham, "Representativeness, Relevance, and the Use of Feeling in Decision Making," *Journal of Consumer Research* 25 (September 1998).

10. This example is based on research conducted by Daniel Kahneman and Amos Tversky. See "The Simulation Heuristic," in Daniel Kahneman, Paul Slovic, and Amos Tversky, *Judgment under Uncertainty: Heuristics and Biases* (Cambridge: Cambridge University Press, 1982).

6. THINK

1. Materials for this case were provided by Siegel & Gale. The principal members of the Genesis ElderCare strategy are: Claude Singer of Siegel & Gale, New York; Bruce Innes, Genesis Health Ventures; and Lynn Madonna, Genesis Health Ventures.

2. Based on company material.

3. David Kirkpatrick, "The Second Coming of Apple," *Fortune,* November 9, 1998, pp. 87–92; Ira Sager and Peter Burrows with Andy Reinhart, "Back to the Future at Apple," *Business Week,* May 25, 1998, pp. 56–66.

4. Jennifer Steinhauer, "The Teach and Sell School of Retailing: Shopping as an Educational Experience," *New York Times,* February 28, 1998, Business, p. 1 and p. 14.

5. Lucy Kellaway, "It's Trendy, It's Smart, It's Corporate Chic," *Financial Times,* July 6, 1998, p. 18.

6. J. P. Guilford, "Creativity," *American Psychologist,* Vol. 14, (1950), pp. 205–8.

7. Norbert Schwarz and Gerald L. Clore, "Feelings and Phenomenal Experiences," in E. Tory Higgins and Ariel W. Kruglanski, eds., *Social Psychology: Handbook of Basic Principles* (New York: Guilford, 1996).

8. Mihaly Csikszentmihalyi, *Creativity* (New York: HarperCollins, 1996).

9. Mihaly Csikszentmihalyi, *Flow* (New York: HarperCollins, 1991), p. 139.

10. Based on information provided by J. Walter Thompson in Shanghai.

7. ACT

1. William C. Symonds and Carol Matlack, "Gillette's Edge," *Business Week,* January 19, 1998, pp. 70–77. James Surowiecki, "The Billion-Dollar Blade: How the Gillette Company Reinvented the Razor—and Itself," *The New Yorker,* June 15, 1998, pp. 43–49. Mark Maremont, "How Gillette Brought Its MACH3 to Market," *Wall Street Journal,* April 15, 1998, sec. B, p. 1. "Gillette Takes Flight with MACH3," *Cosmetics International,* May 10, 1998, p. 11.

2. Jay Schulberg (with Bernie Hogya and Sal Taibi), *The Milk Mustache Book: a Behind-the-Scenes Look at America's Favorite Advertising Campaign* (New York: Ballantine, 1998). "Mustache Hits the Net," *Advertising Age,* June 29, 1998, p. 39. Shuva Rahim, "The Milk's Way to Fame," *Des Moines Register,* March 3, 1998, p. 1. David Orenstein, "Ads Make Milk a Cool Beverage," *The Alameda Times Union,* February 13, 1998, sec. E, p. 1.

3. Kathleen Purvis, "The Joy of Martha: Resistance Is Futile," *The Record,* August 10, 1997. Vicki Cheng, "College Researchers Finding a Lot to Like about Martha Stewart," *Denver Post,* July 3, 1997, sec. E, p. 2. Greg Farrell, "Media Notes," *Mediaweek,* July 6, 1998, p. 1. Donna Boyle Schwartz, "Kmart $10m Bet on Martha," *HFN* (weekly newspaper for the Home Furnishings Network) 71, no. 8 (February 24, 1997), p. 1. Dina Santorelli, "Martha," *Decorative Home,* April 1997, pp. 1, 16–18, and 50.

4. Jens Foerster, "Head Movements and the Encoding of Information," *Journal of Personality and Social Psychology,* in press.

5. Philip Kotler, *Marketing Management,* (8th ed). (Englewood Cliffs, N.J.: Prentice-Hall, 1994), p. 182.

6. John Bargh, "The Automaticity of Everyday Life," in Robert Wyer, ed., *Advances in Social Cognition,* vol. 10 (Mahwah, N.J.: Erlbaum, 1997).

7. Joan Voight, "Leagas Leads Notre Dame Cheers," *Adweek,* September 8, 1997, p. 2.

8. Erich Joachimsthaler, "Branding Challenges for Transitional Economies firms in Local Markets" (paper presented at the conference "Marketing in Transitional Economies: A Davidson Institute Research Conference," William Davidson Institute, University of Michigan Business School, July 24–26, 1998).

8. RELATE

1. Russell Belk, "Possessions and the Extended Self," *Journal of Consumer Research* 15, no. 2 (September 1988), pp. 139–68.

2. Quoted in Anthony Vagnoni, "Creative Differences," *Advertising Age,* November 17, 1997.

3. Kathleen Purvis, "The Joy of Martha: Resistance Is Futile," *Chicago Sun-Times,* December 19, 1997, sec. L, p. 5.

4. Quoted in Richard Teerlink, "Motor Harley Davidson Cycles," @issue: *Journal of Business and Design* 2, no. 1 (1996), pp. 6–13.

5. Henri Tajfel, "Social Psychology of Intergroup Relations, *Annual Review of Psychology,*" 33 (1982), pp. 1–39.

6. Won Choi Hae Won Choi, "Korean Marketers Are Playing IMF Trump to Win Over Patriots," *Asian Wall Street Journal,* January 26, 1998, p. 8.

7. Based on material provided by the company.

8. Steven Pinker, *How the Mind Works* (New York: Norton, 1997), pp. 429–30.

9. *Ibid,* p. 431.

10. Cherie Parker, "Winning the Body Prize," *Washington Post,* October 23, 1995, sec. C, p. 1. Victoria McDonald, "French Bra Ads 'Too Offensive' for UK Woman," *Sunday Telegraph,* October 5, 1997, p. 11.

11. Shalom Schwartz, "Are There Universal Aspects in the Structure and Contents of Human Values?" *Journal of Social Issues* 50, no. 4 (1993), pp. 19–45.

12. O. Yau, "Chinese Cultural Values: Three Dimensions and Marketing Implications," *European Journal of Marketing Management* 22, no. 5 (1994), pp. 44–57.

13. William Swann Jr., "To Be Adored or to Be Known? The Interplay of Self-Enhancement and Self-Verification," in E. Tory Higgins and R. M. Sorrentino, eds., *Handbook of Motivation and Cognition: Foundations of Social Behavior,* vol. 2 (New York: Guilford Press, 1990), pp. 408–48.

14. Michael Martow, "Bijan Aims to Take Michael Jordan to New Heights," *Daily News Record,* June 7, 1996, p. 8.

15. Robert Cialdini, *Influence: The Psychology of Persuasion* (New York: HarperCollins, 1993).

16. Abraham Tesser, "Some Effects of Self-Evaluation Maintenance on Cognition and Action, " in Sorrentino and Higgins, *Handbook of Motivation and Cognition,* pp. 435–64.

17. Susan Fournier, "Consumers and Their Brands: Developing Relationship Theory in Consumer Research," *Journal of Consumer Research,* no. 4 (March 1998), pp. 343–73.

18. Albert Muniz and Thomas O'Guinn, "Brand Community" (working paper, University of Illinois School of Business, 1998).

9. Experiential Hybrids and Holistic Experiences

1. Keith Naughton and Bill Vlasic, "The Nostalgia Boom," *Business Week,* March 23, 1998, p. 587. Chris Reidy, "Beetle-Mania Revival," *Boston Globe,* March 13, 1998,

sec. E, p. 1. Stuart Elliott, "Volkswagen and Arnold Communications Pitch a Beetle with 'More Power' and 'Less Flower,'" *New York Times,* March 13, 1998, sec. D, p. 6. Diane Seo, "VW's Ads Aim to Draw Beetle Buyers Without Bugging Them," *Los Angeles Times,* March 13, 1998, sec. D, p. 3.
2. Based on store visits by Bernd Schmitt and Laura Brown.
3. "It's the Taste, Stupid," *Business Week,* June 1, 1998, p. 6.

10. Strategic Issues of Experiential Marketing

1. Brad Van Auken, "Building and Sustaining Brand Leadership" (presentation at Brand Masters, A Practitioner's Forum, Atlanta, December 10–12, 1997).
2. Based on discussions with Donovan and Green, and a talk by Nancye Green (Donovan and Green), and Sue Meyer (Merchandising Vice President at Hallmark Cards), "Using Emotional Content as the Basis for Store Design: Hallmark Creations" presented at "Branded Environments," conference organized by the Strategic Research Institute, Orlando, Florida, December 3–4, 1998.
3. Based on information provided by DGA consulting.
4. Roger Blackwell, "Case Study: Service Corporation International" (Fisher College of Business, Ohio State University, Columbus, Ohio, 1998).

11. Building the Experience-Oriented Organization

1. Important literature on market orientation includes: John Narver and Stanley F. Slater, "The Effect of Marketing Orientation on Business Profitability," *Journal of Marketing* 54, no. 4 (October 1990), pp. 20–35; Bernard Jaworsky and Ajah Kohli, "Market Orientation: Antecedents and Consequences," *Journal of Marketing* 57, no. 3 (July 1993), pp. 53–70; Rohit Deshpande and John Farley, "Measuring Market Orientation Generalization and Synthesis," *Journal of Market-Focused Management,* 2 (1997), pp. 213–32.
2. Tom Peters, *Thriving on Chaos: Handbook for a Management Revolution* (New York: HarperCollins, 1991).
3. Nigel F. Piercy, *Tales from the Marketplace: Stories of Revolution, Reinvention, and Renewal* (Oxford: Butterworth-Heinemann, 1998).
4. Holly Brubach, "Luxe Populi," *New York Times Magazine,* July 12, 1998, pp. 24–59.
5. Gerald Hirshberg, *The Creative Priority: Driving Innovative Business in the Real World* (New York: HarperCollins, 1998).
6. Conference on "Talking to Teens," Institute of International Research, Fairmont Hotel, San Francisco, June 18 and 19, 1998.
7. Norihiko Shirouzu, "Japan's High-School Girls Excel in Art of Setting Trends," *Wall Street Journal,* April 24, 1998, sec. B, p. 1.
8. Peter Schwartz, *The Art of the Long View: Planning in an Uncertain World* (New York: Doubleday, 1996); Arie de Geus, *The Living Company* (Boston: Harvard Business School Press, 1997).
9. I would like to thank Jacob Goldenberg of the Hebrew University in Jerusalem for discussing these issues with me.

10. Joann S. Lublin, "Climbing Walls on Company Time," *Wall Street Journal*, December 1, 1998, B1.
11. "Headquarters: Prince Street Technologies," *Interiors*, August 1996, Nancy Bearden Henderson, "A Princely War on Waste," *Envirolink*, January 1998.
12. Robert E. Kelley, *How to Be a Star at Work* (New York: Times Books, 1998).
13. "Spirit of Nokia's Human Technology," *Business Times Singapore*, November 24, 1997, pp. 8–9.
14. Richard Branson, *Losing My Virginity: How I've Survived, Had Fun, and Made a Fortune Doing Business My Way* (New York: Times Business Random House, 1998), p. 343.
15. Materials provided by WPP. Mr. Sorrell's quote is from Joseph L. Bower, "WPP—Integrating Icons" (Harvard Business School case No. 9-396-249, 1996).
16. "One-Stop Shops Soiled," *Marketing*, March 5, 1998.

Epilogue

1. For Proustian existential experiences, you may join the thousand of Prousto-tourists to Illiers-Combray, and read *Remembrance of Things Past* on those holy grounds while nibbling on one of the two thousand madeleines sold each month. See Andre Aciman, "In Search of Proust. Why Are More People than Ever Flocking to a Small Town in Provincial France?" *The New Yorker*, December 21, 1998, pp. 81–85.

PERMISSIONS

Photograph of the author in his "Road Warrior" outfit by Gail Van Der Merwe

Times Square photographs by Larry Beck.

ABC ad dismissing rational appeals used by permission.

Cole-Haan is a trademark of Cole Haan and is used with permission. Photo courtesy of Cole Hann. © 1997 Cole Haan.

Coca-Cola photographs courtesy Desgrippes Gobé.

Ad for Jaguar XJR used by permission.

Amtrak photographs used by permission.

Singapore Airlines photographs courtesy Singapore Airlines.

CrossWorlds "Trail Blazer" ad used by permission.

Du Pont ad for Lycra used by permission.

Andersen Consulting advertisement reprinted with permission of Andersen Consulting.

Chocolate design for Richart Classics used by permission.

Volvo advertisement courtesy of Volvo.

Patek Philippe ad used by permission.

Nickelodeon logos copyright Nickelodeon. Used by permission.

Brochure for Philips Satinelle brand used by permission.

Pillsbury advertisement courtesy of Wallace Church Associates, Manhattan-based brand identity and package design consultancy.

The communication program for the 125th anniversary of Zurich Insurance Company has been developed and implemented by Wirz IndentityAG Zurich.

Photograph of Baci dall'Italia plane used by permission.

Nokia advertisement courtesy of Nokia.

British Airways photograph courtesy of British Airways PLC.

Häagen-Dazs photographed by Gail Van Der Merwe.

Promotion for Campbell's Soup used by permission.

Photograph of Victoria Gallegos (with the author) used by permission.

The principal authors of the Genesis ElderCare Strategy are Claude Singes of Siegel & Gale, New York; Bruce Innes, Genesis Health Ventures; Lynn Madonna, Genesis Health Ventures.

Apple billboard photographed by Larry Beck.

Siemens advertisement reprinted with permission of Siemens Corporation © 1998.

Gillette Mach3 advertisement courtesy of Wallace Church Associates, Manhattan-based brand identity and package design consultancy.

Milk Mustache advertisements courtesy Bozell Worldwide, Inc., as agent for National Fluid Milk Processor Promotion.

Palm III advertisement photograph by David Meisel

Beetle advertisement courtesy Volkswagen of America, Inc., and Arnold Communications, Inc.

Photograph of 5S Store used by permission.

Arizona Iced Tea ad and stationery used by permission.

Photograph of SoBe Wisdom bottle used by permission.

Celestial Seasonings photograph © by and used with permission, Celestial Seasonings, Inc.

Perrier photograph printed with permission of The Perrier Group of America.

Photograph of Clif bars used by permission.

Finlandia Advertisement © 1998 ALKO Group Ltd. All rights reserved.

Hallmark store photographs by Donovan and Green.

Photograph of Freq and *Branding Matters* interview used by permission.

Photograph of the author in his "Zen Marketer" outfit by Gail Van Der Merwe.

INDEX

ABOUT THE AUTHOR

Bernd H. Schmitt is an expert in corporate and brand identity, international and strategic marketing, product positioning, and communications. He holds a Ph.D. from Cornell University. In 1988 he joined the Marketing Department of Columbia Business School, where he is a tenured professor and the founder and director of the Center on Global Brand Management. At China-Europe International Business School (CEIBS), China's leading business school, located in Shanghai, he is the chairman of the Marketing Department.

Professor Schmitt has consulted, and given lectures and seminars, in more than twenty countries around the world. He is Associate Faculty Director of Columbia's Marketing Management executive program. He has appeared on CNN, CNBC, and the BBC as well as on other TV channels in the United States, Europe, and Asia and has conducted live satellite executive programs on brand management and experiential marketing.

Dr. Schmitt is a frequent speaker at marketing and management conferences.